'I am more than happy to highly recommend Dele Kogbe's book. This is an outstanding piece of research which breaks new theoretical ground and provides a wealth of new and important empirical data which greatly enriches the field of studies on regional civil society'.

– Professor Cameron Ross, University of Dundee, UK

'With *Rethinking Civil Society Regionalism in Africa*, Dele Kogbe brings into regionalism studies a consideration of civil society organisations and how they shape processes of specific regions. The book provides original theoretical and empirical analyses on Africa, and West Africa in particular, where the literature has tended to ignore African contributions to knowledge and practice of civil society regionalism. Indeed, this is an outstanding book which breaks new theoretical ground and provides a wealth of new and important empirical data which greatly enriches the field of studies on regional civil society. Dele Kogbe provides a very interesting and compelling analysis of an important and largely under-researched topic. As such, this book offers innovative insights for scholars interested in the African security, regionalism studies, as well as regional civil society more generally'.

– Professor Christian Kaunert, University of
South Wales, UK and Dublin City University,
Republic of Ireland

Rethinking Civil Society Regionalism in Africa

This book interrogates the extent to which regional civil society organisations have evolved as actors in West Africa. Examining civil society democratic participation in regional integration and involvement in regionalism of peacebuilding, it rethinks how we study civil society in the Economic Community of West African States (ECOWAS) region. Beyond the functional typology of civil society actors as 'partner', 'legitimiser', 'resistance/counter-hegemonic' and 'manipulator', the book develops a new analytical framework to understand how organisations such as the West African Civil Society Forum (WACSOF) and West African Network for Peacebuilding (WANEP) have evolved. Offering analytical perspectives of the actorship of specific regional civil society actors, the book draws attention to the tendencies in the previous studies of mistaking an action or misdeed that is empirically specific to particular civil society organisations within a region to the generality of the civic space of the region. Providing an alternative perspective aimed at invoking a new intellectual conversation about civil society regionalism, this book advances a new analytical framework of action-based regional identity of civil society, regional presence of activities, regional capacities and societal impact. It will be of interest to academics and scholars of international relations, global governance, African politics and comparative regionalism.

Dele Kogbe, PhD, is a visiting research fellow at the University of South Wales, UK, and co-convenor of the British International Studies Association – Africa Working Group. He has taught politics and international relations at the University of Dundee, where he co-founded the Dundee Africa Research Network. A writer of multiple parts, besides researching African security and comparative regionalism, Dele is a published poet, novelist and playwright who employs a literary medium and social research to interrogate complex issues of politics and societies in speaking the truth to power. He is the author of *The Girl Who Dares the King* (Drama)).

New Regionalisms Series
Series Editor: Timothy M. Shaw

The *New Regionalisms* series presents innovative analyses of a range of novel regional relations & institutions. Going beyond formal, interstate organisations, this interdisciplinary Series builds on over two decades of the pioneering International Political Economy of New Regionalisms series, also edited by Professor Timothy M. Shaw.

New Regionalisms is creative & cosmopolitan, reflecting enquiries from & about the global South & North. It reinforces ongoing networks of analysts in both academia & think-tanks as well as international institutions concerned with micro-, meso- & macro-level regionalisms in the third decade of the 21st century & beyond.

For more information about this series, please visit: https://www.routledge.com/New-Regionalisms-Series/book-series/ASHSER1146

Weak States, Vulnerable Governments, and Regional Cooperation
An ASEAN Case Study
Ştefania Atena Feraru

Constructing the East African Community
Diffusion from African and European Regional Organizations
Mariel Reiss

Region-Building in West Africa
Convergence and Agency in ECOWAS
Emmanuel Balogun

Disruptions and Rhetoric in African Development Policy
George Kararach

Connecting Africa and Asia
Afrasia As a Benign Community
Yoichi Mine

Rethinking Civil Society Regionalism in Africa
Challenges and Opportunities in Democratic Participation and Peacebuilding in the Post-ECOWAS Vision 2020
Dele Kogbe

Rethinking Civil Society Regionalism in Africa

Challenges and Opportunities
in Democratic Participation and
Peacebuilding in the Post-ECOWAS
Vision 2020

Dele Kogbe

Routledge
Taylor & Francis Group

LONDON AND NEW YORK

First published 2023
by Routledge
4 Park Square, Milton Park, Abingdon, Oxon OX14 4RN

and by Routledge
605 Third Avenue, New York, NY 10158

Routledge is an imprint of the Taylor & Francis Group, an informa business

© 2023 Dele Kogbe

British Library Cataloguing-in-Publication Data
A catalogue record for this book is available from the British Library

Library of Congress Cataloging-in-Publication Data
A catalog record has been requested for this book

ISBN: 978-1-032-19000-6 (hbk)
ISBN: 978-1-032-19002-0 (pbk)
ISBN: 978-1-003-25728-8 (ebk)

DOI: 10.4324/9781003257288

Typeset in Times New Roman
by Deanta Global Publishing Services, Chennai, India

Dedication

To My Late Mum
For all her sacrifices.

Contents

List of illustrations

Figure

Tables

List of Abbreviations

AFCDHS	African Centre for Democracy and Human Rights Studies
AFJCI	Association of Women Lawyers of the Ivory Coast
ASEAN	Association of South East Asian Nations
AU	African Union
CAIDP	Commission for Access to Public Information and Documents
CDD	Centre for Democracy and Development
CIDO	Citizens and Diaspora Directorate
CISLAC	Civil Society Legislative Advocacy Centre
CJPC	Catholic Justice and Peace Commission
CJTF	Civilian Joint Task Force
CLHRE	Centre for Law and Human Rights Education
CNGHCI	National Human Rights Commission of Ivory Coast
COSOPCI	Civil Society Coalition for Peace and Democratic Development
CSCI	Ivorian Civil Society Convention
CSO	Civil Society Organisations
DARN	Dundee Africa Research Network
EAC	East African Community
EACSOF	East African Civil Society Forum
ECCAS	Economic Community of Central African States
ECOMOG	ECOWAS Monitoring Group
ECOWAS	Economic Community of West African States
ECPF	ECOWAS Conflict Prevention Framework
EP	ECOWAS Parliament
EPLO	European Peacebuilding Liaison Office
EU	European Union
EYSDC	ECOWAS Youth and Sports Development Centre
FFHC	Freedom from Hunger Campaign
FARE	Forum of Associations Recognised by ECOWAS
FOSDA	Foundation for Security and Development in Africa
GLOBAL IR	Global International Relations
IDEG	Institute for Democratic Governance

IGAD	Intergovernmental Agency for Development
IR	International Relations
LIDHO	Ivorian Human Right League
LWI	Liberian Women Initiative
KAIPTI	Kofi Annan International Peacekeeping Training Institute
MARWOPNET	Mano River Women Peace Network
MDGS	Millennium Development Goals
MERCUSOR	Southern Common Market
MFDC	Movement of Democratic Forces of Casamance
MFWA	Media Foundation for West Africa
NADECO	National Democratic Coalition
NMCL	National Muslim Council of Liberia
NRA	New Regionalism Approach
ONE	National Election Observatory
RADDHO	Rencontre Africaine Pour la Défence des droits de l'Homme
RCSA	Regional Civil Society Actors
RCSO	Regional Civil Society Organisations
REPAOC	Network of West African Nongovernmental Organisations
ROPPA	Network of Peasant Organisations and Producers in West Africa
SADC	Southern African Development Community
SADC-CNGO	Southern African Development Community-Council of Nongovernmental Organisations
SAP	Structural Adjustment Programme
SDGS	Sustainable Development Goals
SERAP	Socio-Economic Rights and Accountability Project
UN	United Nations
UNECA	United Nations Economic Commission for Africa
UNOWAS	United Nations Office for West Africa and the Sahel
WAANSA	West African Action Network on Small Arms
WABA	West African Bar Associations
WACSI	West African Civil Society Institute
WACSOF	West African Civil Society Forum
WADNET	West African Democracy Network
WAEMU	West African Economic and Monetary Union
WAHO	West African Health Organisation
WANEP	West African Network for Peacebuilding
WAPI	West African Peace Institute
WASU	West African Students' Union
WAWA	West African Women's Association
WIPNET	Women in Peacebuilding Network
WOA	World Order Approach

Preface

From the 1990s onward, there have been dynamic changes in regional integration in West Africa. These changes were different from those anticipated in the framework of the Treaty of Lagos that established the Economic Community of West African States (ECOWAS) in May 1975. ECOWAS revised its treaty in 1993 and expanded its governance organs to include the ECOWAS Court of Justice and ECOWAS Parliament and a provision that encourages ECOWAS citizens to promote integration-related activities in the region. It was also in this period that ECOWAS had to engage in peacekeeping and responded to civil wars and violent conflicts within its Mano River Region. While some of these issues have commanded attention in the wider literature, the regional dynamics of civil society organisations in West Africa is one key neglected aspect of these changes that have been overlooked in the mainstream literature. Whether one looks at these dynamics from regional security, regional integration or regionalism discourses generally, civil society movements at the regional levels also manifested in these post-Cold War or post-1990s phenomena of regionalisms in West Africa and are currently begging for serious attention. It is from this perspective that this project interrogates the extent to which regional civil society organisations have evolved to act in regionalist activities in West Africa.

The main activities which this book examines are two prominent areas that are championed by two leading civil society organisations in West Africa. The first is the quest for civil society democratic participation in regional integration championed by the West African Civil Society Forum (WACSOF). The second area is civil society involvement in regionalism of peacebuilding in West Africa championed by the West African Network for Peacebuilding (WANEP). While the study was preliminarily informed by observations, it also critically engaged the wider regionalism literatures through which a New Regionalism Approach was discovered. Although the New Regionalism Approach recognises civil society as an actor, it lacks a clear framework that specifies civil society actorship on the regional level. Moving beyond the functional typology of civil society actors as 'partner', 'legitimiser', 'counter-hegemonic' and 'manipulator', this book develops four analytical concepts used to understand the extent to which WACSOF and WANEP have evolved as actors within their respective areas in regional integration in West Africa.

Methodologically, the study employs qualitative techniques. It combines both primary and secondary data that provides a historical context that affirms the centrality of the agency of the West African people in the pre-colonial movement of pan-Africanism and its manifestation in the regional institutions in Africa such as ECOWAS. The lessons from the evolution of the two case studies draw attention to WANEP as being regionally active and has contributed to reshaping regionalism of peacebuilding in West Africa. WACSOF, on the other hand, has striven over the years to emerge as a regionally active and credible civil society voice in regional integration in West Africa. However, WACSOF has been bedevilled by identity crises with a weak capacity in the region. This has led to an ongoing call to revive WACSOF to take its rightful place in West Africa. While WANEP and WACSOF have evolved as regional civil society actors in their own rights, one cannot overlook the role of regional identities of the two organisations and how they were formed to appreciate their respective standing presently in the region.

Acknowledgement

First and foremost, I give thanks to Almighty God for making it possible for me to successfully complete this project despite the monumental challenges that arose in the course of carrying out the research. I remain grateful to God for His special grace.

I am highly indebted to my late mother, Mrs Wusamot Bolanle Kogbe (nee Ogun), who left the world in April 2018. May Almighty God overlook her shortcomings and grant her the best place in paradise.

Professor Cameron Ross and Professor Christian Kaunert played a very significant role in my intellectual formation as a researcher and I am most grateful to them. I remain grateful to the University of South Wales/the International Centre for Policing and Security for granting me a position of a visiting research fellow shortly after completing my PhD at the University of Dundee. It is a great honour for me to be a visiting member of a centre of excellence with world-leading researchers. I am also grateful to the members of the Africa and International Studies Working Group of the British International Studies Association (BISA-Africa) for electing me in June 2020 as a co-convenor (with Dr Peter Brett) to coordinate the activities of the working group.

I must mention Professor Sarah Leonard, Professor Kurt Mills, Professor Fredrik Soderbaum, Professor Bruce Baker, Professor Valeria Bello, Professor Iheduru Okechukwu, Dr Edzia Carvalho, Dr Toni Haastrup, Dr Scott Brown, Dr Dejan Stjepanovic, Dr Patrick Tom, Rt Hon. Professor Mojeed Alabi, Professor Jide Balogun, Mr. C.J. Maiyaki, Dr Martin Elvins, Dr Abi Abubaker, Dr Ikrom Yakubov, Dr Edwin Ezeokafor, Sheikh Karim Zubair, Buba Ibrahim, Babatunde Okunlaya, Olukokun Adedeji, Dr Alhagi Drammeh, Dr Pontian Okoli, Baheer Elnakla, Dr Nicole Devarrene and members of Dundee Africa Research Network (DARN). I will also like to extend my appreciation to the School of Global Studies at the University of Gothenburg, Sweden, for hosting me as a Guest Researcher in October 2018. I thank all the participants during the fieldwork of my doctoral research for granting me interviews, some of whom have provided me with primary documents or useful links to source relevant data for this research. These include staff of ECOWAS Parliament, ECOWAS Commission, WACSOF regional secretariat, WANEP regional secretariat, WACSI, CDD-West Africa, CISLAC, International Alerts and so on. My special thanks will also go to the

National Universities Commission, Tertiary Education Trust Fund (TETFUND), the Federal Scholarship Board and the Federal Ministry of Education for their respective support at different times of my doctoral journey.

I am grateful to my entire family, particularly my partner, Basirat, and my children, Abdulrahman, Abdulsalam and Muhammad, for their patience, undiminished sacrifices, prayers and love. Words are insufficient to convey my gratitude to you here because you deserve more.

I will be an ingrate if I forget to acknowledge all those teachers who taught me throughout my academic journey. I am grateful to all of them. May this project be of numerous benefits in advancing the cause of peace, security and development for the people and regions in Africa and the world at large.

Introduction

Since the end of the Cold War, the processes of regional integration have increasingly intensified around the world. In the literature, this era of renewed interest has been described as 'a new wave' of regionalism, to differentiate it from the old regionalist scheme (Hettne 1999, Soderbaum 2002, Hurrell 2005, Godsater 2016). There are two distinctive features which distinguish the 'new wave' from the old scheme. These features focus on the actors that drive regionalism and the expansion of policy areas of regionalist projects. According to Soderbaum, the old regionalism was formal and states-led through regional organisations, and its scope was sector specific to trade and security (2016b:31). On the other hand, the new wave combined states and non-state actors as co-drivers and expanded the scope of regionalism to development areas not covered in the old scheme (Soderbaum 2016a, 2016b, Godsater 2013b, 2016). The emergence of civil society in regional integration is often studied in the context of the new wave of the post-Cold War regionalism worldwide.

Although there has been a growing attention on the dynamics of civil society in African regionalism, unfortunately, the bulk of such studies have predominantly focused on Southern Africa and East Africa (Soderbaum 2002, 2004a, 2007, Godsater and Soderbaum 2011, Godsater 2013, 2013b, 2015, 2016). The attempt towards a clear understanding of the extent to which specific regional civil society organisations have acted in given regional policy areas in West Africa is still begging for answers. The inspirational agenda for the previous scholarship about civil society has been shaped by the writings from the Global North. Also, the pre-conceived ideas of civil society in these studies cannot also be taken for granted in terms of the role attributed to civil society actors in African regionalisms. These studies have methodically prioritised how civil society has been traditionally predefined to make sense of it in the African context, rather than what civil society in Africa is, or what it looks like in order to make sense of the context that produces it.

The idea of civil society is contested. The subsequent chapters have devoted attention to explain and situate it contextually. For the purpose of this introduction, broadly, civil society is understood as a space of voluntary associations of citizens and collective action which is based on promoting certain shared interests, purposes and values (Tom 2017, Pouligny 2005 Obadare 2004b, 2016).

DOI: 10.4324/9781003257288-1

These values, shared interests and purposes are manifested in the various actors or groups of individuals that are distinct in their objectives from the functionality of government and private entities. This study looks at the manifestation of these voluntary associations of collective actions beyond the conventional national levels and focus on their regional dynamics and activities within the projects of regionalism. According to Habermas, in Western Europe, the concept of civil society can be traced to 'the emergence of the bourgeoisie and the subsequent efforts by this class to separate private spheres from state action' (1989 cited in Wood 1992:79). The classical inspiration of the idea was to oppose 'monarchical and semi-feudal institutions' that controlled the 'political arena' as 'private realms of the kings and princely estates' (Wood 1992:79). One presupposes that the emergence of civil society was an expression of agency of enlightened citizens in the late 18th and 19th centuries to challenge the age-long patrimonial rule in Western Europe (Wood 1992, Akinrinde 2004, Obadare 2004a).

The concept of civil society re-emerged in late 1989 as a putative discourse in intellectual fora in North America and Europe (Wood 1992). It subsequently gained a heightened prominence in the 1990s in the post-colonial states of Africa (Akinrinde 2004, Obadare 2004). Accepting that some scholars of the New Regionalism Approach (NRA) have specifically focused on civil society in their writings (Hettne et al. 1999, Iheduru 2003, 2015b, Soderbaum 2002, 2004a, Godsater 2013a, 2015, 2016, Fioramonti 2015) is not a surprise. This is because the emergence of the new regionalism scholarship itself coincided with the post-1989 triumphant waves of civil society protest following the exultant struggle against communist rule and military oligarchy in Eastern Europe and Latin America, respectively (Akinrinde 2004:125). This was one of the factors that defined agencies of people in the modern governance of societies following the end of the Cold War. The new shape in the institutional architecture of regionalisms in this era could not afford to ignore the agency of civil society movements. An academic attempt at the time to ignore or exclude increasingly undeniable activities of civil society and other non-state actors would have inadvertently fallen short. Therefore, it would have led to the denial of the post-Cold War new regional order. Even the European Union as an advanced region, '[T]he agenda for consultation of organised civil society was broadened in the late 1990s from definitional issues to include notions aiming at improving legitimacy' (Garcia 2015:16).

Therefore, acknowledging civil society is one thing in the literature. How this scholarship has framed ideas of civil society in the context of African regionalisms is another interesting point that requires a critical exposition (see Chapter 1). After critically examining the existing regionalism literature, this study established that the analysis of the West African civil society has remained at the margin of the debates on one hand. On the other hand, understanding the regional dynamics of civil society organisations and how their actorship is manifested in shaping regionalism or regional governance since the late 1990s has not been explored. The study therefore argues that the existing knowledge on civil society at the regional level in West Africa is still underdeveloped. To have a clear analytical perspective on civil society actors, I posit that it is important to re-examine how we study the regional agency of citizens in African regionalist initiatives. The project therefore builds on the existing body of knowledge on regionalism. And through the four analytic concepts that underpin the framework of this research, the book provides an alternative way of thinking about civil society actors in the study of regionalism or regional integration in Africa.

There is also perceived marginalisation of African intellectual prowess in the mainstream regionalism. The resultant effect of this has manifested in the neglect or marginal treatment of the agency of civil society in African regionalism and its pan-Africanist historical link with the continent's project of regional integration. While African civil society actors are sometimes considered weak (Soderbaum 2016a), alternative empirical evidence shows that CSOs in African regionalism are not just objects of co-option. As we acknowledge their relative weakness, we should not also ignore the fact that some of them have evolved as actors which have earned the respect of states, regional organisations and development partners, in their efforts to drive regionalist activities in Africa in general, and West Africa in particular (Iheduru 2015b).

This introductory chapter describes the research project, its significance and the research question. It highlights the scope of the study, the contributions to the literature, the analytical approach and how the project was developed. The chapter will conclude by highlighting the structure of the book.

The Research Project, the Question and Its Significance

Rethinking Civil Society Regionalism in Africa is an original research project that builds on the critical literature of regionalism, which includes those studies that combine reflectivism and constructivism in the study of regions and regionalism (Hettne et al. 1999, Soderbaum 2002, 2004a, Grant and Soderbaum 2003, Soderbaum and Shaw 2003). The project explores and critically examines the extent to which West African civil society has evolved as an actor in African regionalism with an emphasis on four key *regional attributes* (identities, presence, capacity and impact). The study was first inspired by empirical observations of civil society activities in regional integration programmes in West Africa since the ratification of the 1993 revised Treaty of the Economic Community of West African States (ECOWAS). In that context, it evokes the question: *To what extent and in what ways has regional civil society evolved as an actor in the regionalist activities in West Africa?* The main regionalist activities in this question are specifically focused on two key areas of democratic participation and peacebuilding in regional integration in West Africa. To understand this, the study extensively reviews the existing literature on the role of civil society in regionalism and governance with a focus on Africa (see Chapter 1). The exposition of the previous scholarship allows me to confirm the state of knowledge in this area and to clearly underscore the gaps in the literature filled by this book. These gaps relate to the lack of clarity about the regional actorship of civil society and the empirical treatment of West Africa which has been on the margins of the literature.

In terms of the significance of the study, this book offers new perspectives and empirically enriches the understanding of civil society regionalism, showing the dynamics of wider participation of civil society actors and their contributions in shaping the regionalism of peacebuilding in West Africa. The book represents one of the very few studies that are designed from the context of an African region instead of ignoring the context of the study and prioritise the search for evidence. The emphasis on the African context does not necessarily mean reinforcing the essentiality of Africa's differences without acknowledging its similarity within the world of international relations (Smith 2009). Karren Smith points out that telling African stories is one of the ways of African knowledge production within the study of international relations (Smith 2009). Such stories require affirming the importance of the context to make sense. The complexity of regionalism concepts has consistently compounded the difficulty in appreciating the field of regionalism beyond the limited cycle of its experts (De Lombaerde, et al. (2009). This book moves beyond this limitation by ensuring that civil society regionalism is clearer to researchers, policymakers and laymen/women. As a result, the policy relevance of this project cannot be overemphasised. I have no doubt this book will be useful to African regional organisations, civil society and external actors (both western and non-western). It would help to remind them and deepen their understanding of the historical and continued role of civil society actors in African regionalism. The book will be useful as a source of inspirations for a genuine pan-African role of civil society actors in African integration and development. Overall, based on its focus, one can also affirm its significance to the emerging decolonial ideas about Africa (Ndlovu-Gatsheni 2018) and rethinking of the study of international relations in its regional and global contexts (see Acharya 2014a, 2018, Acharya and Buzan 2019).

The Main Contributions to the Literature

The study contributes significantly to the existing body of knowledge. First, it introduces an analytical framework for the study of regional civil society actors which transcends the dominant tendency of state-centric research on regional integration in Africa. This is an important contribution. For many decades, states have commanded the dominant attention of scholars who study regions and regionalism, particularly in Africa (Iheduru 2015b, Akinyeye 2010). Moreover, the academic study of civil society in regionalism is a very recent development (Hettne et al. 1999, Fioramonti 2015; Iheduru 2003, 2015, Soderbaum 2002, 2004, 2007, 2016a, Godsater and Soderbaum 2011, Godsater 2013, 2015, 2016). Whereas scholars have made attempts to study civil society actors as part of regionalism in Africa, these studies have often tended to downplay the importance of the *regional attributes* of civil society actors. To date, what those studies have provided is a functional typology of civil society organisations in regionalism in Africa. This typology describes civil society as partners, legitimators, resister/counter-hegemonic and manipulators (Godsater and Soderbaum 2011, Fioramonti

2015, Iheduru 2015, Soderbaum 2016a). Unfortunately, the typology does not engage in a deeper interrogation of regional attributes of such civil society actors. Instead of attributing nationally focused civil society movements for regionally active alternatives, this book employs four analytic concepts: identities, presence, capacity and impact to critically reflect on the evolution of regional civil society organisations in the post-1990s West Africa from the context of an ECOWAS regionalism. It also expands the existing debates on civil society regionalism by exploring the experiences of civil society in other world regions. Integrating the four analytic concepts as a guide for the analysis of the empirical chapters is in itself an original contribution to the regional dynamics of civil society in the new regionalism literature.

Another reason the contribution of this book is original is because it focuses on West Africa as a region which has remained largely at the margin of the debate on civil society regionalism. The significance of this is that the initial empirical observations about civil society regionalism were first drawn from West Africa. Before embarking on this research, there has not been a comprehensive study that specifically examined the extent to which key organisations such as WACSOF and WANEP have evolved to influence or shape regionalism in West Africa. The unique feature of this book, which also appears methodological, is that both the analytical framework and West Africa as a region are constitutive in nature. As a result, they interchangeably substantiate each other. Therefore, I can posit that this book is able to draw attention to the key empirical facts that have been overlooked or underplayed in the previous studies. Such lacuna/shortcomings were remedied by situating West Africa at the centre of civil society regionalism for analytical insights.

Overview of the Research Analytical Approach

This research builds on New Regionalism Approach which considers civil society as an actor. Although I consider New Regionalism Approach as plausible, I would argue it is also necessary to reconceptualise its civil society aspect based on the empirical observations of West African civil society context. It is through this understanding that the analytical framework of the book was developed to analyse WACSOF and WANEP. The framework deals with the regional actorship of civil society and is based on a clear understanding of civil society's regional identities, regional presence, regional capacities and societal impact. These analytical concepts are shown in Figure I.1.

As illustrated above, the observation of the West African regional context of civil society is combined with the deduction of the New Regionalism Approach. The study was initially driven by the empirical observation before the New Regionalism Approach was discovered through the exploration of the existing literature. The ideas of identities, presence, capacities and societal impacts of civil society actors in this study emanated first through an inductive process. The initial empirical awareness prompted the author further to uncover if there

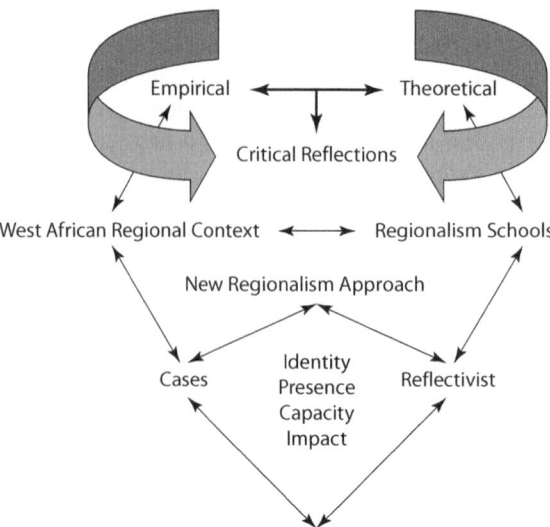

Figure I.1 Contextual illustration of the study. Source: author.

was an existing framework in the literature that could make sense of the evolution of these organisations as actors on the regional levels. In the process, some theoretical ideas were discovered in the regionalism literatures that were closely related to the initial analytic concepts. Although the idea of identities has been used in regionalism literature (Hurrell 1995, Hettne 1999, Soderbaum 2002, 2004, Iheduru 2003, Bello 2011, Checkel 2016), identity has not been included alongside the other concepts which I employ to describe the regional actorship of civil society organisations in West Africa. Second, the idea of regional presence was first inspired through the author's observation, but for a more meaningful interpretation, it was cross-fertilised with the idea of space/levels (macro-meso-micro) in regionalism (Grant and Soderbaum 2003, Soderbaum 2004a, Shaw 2000). The justification for including capacity is to explore the institutional and operational factors that allow civil society actors to engage in various activities in the region. The intent relating to societal impact is to understand the extent to which the two cases have impacted on regionalism in West Africa based on their aspirations. It should be stressed, that these concepts are mainly used as an analytical guide for the development of empirical chapters. In other words, I am interested in how to describe regional identities of these civil society actors, understand their activities across the regional levels, as well as their institutional and operational capacity, and how they impact on regionalism in West Africa. The concepts must be seen in this context, and the aim is to understand the evolution of regional civil society actors in West Africa through the specific organisations analysed in this study. This shared understanding is needed to appreciate the intellectual process of this research.

Development of the Project

Since ECOWAS revised its treaty in 1993, there have been many changes in terms of participation of non-state actors in regional integration. It was during this period that a group of non-governmental organisations in West Africa also began to find a space for their activities beyond their respective states (Iheduru 2003, Olonisakin 2009). Some of these organisations have developed into networks seeking to work with ECOWAS or to lobby to change certain practices on how ECOWAS operates.

This research project is developed based on qualitative methodological techniques to understand the dynamics of civil society in regional integration. The aim of the project is to understand the extent to which these organisations have evolved to act or contribute to regional integration in West Africa. The primary sources of data included observations, ECOWAS treaties, official documents, online documentary evidence, annual reports, policy briefs, newsletters, news articles and a total of 35 semi-structured interviews which were conducted with ECOWAS officials, civil society practitioners, academics and development partners of civil society organisations in West Africa. The study also benefits greatly from secondary sources such as journals and books which also help the researcher to situate the location of the book within the field of regionalism.

According to scholars, civil society groups can be studied as actors in regionalism (Soderbaum 2002, 2004a, Scholte 2015, Fioramonti 2015, Godsater 2015). This project focuses on specific regional civil society organisations rather than to take a broader look at the generality of West African civil society. The historical context of the pan-African origin of West African civil society is also used to provide a contextual background prior to the analysis of the two case studies of WACSOF and WANEP. My intention is that such historical context is necessary, in order to understand the main case studies of this book. The benefits of case studies in social research like this cannot be overemphasised. The case studies method suits the study of regions and regionalism as previous studies in African regionalist programmes have shown (Adedeji 1970, 2004, Adebajo and Rashid 2004, Bedjauoi 2012, Iheduru 2003, 2015b, 2019, Soderbaum 2004, 2007, 2016, Godsater and Soderbaum 2011, Kogbe 2012, Godsater 2013, 2015, 2016, Afadzinu 2015, Zajontz and Leysens 2015). The significance of considering specific cases of civil society actors helps to avoid misleading generalisations of civil society's role in West Africa without delving into the nitty-gritty that defines the boundaries of commonalities and differences among these actors. I have chosen specific organisations even though they may have certain commonalities, but they are also different in terms of their origins, interests, mode of activities across levels as well as how they impact on regionalism in West Africa. These complexities are revealed through empirical findings on both WANEP and WACSOF in the ECOWAS region.

As there is no methodology without its own shortcomings or weaknesses, in developing this project, I constantly reflected on the inherent shortcomings associated with qualitative orientations that rely on the data such as interviews. Data derived from interviews are part of discourse used in perpetuation of powers or influences through the manipulations of words or uses of language in describing or interpreting social facts (Silverman 2011, Bryman 2008, 2016). Because of these intersubjective understandings, I employed aspects of the critical discourse analytic technique in analysing the data used in this study. This intersubjective message that some of these data may carry in them allows me to subject them to scrutiny especially with the use of triangulation techniques – being self-reflective and drawing on multiple sources of data. Especially on the empirical chapter on WANEP where secondary sources are limited, I relied on the alternative perspectives from the interviews with the ECOWAS staff and published reports of external partners to substantiate the analysis. The essence of using multiple sources of data instead of relying on one single source, such as interviews or primary documents is to affirm the validity and reliability of the findings otherwise known as 'trustworthiness and authenticity' (Bryman 2016) in meeting the quality criteria of this qualitative study. These are referred to as 'credibility', 'transferability', 'dependability' and 'confirmability' (Bryman 2016:384). This was duly applied as will be observed later in the development of the chapters.

Organisation of the Book

The introduction provides the background to the study, its rationale, aim, objectives and research question. Chapter 1 presents a detailed critical review of literature on civil society in regionalism, regionalisation and regional governance in Africa. First, it shows that the existing studies, despite their significant contributions to knowledge about regionalism in Africa, have underplayed the importance of regional attributes of civil society as an actor at the regional level. As a result, this book advances an argument for a deeper analytical understanding of regional civil society, underscoring what constitutes civil society actorship in Africa. Second, the review also shows and establishes an empirical gap that West Africa as a region has been at the margin of the regionalism debates when it comes to the study of regional civil society organisations. By filling these important gaps, the study moves the debate further by arguing for a clear analytical framework for making sense of the role of regional civil society actors in West Africa.

Chapter 2 presents the analytical framework of the book. It builds on the reflectivist account of the New Regionalism Approach that acknowledges civil society as an actor (Hettne 1999, Soderbaum 2002, 2004, Grant and Soderbaum 2003, Iheduru 2003). The chapter reconceptualises civil society's aspect of the New Regionalism Approach by suggesting four analytic concepts to analyse the actorship of civil society on the regional levels. Previous studies have created typologies that explain the functions of civil society organisations without uncovering the underlying attributes of some of these actors working at the regional levels. I also draw on such typologies by linking them with regional identities of civil society which is one of the analytic concepts in this study's framework. However, applying it alone cannot help us to understand the dynamics in the evolution of regional civil society actors in West Africa. The chapter provides the initial empirical observations of the West African region (induction) and cross-feeds them with the New Regionalism Approach (deduction), to produce four analytical concepts that undergird the analytical framework of this study. The framework is then used as the guide for the analyses of the case studies.

Chapter 3 is a brief historical context of regional civil society in West Africa that provides the context for the subsequent case-based analyses of the regional civil society organisations examined in the book. This chapter should not be read in isolation from the main case study chapters. Readers will observe that the analytical framework is not applied in this chapter. Because of its contextual purpose, the chapter is primarily meant to aid the understanding of the main case studies. Therefore, it must be seen, as providing a context, not as a separate case study in its own right. The framework is designed to be applied to the case studies. The significance of this chapter is that it clearly shows civil society agency in African regionalism as a continuity of the historical movement of the pan-Africanist movement of solidarity and collective action. The modus operandi of this collective action often depends on the prevailing circumstances of regional order. In the context of West Africa, the current civil society regionalisation cannot be fully isolated from the pan-African struggles that led to the political independence of the modern-day ECOWAS member states.[1] It is acknowledged that historically West African people had a sense of pan-regional identity as a basis for solidarity to promote collective interest against colonial oppression (Obadare 2015). The chapter posits that the post-Cold War civil society movement seeking democratic governance at the national levels also had implication for regional governance in West Africa. Also, the civil wars of Liberia and Sierra Leone helped indirectly to trigger the response of the civil society actors in the region, advocating in favour of human security over regime security of the West African leaders (Iheduru 2003, Olonisakin 2009, Ismail 2011). It is in this context that their involvement in conflict prevention and participation in regional integration could be understood.

In Chapter 4, the first of the case studies provides an analysis of the West African Civil Society Forum (WACSOF), which was established in 2003 for the purpose of democratising ECOWAS. The four analytic concepts discussed earlier are deployed in the analysis. Instead of viewing WACSOF in the context of a functional typology as in previous studies, the analytical framework of this study examines WACSOF based on its action-based regional identity which seeks to democratise regionalism by opening up the space for a wider civil society participation in ECOWAS regional integration. The findings show that the extent to which WACSOF has opened up this space is relatively limited to privileged civil society organisations. This realisation also raises a critical question about the democratic credentials of WACSOF itself. Among other key factors extensively discussed in this chapter, the findings show that although WACSOF may have emerged through the collaboration between ECOWAS Secretariat (Commission) and civil society leaders, it has not evolved as an actor envisioned in its Charter of 2003 which was signed at Accra, Ghana. Part of the explanations for this concerns the top-down approach in forming WACSOF's identity which consequently impacted negatively on its ability to build an active regional presence. This is also evidenced by a waning regional capacity that has resulted in its limited contributions to regional integration as per its quest for a wider democratic participation in regionalism. It is against this backdrop that stakeholders have been calling for the revival of WACSOF as an actor so that it can take its rightful place in regional integration in West Africa.

Chapter 5 focuses on the second case study, the West African Network for Peacebuilding (WANEP), using the four analytic concepts mentioned above to make sense of WANEP as a regional civil society actor in West Africa. This chapter also looks beyond the existing typology of civil society by examining the evolution of WANEP as an actor. Although WANEP was led by two West African citizens, the findings show that the general inspiration behind WANEP at the time might have benefitted from the former Secretary General of the United Nations, Boutros Boutros-Ghali's *Agenda for Peace*. Reason being that it was in this *Agenda for Peace* document that the idea of peacebuilding was first popularised internationally. In a strike difference from WACSOF, the two pioneers of WANEP seemed to have realised the essence of local support. They began WANEP as a form of conversations aimed at socialising a diverse number of groups of non-governmental organisations working for peace into a regional network under one regional secretariat located in Ghana. Although the 15 national chapters have a degree of autonomy, the regional secretariat provides the leadership, coordination and oversights of the chapters across the ECOWAS region. I argue that the bottom-up approach of regional identity formation had a positive impact on the trajectory of WANEP in the region. However, there are other key factors that need to be considered in relation to this identity factor. These include the opportunity that peacebuilding offers to civil society organisations as partners in problem-solving activities of the region. Instead of being radical or counter-hegemonic in relation to the regional institutions of ECOWAS, the stakeholders saw WANEP as a partner and promoter of regional norms in the area of conflict prevention. Coupled with its mode of identity formation, it was possible for WANEP to draw on local and external support to build an active regional presence. Peacebuilding was indeed a scarce commodity at the time. This also explains why WANEP has been able to evolve as a partner in regional integration and opened up the opportunities to small groups of actors in peacebuilding to participate in regionalism through the early warning programmes of the regional network of WANEP. The findings show that there is a great degree of civil society participation in regionalism of peacebuilding in West Africa. Although this is a tentative conclusion, a further study in this area will further undertake the research to determine whether we can aptly describe regionalism of peacebuilding in West Africa as a form of democratic regionalism without counterhegemony.

The last chapter provides the concluding remarks. It summarises the whole argument of the book and draws attention to the emerging challenges and opportunities in the post-ECOWAS Vision 2020. It explains the findings of the study, the contributions of the study to the literature, the limitations, the location of the research within the study of regions and civil society regionalisation, and the potential areas for future research projects.

Note

1 ECOWAS comprises 15 member states, namely Benin, Burkina Faso, Cape Vade, Cote d'Ivoire, The Gambia, Ghana, Guinea Bissau, Guinea Conakry, Liberia, Mali, Niger, Nigeria, Senegal, Sierra Leone and Togo.

1   The Making of Civil Society in African Regions and Regionalisms

Introduction

Many scholars have attempted to explain how civil society works in regions above the state, in the state and beyond the state. Despite their serious commitment, none can be said to have comprehensively captured, fully analysed and concluded what civil society regionalism is and what is not, what constitutes the actorship of civil society organisations at the regional level and clearly explicate what societal impacts have emerged from their social interactions within a given region. It is no longer news to hear about civil society in regionalism, what is rather new in the context of this book is the serious analysis that presents the extent to which civil society organisations have evolved as actors and the impact they make in the region such as West Africa.

This chapter therefore deals with the extent to which regional civil society organisations have evolved as actors in regionalist activities in West Africa. The notion of civil society actors in this study does not imply those organisations that are nationally focused or restricted operationally within their domestic national spheres. 'Regional civil society actors' in this book refer to those civil associations, professional bodies, not-for-profit interest groups, youth associations, women associations, all sorts of non-violent nongovernment organisations, etc. that do work beyond their national boundaries. Their organisations' aspirations or visions are in tandem with inherent issues of regionalisms or regional integration in Africa.

The chapter looks at civil society in African regionalism from a critical perspective and interrogates the relevant studies in the regionalism literature. It demonstrates that the majority of the studies on civil society regionalism in Africa have tilted towards Southern Africa, paying much less attention to an important region such as West Africa. Considering the strengths and limits of the current literature, the chapter argues that a clear framework for regional civil society analysis in Africa is still missing, and as a result, it is highly important to offer one in enriching the regionalism literature on regional civil society. It exposes the academic pitfalls despite the notable contributions of the New Regionalism Approach. As a result, this chapter argues that there are broadly two important academic gaps in the study of civil society regionalism in Africa. One is analytical and the other is empirical.

DOI: 10.4324/9781003257288-2

The first gap is concerned with the analytical aspect of the civil society regionalism literature. It is important to shed light on this claim in relation to the New Regionalism Approach. It can be succinctly stated that the New Regionalism Approach is a theoretical school of a small group of reflectivist writers on regionalism that emerged at the end of the Cold War (Hettne, et al. 1999, Hettne 2005, Hettne and Söderbaum 2000, Grant and Soderbaum 2003, Soderbaum 2002, 2004a, 2007, 2016a, Soderbaum and Shaw 2003, Iheduru 2003, 2013, 2015b, 2016, 2019, Hurrell 1995, Fioramonti and Matheis 2016, Fawcett 2005, Fioramonti 2014, 2015). Their work popularised civil society as co-actors in shaping and reshaping regionalism around the world. Due to the variance in the ontological views of rationalism and reflectivism, the reflectivsit notion of civil society contrasts the rationalist theoretical positions, such as neorealism, neoliberal institutionalism and the functionalist theory of regional integration (Grant and Soderbaum 2003). The functionalists emphasise the pre-eminence of states in the study of regional integration, whereas these reflectivists are critical scholars who draw our attention to the role of civil society in regionalism. Despite the contribution of these reflectivists, especially those who have written on Africa within the last three decades, I argue that there is more to learn analytically about regional civil society in Africa. The extent to which regional civil society organisations have evolved in West Africa is not yet analytically explored. In engaging in such explorations, it may be necessary to have an idea of what makes a given regional civil society organisation an actor. In that sense, an analytical framework may be required as a guide. This must not be seen as a prescription.

The second gap is empirical, as the study of regional civil society in West Africa has remained at the margin of debates in the regionalism literature. This study fills these two gaps. While acknowledging the proponents of the New Regionalism Approach for their recognition of civil society, I also argue that their marginal focus on West Africa has denied the scholarly community an important source of theory building for our understanding of regional civil society actors in Africa. The chapter therefore proceeds in line with the above argument by exploring wider, though brief, perspectives of civil society in regionalism, clarifying the key concepts in regionalism, demonstrating how the scholarship of civil society regionalism in Africa has developed since 1990s. It exposes significant gaps in the existing scanty literature on Africa to justify the originality and significant intervention of this study.

Regionalism and the Advent of Civil Society

The importance of regionalist schemes in international relations has been affirmed extensively in the literature, tracing the first wave of regionalism to the post-Second World War (Hettne 1999, Akinyeye 2010, Bach 2016). Like other scholars, Bach adduces that the first wave was shaped by the Cold War on the template of development programme for the developing world (2016:1). However, the mode of practice of these regional interactions was state-centric in nature. As such, civil society was not prioritised as a significant actor (Hettne 1999, Soderbaum 2002).

Other scholars also posit that the post-1945 order marked 'the growing appreciation of the importance of regional interactions in fostering cordial relations between states and the promotion of commerce, based on shared interest in the pursuit of economic development' (Shaw et al. 2003:196). Bjorn Hettne acknowledges this upsurge in regionalist interests in this putative era but also observes that 'regional integration was not a very fashionable subject, having declined from a rather prominent position in the 1950s and 1960s' (Hettne 1999:7). Broadly speaking, the general literature has classified the above era as a period of old regionalism (Shaw 2000). Soderbaum notes that 'Many regional projects and regional organisations were initiated during the era of old regionalism (1950s–1970s) but were then renewed or re-inaugurated during the new regionalism in the 1980s and the 1990s (often under a new name or with an expanded membership)' (2016b:17). The era of new regionalism broadened the scope of regionalism and acknowledged the roles of non-state actors such as civil society (Shaw 2000, Iheduru 2003, Acharya 2014a). This therefore points to the location of scholarship on civil society regionalism in the revived phase of regionalism in the late 1980s under the label of new regionalism literature (Hurrell 1995, Hettne 1999, Shaw 2000).

Since then, there has been a significant body of literature about civil society participation in regional policymaking and relations with other regional organisations and schemes around the world (Fioramonti 2015). The EU, particularly, has received considerable scholarly attention about civil society participation in its policymaking, most especially in relation to its democratic deficit discourses (Kohler-Koch and Quittkat 2009, Kohler-Koch 2009, Gracia 2015). It is not surprising if so little is accounted for in African regionalism about civil society, let alone the marginal treatment of West Africa in civil society regionalism. Part of the reasons for this is not that West African civil society regionalism is less important as one may assume. This should rather be looked at as part of the broader structural asymmetric relation between the Global North and the Global South in terms of knowledge production (Acharya 2016a, Ndlovu-Gatsheni 2018). The EU has historically remained a dominant pointer in the study of regional integration. The context of its civil society scholarship so far reflects the institutional complexities of the EU itself (Gracia 2015). Spini adds that 'Insofar as it needed to reassess its nature as a fully fledged polity, the official bodies of the EU have reaffirmed the role of civil society, especially as a remedy for the much-lamented democratic deficit' (2011:26). The literature has looked at civil society participation in the EU (Armstrong and Gilson 2011, Spini 2011, Kohler-Koch 2009, Garcia 2015). Those studies do not necessarily seek to understand the key attributes that make civil society a regional actor. This might suggest a gap in the existing literature on the European civil society regionalism. I am not studying the evolution of civil society in the EU. Rather, the aim of this study is specific to Africa and about the lived experiences of regional civil society organisations in West Africa. This requires acknowledging the contexts and everyday experiences of the people and their regions.

Therefore, the agency of citizens and their organised groups in regionalist initiatives in Africa is one important area of study that is still underexplored in the regionalism literature (Fioramonti 2015). It has become a common academic practice to study regionalism in Africa from the perspectives of the state-centric ontology (Asobie 2010, Akinyeye 2010). The structural influence of states and intergovernmental institutions has predominantly dictated how scholars conceive African regions, the underpinning ideas of regions-making as well as their governance (Soderbaum 2016a, Godsater 2016). This is part of the reasons we cannot overstate that some of the regionalist initiatives in Africa today have been dominated by state and intergovernmental organisations. Because states exist and do influence the structure of regions does not necessarily imply that citizens and their organised groups are less important in the contemporary regionalism in Africa (Iheduru 2003, 2015b, Fioramonti 2015). Many critical scholars in the regionalism literature have underscored the need to focus on other actors beyond the states. In a sense, non-state actors like civil society groups can no longer be ignored due to the contribution they have made to region-making and governance in Africa over the last three decades (Iheduru 2003, 2015, Soderbaum 2016a, Fioramonti 2015, Scholte 2015).

Situating Civil Society in the Revival of Regionalisms

The notion of civil society as a regionalising actor is associated with a post-Cold War regionalist phenomenon. Since the reviving surge in practice and theory dated from the mid-1980s, the field of regionalism has been associated with broadening architecturally and theoretically (Hettne 1999, Shaw 2000). This revival was not restricted to a particular region of the world. Rather, it was indeed global in scope (Asante 1997, Hettne et al. 1999, 2000, Bach 2016, Grant and Soderbaum 2003, Soderbaum 2003, 2004, 2009, 2016a, 2016b, Godsater 2016, Fioramonti 2015, Soderbaum and Shaw 2003). Hence, regionalism has continued to manifest itself globally in both policymaking and academic circles (Grant and Soderbaum 2003, Soderbaum and Shaw 2003, Acharya 2014a, 2018). In this era, the European Union was deepened and expanded in scope (Soderbaum 2003:1). The Economic Community of West African States (ECOWAS) was transformed and adopted a revised treaty in 1993 to broaden the ECOWAS regionalism (ECOWAS Commission 1993). A new treaty of the East African Community (EAC) was drafted and signed in 1999 to provide a broader policy base for the reinvigorated regionalism in East Africa (EAC 1999). The Southern African region witnessed a transformation from the Southern African Development Coordinating Conference (SADCC), founded in 1980, into the Southern African Development Community (SADC) in 1992 (SARS 2017), including the transformation of the OAU to AU in 2002.

Traditionally, these regional organisations and their regionalist architectures are clearly different from the post-World War II regional economic commissions of the United Nations system.[1] Unlike the UN regionalist systems, these regionalist initiatives in Africa were led by the states and the African people. Therefore, the regionalist initiatives by states and involvement of other actors such as businesses and civil society have become the means used not only to respond to the myriad effects of globalisation of the post-Cold War (Asante 1997, Van Langenhove 2012). But they have also been mainstreamed into the socio-economic and political aspects of governance where regional centres are being produced, challenged and becoming new units of cooperation and balance of power among various actors (Asante 2016, Adebajo 2016). It is in the realisation of these new forms of cooperation for addressing security and development challenges that one can see a new movement of civil society activities and interest groups (Adejumobi 2016). These groups often identify themselves with the regions and engage in governance issues, acting alongside state actors in regional and global affairs (Armstrong and Gilson 2011).

For Amitav Acharya, regions and regionalism have grown to the levels of sharing practices of regional schemes and actorship (Acharya 2012). Acharya (2018:22) further notes that 'Regionalism has been a key channel for articulating the voices and concerns of weaker actors including non-Western states'. It has become 'a major site of agency in constructing the global order' (Acharya 2018:22). The mainstream conception of agency might have been influenced by materialist interests. The rethinking of agency at the regional level also pays serious attention to the ideational expression, refining or construction or reconstitution of the existing international order (Acharya 2018). This often comes in the form of diffusion of norms (of which civil society is a part) and the spread of regional institutions, especially from the Global South (Acharya 2018, Haastrup 2013b, Yukawa 2018). In the scheme of this, civil society organisations are also taking active parts (Iheduru 2003, 2015b, Godsater and Soderbaum 2011, Godsater 2013a, 2013b, Kohler-Koch 2009, Gracia 2015).

Observably, the ideational significance of regionalism cannot be isolated from the increasing challenges globalisation poses to the traditional Westphalian state systems. The need for region also resonates with the decline in the ability of the states to address the known and the emerging multifarious transnational issues on their own terms (Langenhove 2012, Acharya 2018). This acknowledges the role of private sectors and civil society in this context (Iheduru 2003, 2015a, Adejumobi 2016, Acharya 2018). Global and regional issues include growing economic interdependence, spreading of democratic norms (Stoddard 2017), regional and international human rights regimes (Alabi 2016, Khadiagala 2016), dealing with climate change, addressing cross-border health risks/spreading of contagious diseases such as Ebola, COVID-19, cybercrimes, proliferations of nuclear arms, transnational organised crime such as terrorism, human trafficking, arms trafficking, drug trafficking, and so on (Shaw et al. 2003, Shaw 2016, Bach 2004, 2016). Regionalism has been used for the diffusion of democratic norms (Haastrup 2013b, Genna and Hiroi 2015, Soderbaum 2016a, 2016b, Acharya 2012, Stoddard 2017) as well as numerous economic and social issues that include promotion of regional education policy, regional energy projects, culture, sports, tourism and all sorts of regionalist programmes of cross-border configurations (Asante 2016). Without being state-centric, the evolutions of these regionalist developmental issues are not bereft of involvement of civil society actors in their transnational dimensions. What is varied contextually, however, is how these regional civil society movements evolve as actors in cognisance of the diversities of their regional activities.

In the present time, regional spheres are already integral platforms for both local and international actors in creating order or disorder (Acharya 2014a). It is unlikely today to deny the footprints of regionalisms and activities of civil society in Africa and other parts of the world (Fioramonti 2015, Iheduru 2015, 2016, Soderbaum 2016a, 2016b, Acharya 2018). More importantly, as scholars argue, regionalism may have become a global phenomenon, yet, we should also be aware that it is not automatically a priori meant to be positive (Acharya 2012, Soderbaum 2016:2). According to Soderbaum (2002), regionalism can be good or bad, and so, cannot be uncritically accepted as a positive (or negative) project. The normative responsibility of civil society is an integral component in this scheme. It could potentially reinforce the societal input depending on the space for participation and the responses by the traditional drivers of regionalism. In that view, regionalism like any other project or idea, whether led by states or non-state actors, may either lead to a positive outcome or a negative outcome (Soderbaum 2002, 2016). Therefore, whether regionalism would become positive or negative, irrespective of who drives it, largely depends on the intent and capacity of actors as well as other structural forces affecting a given regionalist initiative. This could be in Africa or elsewhere.

The growing trends of regionalist schemes in Africa are not bereft of proliferations of these regional civil society groups (Acharya 2018, Iheduru 2015b, Godsater 2016). Civil society increasingly manifests itself beyond individual African states towards actorship in the regions by seeking to influence the existing dominant structures of many of the African regional organisations, such as the African Union (AU), the ECOWAS, SADC, EAC, the Intergovernmental Authority on Development (IGAD) and the Economic Community of Central African States (ECCAS). Outside of Africa, examples include the Association of Caribbean States (ACS),[2] Caribbean Community (CARICOM),[3] Organisation of Eastern Caribbean States (OECS),[4] the EU, the Eurasian Economic Union, MERCOSUR in South America and the Association of Southeast Asian Nations (ASEAN).

The context in and the motivation for which African regional civil society began to evolve was not the same as in the EU, although the EU has been of great support in enhancing the capacity of some of these civil society organisations in Africa. Because civil society is integral to critical understanding of regionalism, Acharya argues that 'a broader framework for explaining the evolution and judging the performance of regionalism is warranted; one cannot judge them in terms of whether and to what extent they conform to the EU or any other single model or integration' (2016:123). Notable scholars have acknowledged this and have even warned against associating with the mistaken representations of European regional schemes as models, or the historical root of regionalism (Acharya 2012, 2016, Haastrup 2013b, Soderbaum 2009, 2016a, Yukawa 2018).

We should always be aware that one cannot isolate the contexts that produced regionalism or regionalist projects, in order to appreciate the global diversities of regions and actors that drive them. The same contextual diversity is as well important in understanding the evolution of civil society actors at the regional levels. For instance, in Africa, a large percentage of works on African regionalisms or regional integration in the past have tended to glorify the success of European integration projects (Asante 1997). This explains the tendency that pays less attention to the contexts that produced regionalisms in Africa whether in terms of initiatives or the evolution of actors driving or resisting a given regionalist initiative on the continent (Haastrup 2013b). Soderbaum called for rethinking of the history of regionalism and the tendency of taking a particular region or a regional organisation as exclusively unique, or what they call *sui generis* of the European Union (2016a, 2016b). In her comparative study of the AU and the EU, Haastrup (2013b) acknowledges that many similarities exist in their institutional architecture as well as differences in terms of the motives of the two organisations. One of the illustrative examples cited is the Economic Social and Cultural Council of the African Union (ECOSOCC) which resembles the European Economic and Social Committee (EESC) (Haastrup 2013b:790). She explains further that both ECOSOCC and EESC are forums for including 'civil society' in the governance process of the regional organisations' (Haastrup 2013b:790). For the EU, the EESC is 'a consultative space for special interests groups, particularly trade unions and employers organisations', while the AU's ECOSOCC mirrors the United Nations' design and serves as 'the voice for civil society within the AU from diverse sectors in Africa and the African diaspora' (Haastrup 2013b:790). She also draws attention to pan-Africanism that provides an ideological base for driving regional integration in Africa, whereas the EU's experience is based on economic cooperation. To understand the EU's external role, Haastrup urges scholars to look beyond 'EU integration perspective', by paying 'attention to the international environment, prioritises knowledge of the local environment, and support local ownership as the cornerstone of the EU's Africa policies' (Haastrup 2013b:798). Based on the inter-regional framework that defines the EU and Africa relation, she concludes that the EU is seen 'as a mentor to Africa. It is in implementing mentorship that the EU can serve as a model for regionalism outside Europe' (Haastrup 2013b:798).

Another argument was also developed by Yukawa (2018) in assessing the trajectory of European integration through the eyes of the ASEAN. The conclusion shows that while the EU is considered to have an advanced form of integration, it cannot be a model for ASEAN in the sense that the two organisations' overall intents and modus operandi are not the same. So, it would be wrong to see ASEAN as a failure because it does not follow the regionalist path of the EU and likewise for the EU in the eyes of the ASEAN (Yukawa 2018). Since civil society is integral to this regionalism discourse, we can also relate this to how civil society is studied in the EU regionalism which is context-specific to the EU's democratic institutionalism (Gracia 2015, Kohler-Koch 2009). The discourse of democratising regionalism or regional integration is also applicable to the experiences of African civil society groups. However, these organisations tend to engage in problem solving activities relating to peace, conflict prevention or human security to define their aspirations on the regional levels.

Without a shared understanding of terms, reaching a common understanding or interpretation of a contextual issue may be nearly impossible. This is a problem of regionalism scholarship and one should not expect less when thinking or rethinking civil society regionalism. One particular factor is in definitional conflations of regionalism and regional integration (see Acharya 2012), which seems to have differing perspectives on regions, the role of the states and other societal actors (Van Langenhove 2012). Sometimes, scholars use the two terms interchangeably. There is no doubt that the term 'regionalism' can be 'ambiguous' (Godsater 2016:12) and contested conceptually like the meaning of regions.

Before proceeding, it is necessary to clarify some of the concepts in use in this study and their shared meaning. To understand civil society regionalism or regional civil society as an actor, it is important to show this understanding. The term regionalism becomes complex as an idea when scholars interchange or misplace its intended conceptual meaning. Regional integration in its orthodox context does not seek the same goal as regionalism (Acharya 2012). Both regionalism and regional integration may interweave but they do not imply the same thing even when they are contextualised in relation to civil society. For Asobie (2010:25), 'integration means non-coerced coalescence, or voluntary union of previously independent entities'. The entities Asobie has in mind here are states, to be clear with his centric nuance. For Hettne, 'Regional integration is traditionally seen as harmonisation of trade policies leading to deeper economic integration and with political integration as possible future result' (Hettne 2000: xxi). The notion of trade harmonisation in *Hettnean* enunciation here is also laden with state-centrism. According to Bach (2016:6), 'Regionalism can account for processes of regional integration through sovereignty pooling but … also for groupings that … conceive region-building as sovereignty enhancement'. One needs no haste in inferring that sovereignties in Bach's explanations are sovereignties of the states. However, Soderbaum (2016a:13) has noted that 'Regionalism represents the body of ideas, values and policies that are aimed at creating a region, or it can mean a type of world order'. As a body of ideas, regionalism could bring into perspectives various actors' intentions depending on the given ontology. This sounds persuasive in a sense. For Acharya, two major differences between regional integration and regionalism are succinctly given below:

> First, integration by definition implies loss of sovereignty, voluntary or through pressure. Regionalism does not. This does not make regionalism less important, as some suggest, but it does call for different concepts and approaches to the study of the phenomena … [Second], [i]ntegration studies have always been heavily influenced by the EU's history and experience. The founding theories of integration studies, especially neofunctionalism and transactionalism were drawn heavily from the early life of what is called the EU today.
>
> (2012:12)

Thinking through the above perspective will imply that regionalism may mean different things to different people. One can rightly observe that many of the past studies on African regions or integration in Africa have drawn on the idea of regional integration, rather than regionalism (Asante 1997, Alabi 2016, Akinyeye et al. 2010, Imodu and Igbatayo 2010, Kizito and Patrick 2014, Thonke and Spliid 2012). And because regional integration is narrow in scope, it does not allow a broader space to account for civil society as would be applicable in the broader understanding of regionalism as an ideational tool and as a project. Such analytical perspectives are embedded in the mainstream schools of thoughts of African regionalisms which have progressively resulted in making the contextual realities of actors such as civil society in African regionalism more complex to understand. For them, Africa or West Africa is taken as an object. To make this clearer, the next section interrogates new regionalism in Africa as a part of the post-Cold War global regional waves and exposes the objectification of African ideas of regionalism and perceptions of African actors.

The New Regionalism in Africa as a Post-Cold War Phenomenon

Like other regions, the end of the Cold War had a profound impact on regionalism studies in Africa including views about civil society. A wide range of perspectives on regions and regionalism across the world became evident within academia and in policymaking communities (Asante 1997, Hettne et al. 1999, 2000, Hettne 2005, Hettne and Soderbaum 2000, Soderbaum and Shaw 2003, Grant and Soderbaum 2003, Adedeji 2004, Adebajo 2004, Bach 2004, 2016, Langenhove 2004, Iheduru 2003, 2015, Haastrup 2014a, 2013a, Bøås et al. 2003, Soderbaum 2004, 2007, 2016a, 2016b, Buzan 2003, Akinyeye et al. 2010, Godater and Soderbaum 2011, Godsater 2013, 2015, 2016, Engel et al. 2016, Borzel and Risse 2016, Acharya 2014a, 2014, 2016, 2017, Fawsett 2005, Fioramonti et al. 2015). However, the bulk of such perspectives on African regions and regionalism have focused more on states at the expense of other actors such as civil society organisations, and external actors, despite the new theoretical sensitivity to the multiplicity of actors in regionalist schemes (Adebajo and Rashid 2004, Adedeji 2004, Asante 1997). Some of these studies, especially those with critical perspectives, have given us insights to show that the actors that make and unmake regions are not only states (Hettne et al. 1999, 2000, Soderbaum and Shaw 2003, Grant and Soderbaum 2003, Iheduru 2003, 2015, Langenhove 2004, Godater and Soderbaum 2011, Godsater 2013, 2015, Fioramonti 2015, Scholte 2015). It is in these broader scopes that civil society agency is acknowledged in the manifestation of the popular will against the exploitation of the capitalist order in the age of globalisation (Hettne et al. 1999, 2000, Soderbaum and Shaw 2003, Fioranmoti 2015, Iheduru 2003, 2015b, Godsater 2013, 2015, 2016). One of the key arguments in favour of civil society agency that is attributed to the new regionalism scholars is the extension of Polanyi's ideas on the political role that civil society movement plays in resisting the capitalist order in favour of the people (Polanyi 1957). Commenting on how this idea gained currency, Soderbaum informs us that

> Key theorists in the New Regionalism Approach (NRA) camp such as Bjorn Hettne and James Mittleman build on Karl Polanyi's ideas about the polit-ical role of civil society as a means for the weak and the poor to protect themselves against the exploitative market forces in the context of economic globalisation. In doing so, they emphasise the counter-hegemonic and trans-formative role of regional civil society fulfilled by groups such as pro-democ-racy forces, the women's movement and the environmentalists.
>
> (2016a:133)

Despite the appreciative responses of scholars such as Fredrik Soderbaum, Iheduru Okechukwu, Andrew Grant, Timothy Shaw, Lorenzo Fioramonti, Jan Art Scholte, Andréa Godsater, Zajontz and Leysens and others on the study of civil society at the regional level in Africa, the literature on civil society still remains at the margins of the debate, in comparison to those that focus on states in Africa (Navarro 2010, Dokubo 2010, Imodu and Igbatayo 2010, Akinyeye et al. 2010). This is probably due to the dominant influence of the mainstream and rationalist theories that have maintained the primacy of the African states as the start, the master-planners and determinants of what counts as real regionalist programmes in Africa. However, it is important to critically reflect on the historical role of the organised citizens in the African regionalist projects (Adedeji 1970, Asante 2016, Obadare 2015). Such a state-centric dominance of how regions and regionalisms are studied in Africa is not limited to Africa. It is an epistemic portrayal of the prevailing structural order dominated by the Westphalian states (see Fioramonti et al. 2015). Taking such state-centric ordering without reflective awareness of other actors, such as civil society, would imply a partial perspective in theoris-ing African regions and regionalist initiatives. It is important to acknowledge the significant role of each of the actors in the context of regionalism in Africa. In the new regionalism school, these actors are referred to as states, civil society, the market and the external actors (Hettne et al. 1999, 2000, Soderbaum 2002, 2004a).

The new regionalism scholars have made a significant contribution to civil society research at the regional level. Some of these works seem to reflect a growing importance of civil society as an actor. I would argue that there is a need to also pay attention to the regional attributes of civil society actorship. In addi-tion, West African experience of regional civil society dynamics has been on the margins of the regionalism debates. Being the persistent voice in the new region-alism school on non-state actors in West Africa, Okechukwu Iheduru observes that

> Regionalisation from below spawned by 'popular' civil society and local organised private sector groups indicates the possibility of bridging the

democracy deficit that has been the bane of previous eras of regionalism in West Africa and for fostering novel forms of regional cooperation.

(Iheduru 2003:56 and 64)

What motivated regional civil society actors to go regional in West Africa is as important as what civil society groups do at the regional level, the interest they promote when they conduct their activities, and the impact that can be attributed to those activities. In their individual context, all these are important, and it is vital to gain a greater understanding of them. To say there are numerous works on national civil society movements in Africa is factually undisputable (Baker 2006, Obadare 2013, 2014, 2015, Bratton 1994, 1989, Kasfir 1998, Klandermans, Roefs and Olivier 2001, Landsberg 2006, Lewis 2002, Mamattah 2013, Mercer 2002, Obono 2015, Tagola 2015, Adejumobi 2004, Hearn 2001). For clarity, they are not the focus of this study. Rather, the preoccupation is directed at the lacuna in the literature on civil society actors at the regional level. Soderbaum recently mentions that

> Another limitation of a conventional understanding (and conceptualisation of civil society is related to the notion that civil society operates and consolidates on a 'national' basis (i.e. state-civil society interaction within the nation-state). Such state-centrism needs to be circumvented to escape the Western bias and provide a perspective beyond the nation-state.

> (2016a:135)

This chapter cannot overemphasise this point, as the concept of regional civil society itself is relatively new in the literature. This study transcends the notion of civil society operating within the territorial boundary of a nation-state towards a regional perspective of civil society. For now, the notion of regional civil society is still very new in the African context, owing to the limited literature on the subject in West Africa. One special exception is the continued dedication of Okechukwu Iheduru, who has made empirical contributions to the policy role of organised business entities and associations (Iheduru 2012, 2015a, 2018, 2019). Despite this, there is still a lacuna in the literature on how the so-called regional civil society organisations have evolved and the constitutive elements that qualify them as actors in African regionalism. This will call for a clear understanding of civil society actors across the regional spatial levels. The extant works seem to underplay the spatial levels of these actors and instead prioritise a functional typology that views civil society as 'partner', legitimiser' 'counter-hegemonic force' and 'manipulator' (Fioramonti et al. 2015, Godsater and Soderbaum 2011, Iheduru 2015b, 2015a). While this typology may serve its purpose, it does not offer a framework underlying the regional attributes of the so-called civil society actors. How this typology has been framed is discussed later in the chapter. It is important to clarify the idea of regions as a precursor to the understanding of regional civil society.

Understanding Region to Understand Regional Civil Society

It is near impossible to make a clearer sense of regional civil society without a demonstrated understanding of regions. It is important to shed light on the perception of a region in relation to civil society. In the general literature, the conceptual understanding of a region or regions is a contested one (Hurrell 1995, Godsater 2016). Andrew Hurrell posits that 'there are no natural regions, and definitions of "region" and indicators of "regionness" vary according to the particular problem or question under investigation' (Hurrell 1995:38). For Van Langenhove (2012:14), a region 'is a discursive tool'. A 'region' as a concept has remained unsettled for several decades. Writing about West Africa as a region in 1970, Adebayo Adedeji noted as follows:

> West Africa is not a precise geographical expression, and has no generally accepted definition. One geographer has defined it very broadly as the whole of the area lying west of the boundary between Nigeria and the Cameroun Republic; this would include 19 different countries and several islands.
>
> (1970:214)

If West Africa is seen as a region, it cannot be conceptually accepted as given. For instance, in 1961, the United Nations Economic Commission for Africa (UNECA) adopted broadly the above definition of the West African region, but the islands were not included (Adedeji 1970:214). It is further noted that West Africa as a geographical region of states is a post-colonial and modern creation (Adedeji 2003:22). The idea of region through its multidisciplinary understanding is diverse and fragmented (Van Langenhove 2012:22–23). Also, in October 1945, the Fifth Pan-African Congress held in Manchester, England, called for the 'establishment of a West African Economic Union'. As such, for the congress participants, West Africa meant the British West Africa comprising the territories of Nigeria, Ghana (then Gold Coast), Sierra Leone and the Gambia, which were all British colonies (Adedeji 1970, 2004, Bach 2016). This is not surprising as the conference was predominantly English-speaking (Adedeji 2004). In contrast, before independence (until 1958), the French view of West Africa was premised on what they called French West Africa comprising eight colonies: Mali (then French Sudan), Benin (then Dahomey), French Guinea (now Guinea-Conakry), Cote d'Ivoire, Burkina Faso (then Upper Volta) Niger, Mauritania and Senegal (Adedeji 2004, Bach 2003). No wonder why scholars contest on the meaning of regions, and I think Andreas Godsater is right when he adds that 'the region is constantly contested and renegotiated by different types of actors in a dynamic process of change' (Godsater 2016:11).

Building on the above, there continued to be a growing interest among scholars on how regions are studied (Van Langenhove 2012, Carter and Pasquier 2010, Soderbaum 2004). When we think within the fields of international relations and international political economy, a single universally acceptable definition of region is contentious (Mattheis 2017:37). This contestation is a function of ontological and epistemological orientations, especially between the rationalist thinkers and their reflectivists counterparts (Soderbaum 2004a, 2016a, 2016b, Fioramonti 2015, Godsater 2016). If there is a divergent understanding of region from ontological terms, one should not be shocked about the potential disagreement in understanding regional civil society as an actor because under-standing of regional civil society is predicated on understanding of regions within their contextual peculiarities. For instance, scholars in human geography or politi-cal sociology may have a contrary explanation of territoriality and de-territoriality of regions. Carter and Pasquier, who have taken a political sociological perspec-tive to understand regions, note:

> the region is therefore not viewed as 'unbounded', but as a political space whose multiple frontiers (regulatory, representational) are in a constant pro-cess of being produced and re-produced—including their scope and meaning.
> (2010:287)

What appears prevalent among scholars of regionalism, despite the conceptual contention of the scholars of human geography on ontological and epistemological grounds, is perhaps the constructivist notion which considers regions as not given (Bøås et al. 2003, Soderbaum 2016a, Fioramonti 2015, Van Langenhove 2012). While Carter and Pasquier have a reservation about the de-territoriality of regions, at least they concur that regions are not necessarily passive. For them, regions are subjects – a political space that can be considered as the unit of analysis:

> Studying strategic action of the region as a space for politics is thus not just to study what goes on in the region but to study a variety of regulatory spaces and arenas in which regional actors act.
> (Carter and Pasquier 2010:289)

Carter and Pasquier (2010) may have indirectly conceived regions to have prior existence. The social construction of regions in the new regionalism variants shows that regions do not exist before the actors. It is the activities of actors that give birth to regions (Soderbaum 2016a, Acharya 2012, Godsater 2016). Bøås, Merchand and Shaw posit that 'Regions are not static but changing continu-ously' (2003:204). According to Lorenzo Fioramonti, 'Regions without citizens are unlikely to stand the test of time, especially in times of crises' (Fioramonti 2015:2). Taken as such, according to Hurrell, regions, regionalism and region-alisation are conceptually connected, and they can be ambiguous (1995:38–40). Another closely related notion about civil society regionalism can be linked with the idea of regionalisation which has to do with intensified interactions of various actors (state and non-state actors) in building and management of regions (Hettne 1999, Shaw 2000, Fioramonti 2015, Kochler 2012, Soderbaum 2016a, 2016b, Godsater 2016). Van Langenhove sees 'regionalisation as a project performed by actors that drive region-building' (2012:18–19). These actors comprise states and non-states. It has also been observed that the actors in the process tend to win or lose in regionalist projects (Iheduru 2015a, Soderbaum 2016a). Borzel and Risse posit that regionalisation deals with 'transnational relations involving states and non-state actors' (2016:8). For Soderbaum, within the context of regionalisation, regions may be subject to manipulation by the actors involved, whether in the general idea of regionalism or regional governance (2016a:10). So, civil society's involvement in regionalism, regionalisation or regional governance does not automatically translate into a positive outcome (Scholte 2015). Civil society actors, like any other actors, could be manipulated to become forces for good in the region or be sources of evils or 'plunderers' in regionalist projects (Soderbaum 2007, Fioramonti 2015, Scholte 2011, 2015).

The constructive and inter-subjective understanding of regional and regional agency cannot be taken as a given. As a result, this study has focused on civil society, one of the important actors in African regions and regionalism, in order to understand the extent to which some of these civil society organisations have evolved to act in regionalist activities in West Africa. The next section provides a further analysis of this.

Analysing Civil Society in African Regionalism

Civil society involvement in regional schemes generally, and particularly in Africa, is often seen as a by-product of the post-Cold War phenomena, mostly associated with new regionalism (Soderbaum and Shaw 2003, Hettne 2003, Bøås et al. 2003, Soderbaum 2004, 2007, 2009, Iheduru 2003, 2015, Grant and Soderbaum 2003, Godsater and Soderbaum 2011, Scholte 2015, Godsater 2013, 2015, 2016, Fioramonti 2015). According to Soderbaum and Shaw, 'Civil societies are generally neglected in the description and explanation of new regionalism' (2003:222). The post-Cold War African regionalism has consistently witnessed a boost in regional policy areas within the formal framework of integration across the continent (Adedeji 2004, Asante 1997, Bach 2004, 2015, Grant and Soderbaum 2003, Soderbaum 2004, Iheduru 2015b). Amid these broader regionalisms, the historical role of the pan-African civil society movements in the trajectory of regional integration in West Africa is often not well articulated (Adedeji 1970, Obadare 2015, Iheduru 2015) as if civil society actors are less important in regional programmes in Africa. The credit is given to few critical political economists and scholars of the new regionalism school who have in recent times focused on the study of civil society's role in regionalism. Despite this recent scholarly attention, the actorship of civil society actors at the regional levels has remained underdeveloped, while West African in that context has been on the margin.

Most new regionalism writings on civil society regionalism or the role of civil society in regional governance in Africa have focused predominantly on Southern Africa, with some attention to East Africa (Soderbaum 2004, 2007, 2016a, Godsater and Soderbaum 2011, Godsater 2013, 2015, 2016, Zajontz and Leysens 2015). In West Africa, it cannot be over emphasised that Okechukwu Iheduru has been a lone voice in the new regionalism literature on civil society in the ECOWAS region or what he calls the 'West Africanisation' of CSOs (2003, 2015b:138). On the theoretical front, other contributors, such as Funmi Olonisakin (2009), Opoku (2007), Afadzinu (2015), Eze (2016a) and Bombande (2016) who have contributed to West African civil society, do not engage critically with the new regionalism from a theoretical perspective. However, this limited attention may tend to point at these social actors as empirically insignificant. In fact, they constitute parts of the most active regionalising actors in contemporary Africa (Reinold 2019). As Adebayo Adedeji points out, the call by the pan-African activists to establish the West African Economic Union at the Fifth Pan-African Congress in Manchester, England, in October 1945, was historically significant even before ECOWAS was born (2004:22).

It is also of note that the early activities of organisations like the West African Students' Union, West African Youth League and West African Pilot are sources of historical evidence for constructing a regional identity for West Africa (Obadare 2015:13–14). Prior to 1975, the Federation of West African Chambers of Commerce (FEWAC) made a significant contribution towards the establishment of ECOWAS (Iheduru 2015:142). These are a few practical examples of an early regional perspective on civil society in West Africa but the mainstream literature especially that of rationalism does not regard the agency of civil society in African regionalism as so important. The neglect or lack of attention in the mainstream literature is a reference to the state-centric predisposition of rationalist approaches such as neorealism and neoliberal institutionalism on African regionalisms (Asante 1997, Akinyeye 2010, Adekeye 2004, Adedeji 1970, 2004, Bar 2013, Oosthuysen 1997, Oppong 2011, Sani 2012).

The canon in the rationalist model views states as the primary actors (Van Langenhove 2012). The overemphasis on formal regionalist institutions over informal networks is integral to the approach of the rationalist school (Soderbum 2002). In contrast, according to the New Regionalism Approach (reflectivist type), the social dimension of the new regionalism underscores

> the growth of regional civil society, opting for regional solutions to some local, national and global problems The implication of this is that not only economic, but also social and cultural networks are developing more quickly than the formal political cooperation at the regional level.
>
> (Hettne 1999:10)

The examples of these social networks are reflected in the past works on civil society regionalisation largely in Southern Africa (Soderbaum 2004, 2007, 2016a, Godsater and Soderbaum 2011, Godsater 2015, 2016, Zajontz and Leysens 2015), and to some extent in East Africa (Godsater 2013). The subsequent sections will look at how the few new regionalism scholars have presented regional civil society so far.

What Is Missing in the Literature on Civil Society in African Regionalism?

If we understood the complexities of the regionalisms in Africa, the existing works of Southern African civil society regionalism represents part of the stories of the African regional societal actors. The new regionalism literature on civil society regionalisation has underscored the role of civil society networks in the political economy of regionalism in Southern Africa (Soderbaum 2004, 2007, 2016). These studies have exposed the complexities of civil society regionalisation within the Southern African region which is underpinned by a neo-patrimonial culture of 'inclusion' and 'exclusion' (Soderbaum 2007:330). According to Soderbaum:

> Those forces in civil society that are 'included' are so intimately related to ruling political regimes that their survival is largely contingent upon intimate and informal relationships with governments, which in turn often compromises their performance as civil society actors and their ability to shape the rules that govern social life. In contrast, the more radical critical forces in civil society challenge patrimonial power. These actors are therefore often marginalised or harassed by political regimes and by the main regional organisations in Southern Africa such as SADC.
>
> (2007:335)

Soderbaum further notes that civil society actors are important agents in regionalism despite being marginalised by the state-centric regional organisations (2007, 2016a). For him, they deserve more nuanced analyses in regionalism studies. In furthering this, Godsater and Soderbaum (2011) examined civil society's contribution to regional governance in East Africa and Southern Africa within the development sectors. They concluded that civil society actors in both regions can be classified as 'partners', 'legitimizer', 'manipulator' and 'resister' (2011:152). In a similar vein, Godsater (2013a) conducted a study on the management of the Lake Victoria Region by the East African Community and civil society networks. He showed civil society networks as *problem-solvers* and *critical actors* in regional environmental governance in East Africa. He concluded that civil society can be a source of participatory regional governance (Godsater 2013). Apart from the above studies, *Civil Society and World Regions* edited by Lorenzo Fioramonti (2015) is perhaps the most authoritative volume on the new regionalism and civil society to date. The strength of the book is its global scope of regions with two chapters focusing on Africa: 'West Africa' by Okechukwu Iheduru and 'Southern Africa' by Andreas Godsater. Theoretically, Iheduru's framework divides civil society actors in regional governance in West Africa into three groups (partner, legitimiser and counter-hegemonic) compared with the four categories suggested by Godsater and Soderbaum (2011). According to Iheduru, 'CSOs in West Africa can be partners, legitimizers of the status quo, or counter-hegemonic' (Iheduru 2015b:155). He therefore calls for a more systematic study of civil society's role in regional governance in West Africa (Iheduru 2015b:155). In his subsequent studies, Iheduru (2015a) challenged and departed from the so-called typology of CSOs while examining the policy role of organised business CSOs in regional governance in West Africa. He has now focused on examining the intersections between the development-driven activities of organised private business associations, West African multinational corporations and regionalism underpinned by the philosophy of 'Africapitalism'[5] (Iheduru 2018, 2019). The concept of 'Africapitalism' was developed by Tony Elumelu as an African economic philosophy of capitalism that transcends the traditional Western capitalist ideology preoccupied with profit maximisation. As claimed by its promoters, Africapitalism is embedded in the agency of Africa's development through the collaborative roles between the governments and the private business entities (Amaeshi and Idemudia 2015). Kenneth Amaeshi has been popularising the concept in the emerging academic scholarship of African development. He posits as follows: 'Africapitalism calls on Africa's private sector to play a leading role in the continent's development b*ecause* after all is said and done, the future we all want for ourselves is one of our own making' (Amaeshi 2018). Essentially, Africapitalism embodies a private sector-led approach to solving some of Africa's most intractable development problems (Amaeshi and Idemudia 2015). My view is that Africapitalism may seem plausible a concept. However, serious studies still await the intersection between Africapitalism and African regionalism. Although it is a promising discourse, the idea has not yet been subjected to the rigour of regionalism beyond the states and private business actors. Less is still known about the response of non-business interest NGOs and interest groups in the West African context when we relate Africapitalism to the general questions of regionalisms in Africa.

Furthermore, Zajonntz and Leysens (2015) observe that there is a need for an approach of new regionalism that captures the regionalist phenomena of the developing world, including Africa. They posit that a 'developing regionalism approach' which accommodates the agency of regional civil society is needed. According to the duo:

> The proposed theoretical synthesis between WOA [World Order Approach], an approach specifically focused on social and structural change, and the NRA [New Regionalism Approach], which offers a comprehensive, agency-oriented framework with which to understand regional dynamics, is well suited to the changing nature of developing regionalisms. It also serves as a theory-building enterprise that leads to the necessary re-evaluation of exiting approaches. [It] offers a theoretical 'entry-point' to a widely neglected, but increasingly important sphere of regional activity, viz. regional civil society.
>
> (Zajonntz and Leysens 2015:317)

Despite Zajonntz and Leysens's emphasis on regional civil society, their proposed approach offers no new analytical framework. Rather, they emphasise that 'An analytical focus on actors, agendas and strategies within regional civil societies and changing politico-economic dynamics on the continent [Africa] is timely and can develop into a productive research agenda' (Zajonntz and Leysens 2015:317–318).

Due to the academic gap, Andreas Godsater added a volume to the literature in 2016 entitled, *Civil Society Regionalisation in Southern Africa*. This book is perhaps the most revealing of his contributions so far. Developed from the New

Regionalism Approach, the book provides a well-thought out framework for the study of regional civil society and focused on two main policy areas: Trade and HIV/AIDS in Southern Africa. However, like many other scholars, Godsater (2016) attributes a collective identity to civil society and considered SADC an external actor, like donor agencies. Many scholars have taken collective identities to describe the kind of identities that civil society actors construct on the regional levels (see Scholte 2005, 2012, 2015, Fioramonti 2015, Godsater 2015, 2016). Valeria Bello (2011), however, suggests sociological differences between what is taken as 'collective identity' from 'social identity' (Bello 2011), positing that social identity is an action-based identity commonly constructed by civil society groups based on shared values. For her, collective identity is structure-based, fixed or geographical. If civil society regionalisation is constructed from below (Godsater 2015), it implies that it is horizontally oriented. As a result, Bello (2011) relates it to social identity. Whereas the identity constructed vertically is otherwise known as collective identity (Bello 2011). It is still an open question in the literature to determine what kind of identities do civil society actors construct at the regional levels and for what purpose? In building on the above, the next section clearly presents the major gaps that are interrogated and addressed by this study.

Emphasising the Gaps: Bringing West Africa to the Centre

West Africa, whether taken as given or not, is presently at the margin of the new regionalism debates even though it remains one of the most prominent regions today in African regionalism. Often defined by the scope of ECOWAS, I argue that activities of regional civil society actors in West Africa can help enrich our understanding of civil society agency in the new regionalism literature.

The Direction of the Study

This chapter has acknowledged the significant contributions of authors in the study of civil society actors in African regions and regionalism. It has not only showcased the state of the literature in civil society and regionalism in Africa, the chapter also critically analysed the key literature relating to this research, showing their inherent strengths and weak points as highlighted above. One important lesson from this analytic critique is the fact that scholars who write about civil society in African regionalism are relatively few. Nonetheless, they have conducted excellent research at least in moving beyond state-centric scholarship that often stiff against innovative thinking when it comes to knowledge production about regionalism in Africa. However, despite the significance of the previous studies, we should not close our eyes to the apparent shortcomings in the framings and regional preferences of such studies. First, this chapter uncovers that the bulk of previous studies are predominantly located in the reflectivist school of regionalism (New Regionalism Approach) but unfortunately, they have not succeeded in providing a clear framework to make sense of regional civil society as an actor in Africa. Second, there is a tilted predisposition towards Southern Africa in civil society regionalism at the expense of other regions such as West Africa. This chapter has no doubt that West Africa commands a credible scholarly attention in state-centric scholarship of regionalism or regional integration, but unfortunately it falls at the margin of the debate when it comes to the critical literature about civil society regionalism in Africa. Third, the notion of regional civil society seldom appears as the main focus of analysis in the previous studies. In contrast, the concept of regional civil society is the main focus of this book and the aim is to uncover its descriptive analytical attributes for actorship in the regionalism literature. In line with the above, this chapter has succeeded in establishing the gaps and advanced our knowledge of regionalism by filling these gaps based on the development of the subsequent chapters.

The next chapter therefore presents the analytical framework of this book. It extends the debate by offering a new analytical framework for the study of regional civil society actors with four integrated concepts: regional social identity, regional presence, regional capacity and impact. The integration of these concepts is new, original and helps in broadening our understanding of regional civil society actors in African regions and regionalism literature.

Notes

1 There are five Regional Commissions of the United Nations; The UN Economic Commission for Europe (UNECE) was established in 1947. Details available online: http://www.unece.org/mission.html [accessed 6/05/2018]. The UN Economic Commission for Africa (UNECA), established in 1958. Details available online: https://www.uneca.org/pages/overview [accessed 6/05/2018]. The UN Economic and Social Commission for Asia and Pacific (UNESCAP), established in 1947. Details available online: http://www.unescap.org/about [accessed 6/05/2018]. The UN Economic Commission for Latin America and the Caribbean (UNLAC), established in 1948. Details available online: https://www.unsceb.org/content/united-nations-economic -commission-latin-america-and-caribbean [accessed 6/05/2018]. The UN Economic Commission for Western Asia, established in 1973. Details available online: https://www.unescwa.org/about-escwa [accessed 6/05/2018].
2 ACS was established in 1994. ACS has 25 member states and 12 associate member countries. Details available online: http://www.acs-aec.org/index.php?q=about-the-acs [accessed 6/05/2018].
3 CARICOM was established in 1973. Details available online: https://caricom.org/about-caricom/who-we-are [accessed 8/05/2018].
4 OECS was established in 1981. Details available online: http://www.oecs.org/home-page/about-us [accessed 8/05/2018].
5 Details available on Tony Elumelu Foundation website at: https://www.tonyelumelu foundation.org/research-publications/africapitalism-rethinking-the-role-of-business-in -africa-by-prof-kenneth-amaeshi [accessed 1/11/2019].

2 Analytical Framework

Introduction

This chapter is developed based on an inductive-deductive process. The reason for a claim of induction is borne out of the fact that I did not begin this study with a theoretical tool of regionalism. Rather, it was the empirical observation of the West African civil society organisations on the regional levels that prompted my curiosity to find out the extent to which these organisations have evolved to act in the region. This curiosity led to the uncovering of the New Regionalism Approach which also has something to say about civil society agency. I found the New Regionalism Approach as the closest guide for this study. However, for the New Regionalism Approach to be applicable, there is a need to reconceptualise its civil society aspect in order to address the problem of this study. This is where analytical induction of the West African context is combined with the deduction from the New Regionalism Approach. This inductive and deductive marriage provides the basis for the new framework suggested in this chapter.

Through the shared understanding of the context and social construction of realities by these civil society activists, the chapter conceptually frames who are regional civil society actors (identity question)? At what regional levels do they act (presence question)? What capacity do they have (actor's capacity question)? And what has been the outcome of their evolution in West Africa (normative impact question)? The analytical framework is explained through the existing regionalism literature and subsequently advanced as a guide to understand the extent to which these organisations have evolved to act in West Africa. The overview of the chapter is given below.

How the Chapter Is Structured

The chapter is divided into five sections. The next section revisits the actorship of civil society in the reflectivist understanding of the new regionalism. This enables the author to underscore the deduction of the New Regionalism Approach. I also discuss how the idea of human security and democratic participation is factored into the framework as the basis of identity formation for civil society in regionalism in West Africa. After establishing this important preliminary understanding,

DOI: 10.4324/9781003257288-3

I discuss the analytical framework, clarifying the use and shared understanding of the four analytical concepts. In conclusion, I discuss why the analytical framework is important to the context of this study and the issue of democratic knowledge production about African regionalism.

From Revisiting Civil Society Regionalism to Analysing Its Actorship

There is a connection between approaches used in studying international relations and regionalism. Hurrell (1995:37) posits that 'The theoretical literature on regionalism is enormous, but it is also uneven and fragmented'. This is broadly true, however, such theoretical literature on civil society regionalism is relatively limited partly due to the recent interest in civil society in regionalism theories and practice (Godsater 2016, Fioramonti 2015, Scholte 2015). My focus here is limited to the New Regionalism Approach in the reflectivist understanding of regionalism. The New Regionalism Approach is based on the perspectives that see 'regionalisation as a multidimensional process, occurring in many sectors and on different levels simultaneously, and driven by a variety of state and non-state actors' (Godsater and Soderbaum 2011:149). My aim is to develop an analytical framework that focuses on the civil society component of the New Regionalism Approach. According to Hettne, 'there is a need for a strong civil society on the level of the region' (Hettne 2003:37). Another perspective sees civil society as a 'possible avenue for people to (re)make regions' (Scholte 2015:11). Apart from the expansion of scope of regionalism, the civil society idea has conceptually formed one of the key pillars of the pluralist perspectives of regionalisms (Bøås et al. 2003:204).

As noted in the introduction, civil society as a term is bereft of a conceptual precision like many social science concepts. Theorising the concept in the regional context has also become problematic. Conceptually, for Jensen (2006:39), civil society is 'vague'. Scholte (2015), a prominent thinker on globalisation, expresses doubt if there will ever be a universally accepted definition of what civil society is. His concern is expressed below:

> In some usages civil society refers to a society that is civil: open, tolerant, democratic, [and] virtuous. From other perspectives civil society is a public sphere of deliberation. In other understandings civil society encompasses the whole of associational life outside of official, commercial, and household circles. In other interpretations civil society is synonymous with NGOs. There is little prospect that these diverse conceptions will ever converge on a universally agreed definition.
>
> (Scholte 2015:19)

Scholte further posits that researchers are at liberty to determine which notion of civil society is apt and applicable to the context of their analyses (2015:20). This is probably why Obadare observes that 'despite universal employment, civil society's meaning remains frustratingly ambiguous' (2016:10). Looking beyond the traditional state system, Fioramonti (2015:2) opines that 'Regions without citizens are unlikely to stand the test of time, especially in the times of crises'. Fioramonti tends to reinforce the importance of organised groups of citizens in giving life to regions and regionalist sustainable initiatives. The conceptual understanding of civil society and its uses are undoubtedly and increasingly becoming evident beyond the Westphalian state system (Hettne 1999, Armstrong and Gilson 2011, Soderbaum 2007, 2016a, Iheduru 2015b, Godsater 2016).

As a sphere or a collective manifestation of civic organisations, civil society application has transcended the traditional notion of the state system (Spini 2011, Fioramonti 2015). It is now being studied in relation to regions/regional governance, including in the context of globalisation and global governance institutions (Hettne 1999, Soderbaum 2004a, Scholte 2012, 2015, Iheduru 2015a, 2015b, 2018). While the idea of national civil society is not as new as the idea of regional civil society, Soderbaum adduces that in regionalism or regional governance, 'the general neglect of civil society in the literature is a conceptual, theoretical and methodological problem' (2016a:132). However, according to Fioramonti,

> civil society is an open arena of participation, generally located outside the fuzzy boundaries of state and market, in which different types of individuals and groups cooperate or compete for visibility and relevance, in the pursuit of collective (though not necessarily shared) political and social goals and animated by a variety of values and interest.
>
> (2015:5)

From the above, the 'open area' seems to point to the space or sphere where different people and groups partake in the activities often through cooperating together where common values and interests are shared. They may as well compete for visibility in pursuance of their social goals. Fioramonti's (2015) description is conceived as a working definition for his edited book. The definition offers a perspective within civil society's multiple interpretations earlier observed in Scholte (2015:19). My observation is that Fioramonti's definition rather offers a general idea about civil society. The notion of regional civil society remains conceptually hidden. Within the regional arena, civil society actors are often described as partners in regional governance. They also participate to legitimise regional governance (Acharya 2018). On other occasions, they can as well resist the drive for regional governance or manipulate the regulatory framework of regionalism to serve other interests outside the professed values of civil society (Godsater and Soderbaum 2011, Fioramonti 2015, Iheduru 2015b, Soderbaum 2016a). Jan Aart Scholte lists examples of these actors within civil society as non-governmental organisations (NGOs), faith groups, foundations, labour unions, business forums and social movements, and wonders whether they can 'reinvent region for better: culturally, ecologically, economically, morally, politically [and] socially' (Scholte 2015:12). While the typology of civil society actors may offer insights into their mode of engagement in regional governance, it is also analytically important to understand what is *regional* in these actors. Sometimes, civil society actors do not necessarily need to be regional before they can contribute to regional governance (Scholte 2015). Depending on the aim of study, the regional levels may also constitute a key analytical glance to address the main problem of the study. To understand the extent to which regional civil society actors have evolved, regional levels of these civil societies become analytically important. Soderbaum once observes that the space (or levels) are important for reflectivist writers because it enables them to unbundle rationalists' heavy emphasis on state and global levels (2013:11). For him, such a tendency 'leads to a weak, even superficial, conceptualisation of "regional space"' (Soderbaum 2013:11). What Soderbaum accentuates here is, if the national space (including national civil society) is not taken for granted, researchers can problematise it to open space for the recognition of other spaces and scales (2013:11).

The implication of this is likely to reinforce the importance of regional spatial levels as regional arenas, where different types of individuals and groups engage in regionalism, or where they seek to influence regional policy (Reinold 2019, Godsater 2016). These groups may include civic organisations, youth movement, student movements, interest groups, trade unions, non-governmental organisations, think tanks, women associations, faith-based organisations, community associations and so on. They are likely to be acting in cooperation or competing based on certain values and interests aimed at initiating regionalist programmes. They may as well choose to respond to the existing regional policies or framework across regional levels without necessarily aiming at taking over political power. Although focused on the states, Kasfir observes that 'Patronage-based political economies (of states) produce incentives for civil society actors to organise platforms for gaining power rather than creating reform' (Kasfir 1998:126). This may hold true at the local level. The motivation of civil society in African regional integration can also partly reflect this assumption. Unlike what plays out at the national levels, the essence of civil society regionalisation tends to focus more on the influence or transformation of the statist approach to regionalism to a participatory one with focus on the general interest rather than the few interests of the political elites. While being conscious of the above, this may sometimes be influenced by neo-patrimonial relations as Soderbaum (2007) indicated in the Southern African experience. However, the main point here is that civil society can exist at the national and regional levels based on self-serving interests as against the normative aspiration for change or accountability in regional governance or policymaking (Scholte 2015, Godsater 2016). That is why it is important to exercise caution that the involvement of civil society in regionalism must not be taken for granted as positive. Researchers should not also be blind from pointing out the positive role played by civil society in regional integration (Scholte 2015, Godsater 2016, Soderbaum 2016a).

Understanding the extent to which regional civil society has evolved in West Africa can renew the conversations on the agency of civil society actors in relation to other identified actors in the New Regionalism Approach. This chapter specifically reconceptualises the actorship of civil society based on the New Regionalism

Approach's understanding. We should be reminded that the New Regionalism Approach identifies three main actors: the state, the market and the civil society (Hettne 1999). The significance of external actors as part of this category became more pronounced in Soderbaum (2002, 2004a). These four actors are posited as region builders or relevant actors in the making of a region (Grant and Soderbaum 2003, Soderbaum 2004a, 2016a). The problem this study identified is not the lack of acknowledging civil society in the New Regionalism Approach. Rather, it is the fact that the idea of *regional civil society agency* is still under construction. I found that civil society actorship in New Regionalism Approach needs rethinking in a way that brings out the regional attributes of civil society as an actor. It is by understanding these attributes that would enable us to analyse the extent these actors have evolved in West Africa. I will discuss the New Regionalism Approach in reflectivism before moving to explain the analytical concepts under consideration.

Framing Civil Society Actorship through Reflectivism of the New Regionalism

Reflectivism is a school of regionalism that rejects the positivist positions of rationalism. Instead of settling on the rational-choice tendencies and accepting interest, ideas and identities as given phenomena, the reflectivists argue that these interests, ideas and identities are neither given nor could they be taken for granted as objective realities (Keohane 1988, Shaw 2000, Soderbaum 2002, Iheduru 2003, Acharya 2014a, 2016a). The rejection of the positivist stance and statist worldviews of rationalism allows reflectivism to account for other actors such as civil society (Acharya 2014a, Fioramonti 2015, Scholte 2015). In this account, reflectivism lays a claim to the significance of inter-subjective frames, practices and the social interactions of actors that give meaning to what appears to the rationalists as an objective truth (Soderbaum 2002). These reflectivist approaches comprise social constructivism, critical theory, post-structuralism and the New Regionalism Approach (Hettne et al. 1999, Soderbaum and Shaw 2003, Soderbaum 2003, 2004, 2016a 2016b, Grant and Soderbaum 2003, Iheduru 2003, 2015a, 2015b, Acharya 2014a, Fioramonti 2015). These were the radical/critical approaches that emerged in the post-Cold War era in order to grapple with the growing and worldwide manifestations of regionalism and the regionalisation of civil society (Shaw 2000).

I find the New Regionalism Approach as a plausible guide to understanding civil society. However, its applicability to address this problem in this study also requires that I integrate the four regional attributes of civil society actors for the analysis. According to Acharya (2016), the New Regionalism Approach has broadened the study of regionalism by including non-state actors and multiple sectors of regional projects, even though it is not completely free from EU-centric views. Acharya's observation appears true even though some scholars who follow the New Regionalism Approach have the tendencies of advancing their arguments based on the EU-centrism of the old regionalism approaches in order to justify the usefulness of new regionalism analytical relevance. Soderbaum (2016a) has cautioned scholars against such tendencies perhaps to sustain the continued relevance of the approach. Acharya (2016) also argued that today, new regionalism may have developed beyond what its proponents intended (Acharya 2016), but the fact remains that new regionalism cannot completely isolate itself from being EU-centric when we uncover its preliminary conceptual foundations. Citing the foremost conceptual text of new regionalism in Hettne and Inotai (1994:12), Acharya reminds us of what Hettne and Inotai declared as the research paradigm of the New Regionalism Approach:

> Europe represents the most advanced regional arrangement the world has seen, and it will consequently serve as our paradigm for the new regionalism in the sense that its conceptualisation eagerly draws on empirical observations of the European process.

(2016:119)

The reference above only points to the preliminary paradigm but the scholarship of the New Regionalism Approach has moved beyond that ethnocentric trap. One of the most relevant parts of this scholarship to this present study is what Soderbaum (2002, 2004a) described as reflectivist constructivism of New Regionalism Approach that emerged from his study of Southern Africa. This is the approach that this book builds upon. It is a version of the New Regionalism Approach that emphasises a sociological context of agency and structure in our understanding of regions and various actors in region building including civil society (Soderbaum 2002, 2004a). However, the approach does not offer perspectives on the regional attributes of civil society – a key limitation.

We should be aware that distinct characteristics of regionalisms around the world are partly cultural, and therefore it is incumbent to understand the motives in which regions and actors are being analysed. In fact, Acharya (2016) argued that, now, there is no universally accepted theory of regionalism that provides the cause-and-effect explanation of various regional integration schemes around the world. In *The Oxford Handbook of Comparative Regionalism* edited by Borzel and Tanjel (2016), governance is suggested as a tool to incorporate various actors that are considered important in the study of regionalism, especially in a comparative sense. It was a timely intervention and provided excellent insights about the regionalism. One can observe that the book not only lacks a single chapter on civil society, no single African scholar contributed to the book.

Beyond these observed shortcomings, governance, because it is also compatible with new regionalism scholarship, may be an integral tool in analysing regional civil society organisations not only in West Africa but also in other world regions (Armstrong and Gilson 2011, Soderbuam 2004b, Godater 2013a, Iheduru 2015b, 2015a). One should not ignore the fact that governance as a form of regulatory activity can be considered along the regional attributes of civil society as an actor. In fact, there is perhaps no difference between the inherent functional typology (legitimiser, partner, counter-hegemonic and manipulator) of civil society (see Godsater and Soderbaum 2011, Godsater 2013, 2015, 2016, Iheduru 2015b, Fioramonti et al. 2015) and the expected role of civil society actors in regional governance (see Armstrong and Gilson 2011:5). Armstrong and Gilson (2011) posit the following typical activities of the civil society in regional governance include: (i) promoting transparency (making information available for public scrutiny); (ii) demanding justifications for policies (creating a civic space to prod the reasons for actions taken, especially by the organisation/institutional leaders); (iii) ensuring compliance (monitoring and evaluations of actions taken) and (iv) acting for enforcement of rules/law (sanction when the actions are inconsistent with policy objective). These are the conventional understandings of civil society at the national levels. A critical examination of this list of activities shows that it reflects a view of civil society participation in EU policymaking, based on democratic participation. However, the points noted in the list may not be taken as the totality of what civil society actors do. The underlying logic is based on democratising governance whereas there is also a need to show due cognisance of other roles played by non-Western civil society actors based on their respective regional contexts in terms of problem-solving (Godsater and Soderbaum 2011). For instance, civil society has been known for its involvement in conflict prevention/peacebuilding in West Africa. This involvement is often framed in the context of human security (Iheduru 2003, Ismail 2011, Olonisakin 2009). It is important to take this also into consideration to understand the extent to which such civil society actors have evolved in the ECOWAS region.

Democratic Participation and Human Security

The idea of democratic participation and promoting human security is normatively central to civil society's involvement in regionalism or regional governance, especially in non-Western regions. It should be noted that there have been some attempts in the regionalism literature to link the activities of civil society to human security based on the particular problems to be found in Africa (Iheduru 2003, Shaw et al. 2003 and Van Langenhove 2004). So far, the scholarship has not seriously considered human security as a key justification for civil society's identity formation in regional integration specifically in West Africa. My aim is to explore this important notion of human security and integrate it with democratic or popular participations as key factors in understanding the motivation for civil society's identities in regional integration. First, the understanding of human security as a human-centred approach is often traced to UNDP (1994:23). The UNDP report stresses that 'How individuals regard security depends very much on their immediate circumstances' (UNDP 1994:23). The centrality of human security is based on putting the protections of the people at the heart of security discourse and practice. Because of this, human security

> is not a defensive concept – the way territorial or military security is. Instead, human security is an integrative concept... It is embedded in a notion of solidarity among people. It cannot be brought about through force with armies standing against armies. It can happen only if we agree that development must involve all people.
>
> (UNDP 1994:24)

Its conceptual compatibility with New Regionalism Approach relates closely to recognition of the people as co-participants in the affairs that affect them (Iheduru 2003). Its seven components – economic security, food security, health security, environmental security, personal security, community security and political security (UNDP 1994:24–25) reflect some of the challenges observed in civil society's activities in non-Western regions such as West Africa (Shaw et al. 2003, Olonisakin 2009, Ismail 2011).

Thus, one cannot overemphasise that some of these regional civil society actors or networks in West Africa, tend to associate their regional engagement or aspiration to contribute to regional governance within this framework of democratising regionalism and promoting human security/conflict prevention in the region. Some scholars have attempted to link the post-Cold War regionalism in Africa with the notion of regional human security driven from below, although the idea has not been given serious attention (Shaw et al. 2003, Van Langenhove 2004). This idea occupied a considerable space in the concluding chapter of the volume, *The New Regionalism in Africa* of 2003. In it, Timothy Shaw and others posit that the framework of the NRA (New Regionalism Approach) is 'compatible with notions of human security and development in which a range of human concerns is privileged, not just "national" or "regime" security and development' (Shaw et al. 2003:201). This is exactly what tends to define the aspiration of new emerging regional civil society groups in West Africa from the late 1990s onwards. Van Langenhove (2004) also suggested that regional integration in Africa should be linked to human security. Van Langenhove tended to advance another understanding of human security that was based on a transformation of regional security complex theory of Barry Buzan into what he then proposed as 'regional human security complex' (Van Langenhove 2004). According to him,

> A regional approach to human security only makes sense if it is linked to the idea of a transnational (regional) civil society. Only in that way a sense of regional identity can flourish and also gives prospects for the development of so-called informal or bottom-up regional development.
>
> (Van Langenhove 2004:15)

While Van Langenhove's (2004) perspective on regional approach to human security seems relevant to the contextual purpose of this chapter, his suggestion of a regional human security complex does not correspond to the state-centric underlying logic of security complexity and its restrictive sectoral scope. Van Langenhove also acknowledges the state-centredness of regional security complex of Barry Buzan and Ole Weaver (2003). He nevertheless believes that it can serve as a basis for understanding regional dynamics of human security in Africa if it includes civil society participation. He therefore clarifies that

> The problem of Buzan and Weaver's regional security complex theory is however that they primarily focus on state security. But their arguments for a regional approach hold even more when thinking in terms of human security.

So, the challenge is to explore how a regional human security complex theory can be developed.

(2004:10)

But the question to Van Langenhove relates to the extent to which the assumptions of regional security complex theory embraces the concept of human security – an idea Buzan himself is emphatically sceptical about. According to Barry Buzan,

> I remain sceptical about human security. It proliferates concepts without adding analytical value. It also both drives towards a reductionist understanding of international security and reinforces a mistaken tendency to idealise security as the desired end goal. If the referent object of human security is collectivities, then the job it is trying to perform is better done by societal or identity security. If the referent object of human security is the individual, or humankind as a whole, then little if anything differentiates its agenda from that of human rights.
>
> (2004:369–370)

Buzan's rebuttal as reflected above shows a clear disconnect between Van Langenhove's proposed conceptual marriage. This has therefore stifled its contextual relevance. While a regional security complex covers the sectoral approach – 'economic', 'environmental' and 'societal' (Buzan 2003:140), the theory has attempted to address its state-centric weaknesses by employing a version of constructivism. According to Barry Buzan, 'Rather than basing regional security complexes purely on the state, one will need to allow in other types of actors and referent objects as well' (2003:159). Despite this, Buzan still argues that the broad scope of human security has a clear weakness and lacks 'analytical value' (Buzan 2003). Buzan's rebuttal does not necessarily render human security's concept analytically inapplicable. It is also important to underscore that many other scholars have also pointed at the weakness in Buzan's position while embracing the significance of human security especially in non-Western regions such as Africa. Soderbaum (2016a) for instance is one of the scholars who drew attention to the neorealist orientation of the regional security complex and its selective focus in application. Sodeabaum explains that

> Buzan still shares the conventional neorealist conviction that strong states make strong and mature regions (cooperative anarchies), whereas in their quest for power and security, weak states tend to create (regional) conflicts and immature regions. It follows for Buzan that Western Europe is an example of a mature region, whereas the weak states in Africa create immature or weak regions. Again, neorealism and the security complex theory are based on foundations that make them more applicable to some parts of the world rather than to others, especially those parts where Westphalian state-building prevails.
>
> (2016a:39–40)

For this study, a broader context of human security provides a comprehensive understanding within the context of regional civil society's role in African regionalism and regional governance. According to Acharya (2018), the idea of national security or security that has the state as its core is an American idea and reflects the realist precautionary ideals of safeguarding 'nation states' from external aggressions. Robert Keohane and Joseph Nye contribute to the underlying logic of the neorealist view of security, its origins and relevance within a given historical location:

> [n]ational security symbolism was largely a product of the Cold War and the severe threat Americans then felt. Its persuasiveness was increased by realist analysis, which insisted that national security is the primary national goal and that in international politics security is permanent.
>
> (Keohane and Nye 2012:5–6)

The aftermath of this, is the transformation of the interpretation of security to one which is people centred. And it has gained international popularity since the end of the Cold War in Africa. So, it is contextually relevant to acknowledge this in the regionalisation of civil society in West Africa. Since year 2000, Toni Haastrup explained that a new idea of security with development as its undercurrent has been evident in the transformation of relations between Africa and the EU (see Haastrup 2013a). Embracing the analytical and policy usefulness of human security in the non-Western worlds, Acharya also persuades us that

> The ideas of comprehensive and cooperative security formed an importance backdrop to the emergence of human security as a key alternative notion of security for the post-Cold War era. Emerging in the 1990s, the idea of human security rekindled the debate over what security means and how best to achieve it. It not only represents the most powerful challenge to date to the idea of national security, it also highlights the ideational and normative agency of non-Western scholars and contexts.
>
> (2018:137)

The popular thrust of any security conversation in the non-Western societies must underscore not just the importance of human security as a set goal of both states and non-state actors, but also as a defining current of development. The set goal of alleviating endemic poverty speaks of human security from economic sense just as food, political, environmental, community, personal and health security form a holistic, comprehensive and encompassing picture of a conducive, safe and admirable condition for human existence. The thinking that human security lacks analytical significance is not only ethnocentric in understanding, it portrays a seeming ignorance of contextual reality of other societies outside the West. An average person who does not live in poverty may lack a basic understanding of what it means to be poor; to be a graduate of more than ten years without a job; to be hungry; to be internally displaced and become a refugee; to be orphaned by civil war or violent conflict; to be abducted by terrorists, raped, forcefully married and impregnated by the rapist. This is in addition to everyday abuses by police brutality and perpetual condition of living in penury. How can one imagine security in that context? Even if it is regarded as a vernacular security, because one does not experience it personally does not necessarily mean s/he should deny the affected people's ordeal and quest to be free from wants and hunger. The contemporary Western privileges resulted from historical imperialism and mass plundering of wealth of nations have continued to subjugate politically, ideologically and economically through the neocolonial framework. The real thinking of security perhaps outside the dominant Western framework in regionalisms underscores the importance of inclusive or democratic participation that accommodate civil society/non-governmental organisation's activities in regional integration and provision of security.

As Acharya (2018) observed, the post-Cold War understanding of security that focused on humans rather than regime, can also account for the popular participation of civil society actors. The EU's civil society (interest groups) activities as demonstrated in the works of Garcia (2015), Spini (2011), Armstrong and Gilson (2011), Kohler-Koch (2009) have exemplified civil society participation in promoting democratic regional governance. Apart from this democratic participation, the interests of non-Western civil society actors also include problem-solving (human security) in regional governance (Godsater and Soderbaum 2011, Collins 2015). One may posit that engaging in problem-solving popular activities is likely to create opportunities for civil society groups to overcome some of the structural hurdles in contributing to regionalisms. This also depends on the prevailing norms at the regional levels. There could also be resistance either from the regional organisation or from a given regime at the national level. However, in a region where civil society groups enjoy a cordial relationship with both regional organisation/policymakers and member states, especially when such member states are committed to regional demands, the impact of such civil society in terms of contribution to regional policy development or norm is likely to be felt in the region. It is otherwise hard when such a mutual understanding is lacking in the region, especially where the will of the national regime is the determinant of the regional norm, instead of the other way round where the regional organisation is more influential in shaping the national preferences through its regional instruments and norms (such as democratic conditionality as a basis of membership). In this particular scenario, civil society, especially regionally active ones, are often seen as critical partners of the regional organisations in dealing with the prevailing challenges of their respective regions (Iheduru 2003). From the observation of the West African context, there tends to be an aspiration among civil society actors interested in regionalism under their umbrella organisations to seek participatory space for their members to contribute to the regulatory framework of regionalism or regional governance. This can be seen as a channel towards popular participation in the context of democratising regionalism and promoting human security at the regional level. However, there is a caveat. Many of these civil society organisations may frame their aspirations in terms of representing the popular interest of the generality of the people in regional governance, serving as a watchdog to regional policymakers and engage in social service provisions. This does not mean that there are no self-interest-seeking organisations that often parade themselves as promoters of popular interests (Soderbaum 2007). Apart from the above, it is also important to acknowledge how the regime types of member states of regional organisations as well as the prevailing regional norms can either constrain or enable this kind of popular participation of these civil society groups in regional integration. The next section attempts a brief discussion of these factors before moving forward to discuss the four analytical concepts.

Regime Types versus Regional Norms and Civil Society Participation in Regionalisms

While the regime types can enable or constrain civil society participation on the regional levels (Hulse el al. 2018, Reinold 2019, Soderbaum 2007), the prevailing regional norms can as well engender access for civil society at the same time (Glas and Balogun 2020, Reinold 2019). In their empirical studies of Southern African civil society, Hulse et al. (2018:17) observe that 'levels of civic participation tend to be relatively high in the more democratic states, civil society faces serious (and increasing) constraints in the less democratic regimes' (2018:17). Hulse et al.'s (2018) observation is right. However, it should be pointed out that the authors did not acknowledge the impact that the regional norm has on the civil society participation. Second, the claim of the author is compatible with the context of the Southern African region they studied where there is more resistance against civil society at the national levels unlike in West Africa. The study was based on the Bertelsmann Transformations Index (2018).[1] One of the challenges includes difficulties in terms of legal registration of regionally focused CSOs in member states with less democratic credentials. In another recent study, Reinold (2019) also posits that civil society actors in both the Southern African Development Community (SADC) and the East African Community (EAC) are less active when compared with the civil society in the Economic Community of West African States (ECOWAS). Her explanation was based on the influence of the member states in both SADC and the EAC but such influence is less in ECOWAS. Glas and Balogun (2020) examine the evolving people-centric governance norm in both ECOWAS and ASEAN. They suggest that regional norms that focus on the people and popular participation tend to give opportunities to civil society as partners of regional organisations like ECOWAS, especially in the context of an ECOWAS of the People. The authors conclude that civil society actors are able to participate more in ECOWAS because of partnership relationship that currently exists between ECOWAS and CSOs unlike ASEAN which tends to exhibit elitist culture despite professing a People-Oriented ASEAN (Glas and Balogun 2020).

So, the ability of civil society organisations to act or contribute to regional governance can be enabled or constrained depending on the regime types of member states of a given regional organisation (Collins 2015, Reinold 2019). Regionalism can also be a tool in the hand of member states to promote their national interests (Bach 2016) or what Soderbaum (2004b) describe as sovereignty-boasting regional governance. The preferences of these states on the regional issues include their influence on civil society participation. The openness or otherwise of a given region or regional organisations can depend considerably on how democratic or otherwise these member states are (Hulse et al. 2018). For those interested in the state behaviour towards regionalism, Theresa Reinold (2019) has emphasised the need to acknowledge political characteristics of member states of regional organisations on how civil society actors participate in governance at the regional levels. My argument is we should not however ignore that the prevailing institutionalised norms of regional organisations such as protocol on democracy and good governance can also create opportunities for civil society actors to participate and shape regional governance (Glas and Balogun 2020). This chapter does not dispel the influence of regime types on the capacity of civil society actors to act on the regional levels especially when civil society groups tend to challenge the status quo. Although regime types often aim to explain the cause and effect of states' behaviours on integration projects (see Kirschner and Stapel 2011), the context of its application in this study is to acknowledge the extent to which the regime types of member states also enables or constrains the ability of civil society actors to act and make impact in the region (even though the ECOWAS region is more receptive to civil society at the regional levels compared to other regions in Africa). The observation in ASEAN has shown that regime types matter as they could constrain or enable civil society participation in regional governance (Glas and Balogun 2020, Collins 2015). The study by Allan Collins (2015) on ASEAN civil society confirms that regime type may constrain the tendency towards counter-hegemonic civil society movement unlike those groups who engage in problem-solving in regional integration. Member states of African Regional Economic Communities (regional organisations) are likely to be hostile or friendly towards civil society in regional integration depending on their respective regimes in terms of being democratic, authoritarian or hybrid democracies (Reinold 2019). While the influence as regards regime types is noted, the prevailing regional norm also matters as civil society organisations can as well serve as a cover for the bureaucrats of regional organisations as promoting agents of regional norms at domestic levels often with external support. These can offer insight into the extent to which civil society actors are able to participate in regional governance. In democratising regionalism and promoting human security in the context of popular participation, the evolution of regional civil society actors is arguably predicated on the shared understanding of their action-based regional identities, regional levels of activities (presence), regional capacity to act and societal impact. These are the analytical concepts upon which the development of the empirical chapters/case studies is organised. The next section explains what each of the analytical concepts mean and their common interpretations in the regionalism literature.

The Analytical Framework for the Book

This section discusses the four analytical concepts – regional identity, regional presence, regional capacity and societal impact/contributions – put forward to understand the extent to which regional civil society has evolved as an actor in West Africa.

Regional Identity

The idea of identity in this context distinguishes an idea of identity that is action based from the overall collective identity of the region (see Bello 2011). According to Hurrell, 'regional identity' is imprecise and fuzzy, yet it is considered one of the important concepts in the regionalism analysis (1995:41). If the research is driven by agency, not the structure per se, it is highly unlikely that we can truly grasp regional civil society as an actor analytically without a clear analytical understanding of regional identity. Godsater admits that regional identity can spur regionalisation (2013a:224), even though the so-called identity making on the regional level may appear complicated (Bello 2011, Armstrong and Gilson 2011). The idea of identity as a key concept is highly important as the main thrust of this book speaks to the agency of civil society movements and how they have evolved to act over time in the region. Whether one looks at an identity as an interdisciplinary term with a baggage of interpretations (Semian and Chromy 2014), its common meaning is related to perception of self in relation to others. Identity is also conceived as how others perceive who we are within the social context of inclusion and exclusion (Stets and Burke 2000:226–227). Regional identity may imply the selfhood of region or what or how a region perceives itself in terms of its values, history, language, norms and mores, in comparison or in relation to other regions (Paasi 2010, Bello 2011). Identity has been associated with the emergence of a region as a security community (Adler and Barnett 2000, Checkel 2016). However, regional identity can as well comprise common regional symbols, regional citizenship and socio-cultural practices and conventions of members of certain regional organisations (Bello 2011). For instance, the issuance of common ECOWAS passports to the nationals of the fifteen-member states is one symbol of collective identity. Others include the ECOWAS anthem, ECOWAS biometric cards, the ECOWAS policy on freedom of movement and settlement within the ECOWAS community. The directive of the Council of Ministers of the East African Community, at its 35th meeting in 2017, which stated that all member states should start issuing East African e-passports, is another symbolic case of identity representation of the region and its citizens (EAC 2017).

Another example is what Acharya (1997) calls 'the ASEAN Ways' as bases of regional identity and regional institution building based on informal regionalism. 'ASEAN Ways' is characterised by the shared values and norms of human rights and democracy in regionalist consensus practice among the leaders in the South East Asia (Acharya 1997, Yukawa 2018). While identity has never been a wanting concept in the regionalism literature, its interpretation is elusive since no single definition of region applies in a universal context (Checkel 2016, Godsater 2016). Therefore, speaking of the identity of regions or regional identity will be out of context without a clear understanding of regions that exist in practice or in our imaginations. For this purpose, the spatial context of region in this study is transnational in nature and intertwines with the agency at the local level. According to Acharya, 'An important part of the consideration of agency in global order lies in recognising where its key ideas and norms came from. Many *global* (and regional) ideas and norms are local in origin' (2018:20, emphasis in original). From this perspective, we can gain a better understanding of how identity is formed and animated within the region (Acharya 1997, Bello 2011, Soderbaum 2002, 2004, Börzel and Risse 2020).

Regional Collective Identity *versus* Regional Social Identity

I build on Valeria Bello (2011:36) who provides a clear distinction between 'collective identity' and 'social identity'. Bello's understanding of collective identity is based on the sense of belonging and attachment to a given community (2011:40). It can also relate to the existing structure of regional organisations often set up by states which could be represented by the EU, ASEAN, EAC, ECOWAS and so on. In contrast, the understanding of regional social identity is based on an action or agency, the essence of which is to undertake activities to respond to the issues emanating from the region. According to Iheduru, 'CSOs seek to construct a regional identity and frame the values, norms and ideas that could change the way the region works' (2015b:140). Most new regionalism scholars seem to underplay the differences between collective identity and social identity at the regional level. Although Godsater posits that 'issues are never framed and identities never constructed apart from social structure' (2013b:62), the existing analyses often do not distinguish between those whose identities that are social and those identities that are collective. This lack of clarity makes an agency-based analysis of civil society actorship difficult to undertake.

A sociological view of collective identity closely conforms to the view of the existing regional structure. Bello explains that 'collective identity is a term which suggests vertical, top-down processes of identity construction set up by a collective actor or dominant group, which people can then choose to identify with' (Bello 2011:36). Adding to the debate on the structural influences on the governance of regions, which are characterised by 'social hierarchies', 'capitalist production' and 'modern-rationalist knowledge', Fioramonti notes that 'nationalism is a powerful governing structure of collective identity' (2015:18). What Fioramonti meant in a regional context is the influence of the neoliberal order of institutions through the expression of the Westphalian states. In contrast, social identity is agency based, its construction is horizontally oriented. It involves the responses of citizens and interest groups to the existing region through a 'spontaneous process ... and interaction' (Bello 2011:36).

While I understand that there are various ways of interpreting identities, my attempt here is not to prescribe a particular interpretation of identities that defines the activities of civil society actors in regional governance. For the purpose of this study, I posit that collective identity can represent the supranational identities of regional organisations such as ASEAN, ECOWAS, the EU, SADC, the EAC, the North Atlantic Treaty Organisation (NATO), the AU and so on. On the other hand, social identity is not structure based but dynamic in the sense that the essence of the citizens' movements or civil society organisations or networks is to respond to the overarching issues that arise from the region. As they create these norms and values (Iheduru 2015b:140), they also work as groups to protect those values (Soderbaum 2002, 2016a). Typical examples are evident in the establishment of various regional civil society organisations, formal and informal networks across the world regions (Acharya 2018:182). These are the organisations that give expressions to the agency of citizens and interest groups in regional governance and global governance (Shaw et al. 2003, Armstrong and Gilson 2011, Iheduru 2015b, Godsater 2016, Fioramonti 2015, Acharya 2018, Soderbaum 2016b).

In this process, civil society actors engage regional governance institutions, as partners in addressing social, political and economic issues considered crucial to their members or the regional public (Fioramonti 2015, Adejemobi 2016, Khadiagala 2016). Typical examples of their activities include regional health governance, for example, responding to Ebola pandemic in Mano River Region or the COVID-19 pandemic and its variants such as Omicron; regional peace and security governance through the West African Early Warning System (WARN/ECOWARN) in collaboration with WANEP, and promotion of regional human rights by the Media Foundation for West Africa through the ECOWAS Court of Justice. Empowering women and youth through the activities of the West African Women Associations (WAWA) is another example. Other regional civil society actors include the West African Civil Society Institute (WACSI), the Centre for Democracy and Development (CDD-West Africa) and so on.

The foregoing suggests that most of the regional civil society organisations emerge by constructing their social identities in response to the prevailing socio-economic and political issues or development challenges within the communities of regional organisations. They tend to manifest themselves in a variety of areas such as peacebuilding, trade, participatory democracy, environmental protection, human rights, human security and development in general (Iheduru 2015b, Khadiagala 2016).

In this view, regional social identity is interpreted as the identity constructed by civil society movements, organisations and networks which engage with regional institutions, in order to contribute to regional governance, either as partner, legitimiser or counter-hegemonic force. Perhaps, this is where Godsater and Soderbaum's (2011) typology of civil society resonates contextually. It is the interest that underpins the social identity of these civil society actors that will determine whether they may be partners, resister (counter-hegemonic), manipulators or legitimisers in the region.

Thus, the image and activities of these civil society actors are located within the regional space. Their activities can be physical or existential on one or more regional spatial levels. In this context, the understanding of regional presence of these actors is also very important. To understand the extent to which these organisations have evolved, it is analytically important to explain the manifestations of their activities on regional levels.

Regional Presence

I used the idea of presence here as an adaptive understanding of three regional levels where regionalisms take place from the reflectivist literature. These levels are otherwise described as micro, meso and macro (Soderbaum 2002:55–56). However, presence/level has not been previously used to understand civil society actors. Given that, what is *regional* is not objectively deterministic, regional presence is equally fuzzy, particularly because scholars of regionalism have continuously disagreed 'on the demarcation of what is regional' (Grant 2017:152). Depending on conceptual nomenclature, the regional presence in this framework focuses mainly on three levels: the macro, the meso and the micro levels. A shared understanding of these levels can also be found in Soderbaum's (2002, 2004a) work on *the Political Economy of Regionalism in Southern Africa*, where Soderbaum argues in favour of three levels of regions within Southern Africa. Acharya (2014a, 2018) also affirmed the influence of the agency of actors at the local, regional and global levels. However, such levels have not been conceived in making sense of the actorship of regional civil society.

Therefore, one can posit that there are three basic regional levels for the manifestation of civil society's action-based identity in a given region (if we don't enter the realm of interregionalism which can also provide an insight to another regional sphere). These can be on a macro level, a meso level and/or on a micro level. The prevailing regional presence of these actors will, to a large extent, depend on the interpretation of a reflective researcher or actor on what a region is to him/her. A regional civil society analyst will contextually miss out the real issues if s/he ignores the significance of regional presence in explaining or analysing the phenomena of regional civil society organisations. The extent to which West African civil society has evolved cannot be isolated from these three levels. Each of these levels may overlap as the analysis below shows. However, they are important and needed to be accounted for. I shed light on each of these levels below, starting with the *macro-regional level*.

Macro-regional Presence

A macro-regional presence is a type of presence of civil society actors on the regional level. This is often seen as a bigger regional level and civil society actors are found at this regional level. But what does macro-regional level entail? The conception of regional space as it applies to macro-regional spatial level rests largely on the inter-subjective meaning that scholars or researchers attach to it. Grant and Soderbaum explain that '[I]n IR, macro region has been the most common object of analysis. Nevertheless, it must be recognized that regions exist at different spatial levels' (2003:5–6). As earlier explained, a region has a sub-jective interpretation based on the ontological angle of theorisation. While it is acknowledged that this can be explained in different ways, at this level, the critical underlining note should point to the socially constructed notion of a bigger region (Hettne 2006). While the general assumption may view 'macro-regions ... as con-tinents or as supranational formations of countries sharing a common political and economic project and having a certain degree of common identities' (Hettne 2006:544), it is further understood that regions or regional spaces are subject to interpretation of political actors depending on the purpose of usage (Hettne 2006, Soderbaum 2004, Soderbaum and Taylor 2008, Grant and Soderbaum 2003). Grant and Soderbaum (2003) point out that we can conceive the African Union as a macro-regional level. This is because it is a grouping of sub-regional levels or meso-regions of the continent. They also aver that Southern Africa can also be regarded as a macro-region because it can boast of the presence of sub-regions and regional spatial levels within it. They posit that 'Southern Africa is most fre-quently considered a macro-regional space in its own right, thereby encompass-ing distinct sub-regions, such as Southern African Custom Union (SACU) area' (Grant and Soderbaum 2003:6).

From the constructivist postulation, region is not taken as given. SACU may have a long historical existence. With such constitutive assumptions, it means that West Africa can be seen as a macro-region since the conception of 'sub regions will only make sense when they are related with larger macro regions' (Grant and Soderbaum 2003:6). Within West Africa, there are sub-regions such as the West African Economic and Monetary Union (WAEMU), West African Monetary Zone (WAMZ), Mano River Region and so on. In this view, the ECOWAS can be seen as a macro-region. When we study the AU, it becomes a macro-region, and ECOWAS becomes a meso-region, while individual member states could be seen as micro-regions. These are all inter-subjective definitions, depending on the subject as well as issues that a reflective researcher seeks to study (Hurrell 1995). For this study, ECOWAS is the macro-regional level.

Meso-regional Presence

A meso-regional presence represents a middle ground between the macro- and micro-regional spaces (Soderbaum 2004, Grant and Soderbaum 2003:6, Soderbaum 2003:6, Jossop 2003:186). It is claimed in the reflectivist constructivist thesis of the new regionalism that macro-micro emphasis in the mainstream international relations theories has resulted in the neglect of the meso-regional level (Soderbaum 2004a:52–53). This is one of the theoretical shifts in the New Regionalism Approach. In Africa, there is recognition of those middle-ground regions as impor-tant components of the overall regional integration projects (Asante 2016). Most often, it is the African Union that is taken as a macro-region, whereas other regions are seen as sub-regions (Sani 2012, Salih 2013, Nzewi 2014). By taking the African Union as a given macro-region in Africa, other regions may be known as sub-regions or meso-regions, for example, West Africa, Southern Africa, East Africa,

North Africa and Central Africa. For reflective scholars, these regions are dynamic in nature and do not exist in isolation from the regionalisation processes. For an analyst who takes ECOWAS as a macro-region, the meso-regional presence will emerge in the process of analysis. These meso-regions may include the Mano River Union, if the analysis focuses on the states. A meso-regional level can also represent the level of civil society actors, such as the Mano River Women's Peace Network (MARWOPNET) or de-territorise the state in its given sense and consider a national level as a meso-regional level. For instance, WANEP regional office represents the macro level, comprising the 15 national offices, whereas a WANEP national office may represent the meso-regional level depending on the analysis. Two or more national offices of WANEP can represent such a meso-regional level. In theorising regional civil society, the national platforms of both WACSOF and WANEP fit in analytically as meso-regional levels in West Africa. To put it differently, the choice of national levels as meso-regional levels in this study is not fixed or pre-determined, and this approach recasts the conventional way of viewing the state, as something unchanging, rather than seeing it as a product of social construction (Soderbaum 2002, 2004). A reflection on the emergence of meso-regional spaces within the ECOWAS community and beyond, especially concerning the regional activities of a variety of civil society actors would point to the fact that these regions are becoming the centres of regional civic engagement (Iheduru 2003, 2015b). The meso-regional space is becoming a centre where most civil society actors and other normative non-state actors mobilise regionally in order to protect 'crucial values' that are centred on popular participation (Iheduru 2015b, Soderbaum 2004a). According to Soderbaum,

> the NRA highlights the possibilities of political regionalism. ... regionalism will emerge in order to achieve and protect crucial values, such as economic development, ecology and peace due to the fact that these values are not necessarily ensured by the state.
>
> (2004a:53)

The agency of meso-regional space, especially of civil society also takes cognisance of the political struggle to protect 'crucial values' and extend its tentacle across the micro-, meso- and macro-regional social spaces. The regional context and national levels can serve analytically as meso-regional levels depending on the issues at hand. Thus, for this study, the national offices of WANEP and national platforms of WACSOF are the meso-regional levels in this analysis emphasising the fact that a meso-regional level of civil society does exist and can be accounted for. Subsequent research may take a meso-regional level to mean Mano River Union or West African Economic and Money Union; it all depends on which regional civil society actor is being analysed or investigated.

Micro-regional Presence

The micro-regional presence of civil society is the smallest of the regional space/ levels in the new regionalism theoretical construct, depending on the subjective interpretation of authors and actors. It refers, however, to those regions and sub-regional spaces that are within the larger national space or a part of cross-border areas or regional corridors. Those regions at this level are not left unconsidered in the regionalisation process. According to Grant and Soderbaum,

> micro-regions refer to a space between 'the national' and 'the local'. Historically speaking, micro-regions have primarily existed within particu-lar states (i.e., subnational micro-regions). However, in the post-Cold War era and in the context of globalization and regionalization, micro-regions are becoming increasingly cross-border in nature.
>
> (2003:6)

To view this from a regional governance angle, a micro-regional level refers to the subnational regions within the national context (Vleuten and Eerdewijk 2014, Grant 2017). The African regional social space will therefore be incomplete with-out showing how civil society activities are manifested at various regional spatial levels in Africa. The micro-regional space as an integral part of the spaces in the new regionalism theory is demonstrated in the study of the Maputo Development Corridor by Soderbaum (2004, see also Soderbaum and Taylor 2008). It is neces-sary to rethink civil society actors in this local presence to understand their role in regional governance. The post-Cold War positions of contextualising micro-regions as development corridors and issues of cross-borders are understandable. The neglect of micro-regional levels as integral parts of analytical understanding of societal actors in regionalism in West Africa is merely a theoretical problem (Soderbaum 2002, 2004a). These subnational regions or grassroots regions are part and parcel of regionalist activities of civil society in West Africa. It is there-fore important to acknowledge their presence at this level in order to account for their regional activities. One example is the WANEP community monitors who gather open-source data on early warning within local communities and feed the reports into the national office of WANEP. Thereafter, the national office collects the reports across the subnational regions and develops its national early warning report and feeds it into the regional secretariat of WANEP in Accra. Thus, we can-not underplay the local presence of these regional civil society actors. Their local presence needs to be visible in our analysis because these are always linked to regionalisation and development of regional projects from below. The localness of this form of regionalising activities does not undermine its relevance as part of the world order (Acharya 2018). It can be a source of problems as well as a source of the solutions. As James H. Mittleman (1999:47) has argued, 'it is clear that focusing too heavily on macro level underestimates the importance of the micro issues' (1999:47). It can be argued that it is these micro-regional issues emanating from local politics, mis-governance or maladministration, insurgency, unemploy-ment, poverty and so on that are forming parts of the agenda for regional and global governance. According to Okechukwu Iheduru,

> [w]hat is important in a region like West Africa [...] is not necessarily the strength or feebleness of these democratic forces. Instead, the focus should

be on their potential to create new (or deepen old) regional cultural identities as they grow and opt for regional solutions to some local, national and global problems.

(2003:51)

While civil society actors across all regional spatial levels including the micro, are not immune from showing negative tendencies (Acharya 2014b, Soderbaum 2007, Iheduru 2003), the awareness of this is important at least to remind us that civil society can sometimes serve popular interest or work against it depending on their motivations and orientation towards the region. Nonetheless, regional responses provide an opportune ground for understanding how different actors from the local-regional to the global-regional levels rise to address human challenges and insecurity in the 21st century, and how such responses by multiple actors including civil society in this sense, are contributing to the regionalist activities in Africa (Acharya 2018, Godsater 2013b, 2016). So, this chapter reaffirms the importance of regional presence of civil society actors as parts of the analytic concepts in this framework. I therefore focus on regional capacity in the next section.

Regional Capacity

To understand the extent to which regional civil society actors have evolved, I consider it important to also examine their capacities/capability on the regional levels. I introduce regional capacity of civil society actors to denote the ability of the regional civil society organisations and networks to act in building regions, in expressing their agency and contributing to regional governance. According to LindVall (2017), when we talk of capacity, we refer to key factors in determining effective implementation of public policy. Olowu (2003:1–6) sees capacity as the ability of both states and non-state actors when implementing development policies and governance. This is a very important concept that helps us to make sense of how civil society actors are enabled (or otherwise) to transform the interests that characterise their action-based identities into relevant activities/contributions in the region. Region does not seem to exist without a normative value (Genna and Hiroi 2015:152). Analysing regional capacity of civil society actors injects a critical perspective on actorship of civil society on the regional level. It does not necessarily reject civil society actors but moves further to engage critically with what enables them to act in the region. There is a tendency to become uncritical if we fail to unravel what enables or constrains the so-called regional civil society organisations to act. Do civil society actors at the regional levels have the capacity to act in the region? Having capacity does not mainly refer to material aspects alone. It also underscores the relevance of ideational factors embedded in it. In considering the presence or absence of these important agential ingredients, we will be able to identify responsible factors that aid or undermine the expression of their agency in the region. Because the capacity is very important for any given actor, this needs to be accounted for in the analysis of regional civil society actors either in Africa or elsewhere.

There are CSOs in the African regions interested in peace and security, human rights, environmental activism, poverty alleviation, regional and interregional trade promotions, women's empowerment and so on (Iheduru 2003, 2015b, Acharya 2018, Godsater and Soderbaum 2011). What is the level of their operational and institutional capacities in promoting or realising their social goals at the regional levels? Do they rely on other actors in the New Regionalism Approach such as state, market/business entities and external actors before they can act? If they do, how does it reinforce civil society actorship in the region? This needs to be problematised. My argument is that constructing a regional identity is one thing; the ability to act based on that action-based identity is another thing. This needs to be accounted for in the evolution of these actors in the region. The understanding of this capacity can also reveal some vital details in relation to the contribution or impact of these organisations at the end of the day. This leads to the fourth analytic concept which focuses on societal impact.

Societal Impact

I introduce societal impact to describe the specific contributions of civil society actors in regional integration/regionalism. Some of these organisations have the aspirations to democratise regionalism based on their activities. This analytical concept makes it possible to find out whether there is a trace of a democratic input based on the activities of a given civil society actor. For those civil society actors aspiring to promote human security or conflict prevention in the region, an analytic concept like this makes it possible to find out whether there is a related contribution as a result of the activities of such a civil society actor in the trajectory of regionalism.

Generally, societal impact focuses on the contributions on the regional levels, as a result of civil society's identity, presence and capacity. Although this has not been considered in the regionalism literature, the concept is important as it helps us to understand what constitutes civil society's actorship in the region. Due to civil society's normative tendencies, societal impact could be one that is positive to the popular aspiration of the people, for example, reducing the frequency of violent conflicts, as a result of conflict prevention activities or peacebuilding. It could be nominal without significant impact or negative when the activities of civil society create more problems leading to more unrest or anxiety for the people. This occurs especially when civil society activists take laws into their own hands and engage in anti-social activities and abuses of the civic space. The notion of societal impact may resonate with the inherent question in the new regionalism discourses that interrogates the question, regions for whom, or whose regions (Hettne 1999, Soderbaum 2002, Boas, Marchand and Shaw 2003).

The context of this framework closely connects with the aspiration of the ECOWAS policy makers who now emphasise the need to transcend the existing state-centric emphasis in ECOWAS affairs in order to create an ECOWAS with less focus on the states as drivers, and more focus on an ECOWAS that is actively driven by its citizens (ECOWAS Commission 2008, 2011, Kogbe 2012,

Iheduru 2013, 2015b, Ismail 2011, Afadzinu 2015). That is what is termed 'the ECOWAS of the People' (ECOWAS Commission 2008:9). Societal impact analysis is an important tool to assess whether civil society and other non-state actors' activities in the governance of regions do have positive, nominal or negative societal impact. The outcome of a qualitative analysis of societal impact will surely depend to a great extent on (1) what kind of social identity underpins their agencies, (2) at what regional spatial levels does the given civil society actor engage and (3) the capacity, such as institutional and operational, that enables it to act. All these are predetermining factors which must be taken into consideration, before a reasonable impact can be made. For regional CSOs to transform the interest that underpins their social identity into a concrete outcome, it becomes important to reflect critically and pay a serious attention to the points made above.

The above explanation tends to shift the focus from the states as the referent objects of regionalism or regionalist projects. In fact, this is gradually becoming a reality in a region such as West Africa, with the example of the ECOWAS community (Iheduru 2003, 2015, Asante 2016). ECOWAS has begun to reframe its regionalist programmes in reference to human security in the region and to consider regional CSOs as credible participants in that transition (Opoku 2007, ECOWAS Commission 2008, Iheduru 2003, 2016, Ismail 2011). Therefore, the impact as part of the framework seeks to uncover key contributions of these actors on the regional levels. It also seeks to determine whether such contributions resonate with the interest that regional CSOs often claim to represent. Societal impact can, however, be very elusive to analyse but it is one of the most important factors to consider in studying regional civil society actors, in order for us to determine whether they have the capacity to do what they have promised to do. And where capacity is not an impediment, it will also help us to consider whether they are doing what they have claimed to do in the governance of a region or not. In addition, the framework will also provide an opportunity analytically to find out the factors responsible for the ability and inability of civil society to contribute to regionalist activities and the impact they make at the end of the day.

I have represented the analytical framework explained above in a succinct and clear tabular representation in Table 2.1.

Conclusion

In summary, this chapter has showed how civil society is understood in regionalism. It identified the New Regionalism Approach and integrated the proposed regional attributes of civil society actorship as an analytical framework. The developed framework will therefore serve as the analytical guide to understand the extent to which civil society actors have evolved to act on the regional levels in West Africa.

Two forms of identities presented in this study are analytically linked to understanding civil society actorship. Accounting for the regional levels where these actors are present (or absent) helps us to see whether they are truly regional in terms of their activities. Both concepts of capacity and societal impact are keen

Table 2.1 Tabular Representation of the Analytical Framework

Typical Regional CSOs	Regional Identity	Regional Presence	Regional Capacity	Societal Impact
Regional CSO 1	e.g., Action-based identity for democratising regionalism	**Levels:** Regional/macro National/meso Subnational/micro	(+ / -) Ideational factors. Institutional factors. Collective alliance. Internal and external support.	(+/-) Overcome state-centric regionalism. Wider participation of civil society in regional policymaking. Mainstreaming civil society in regionalism and influencing the trajectory of regionalism in the interest of the people.
Regional CSO 2	e.g., Action-based identity for conflict prevention in regionalism	**Levels:** Regional/macro National/meso Subnational/micro	(+/-) Ideational factors. Institutional factors. Collective alliance. Internal and external support.	(+/-) Mainstreamed civil society inputs in regional conflict prevention. Reduction in frequency of violent conflicts in the regions. Recognition as a partner. An institutionalised structure for participatory regionalism in peacebuilding.

Source: author.

elements to juxtapose normative claims with the actions on the regional levels. It is a Coxian observation that 'Theory is always for someone and for some purpose' (Cox 1981:128). As applicable to other social sciences, the field of regionalism or comparative regionalism is characterised by divergent perspectives (often alien to African reality) which have stemmed from varied ontological and epistemological orientations over the last 70 years. Samuel K. B. Asante explains that the African experience of 'region-building and regional integration actually started off as aspects of the pan-African movement' (2016:127). He further points out that the centrality of this regionalist pan-African movement was anchored essentially to unify 'African forces against imperialism and colonial domination' (2016:127). However, the mainstream scholarship has tended to look at the so-called domination, from what is obtainable in the policy cycle and political economy of the continent. Unfortunately, there is a pervasive tendency that seems to overlook the intellectual domination of Africa's understanding of itself, as against the normative templates of exogenous intellectual forces that contemporarily define the strength and limits of African regionalist initiatives.

I therefore argue that the academic understanding of regionalism and regional integration hitherto in Africa tends to originate from that which is most often imposed or informed from outside. Such exogenous templates have great impact on the understanding of African regionalisms and how the knowledge is produced. This chapter underscores this fact and puts forward the above framework to understand the case studies of this research.

Theory as an analytical lens of a social researcher is meant to describe, explain or predict the phenomena of the world (Balogun 2011, Ndlovu-Gatsheni 2018, Heywood 2011). It should be cautiously noted that the framework proposed in this chapter is not a theory in a positivist view of what a theory is. The framework proposed is meant to guide the researcher to describe (and partly explain) the extent to which regional civil society has evolved as an actor in West Africa from the experiences of the people and groups who are partaking in regionalist activities. This must be seen as a story of African civil society regionalism through the perspectives of the actors themselves.

Note

1 Of the 13 member states of SADC, three (Botswana, Mauritius and Namibia) are consolidating democracies, four (Malawi, Tanzania, South Africa, and Zambia) are defective democracies, two (Lesotho and Madagascar) are highly defective democracies, and two (Angola and Mozambique) are moderate autocracies, while two (Democratic Republic of Congo and Zimbabwe) are classified as hard-line autocracies (Hulse et al. 2018:18).

3 The Contextual Understanding of the Evolution of Regional Civil Society in West Africa

Introduction

This chapter provides a historical context and symbiotic relation between regional integration and the agency of civil society in West Africa. The structure of this chapter comprises the history of regional CSOs in West Africa, the colonial and post-colonial perspectives of civil society regionalism in the region, the influence of the West African political regime, the inspiration behind regional CSOs formation in West Africa, aimed at promoting democratic participation and human security/conflict prevention in the region, and discussions of the analytical framework.

The History of Regional CSOs in West Africa

This section takes a brief look at the recent history of regional civic associations in the West African region. Geographically, the conception of West Africa is a modern construct (Adedeji 2004). The given understanding of the West African space comprises 16 countries: five Anglophone (Nigeria, Ghana, Gambia, Sierra Leone and Liberia), nine Francophone (Senegal, Côte d'Ivoire, Benin, Mali, Guinea, Burkina Faso, Niger, Togo and Mauritania) and two Lusophone (Cape Verde and Guinea Bissau). (Now, it is just 15 for the ECOWAS region excluding Mauritania). However, many observers would have assumed that the historical antecedent of regional civil society organisations in West Africa took its root after the establishment of the Economic Community of West African States (ECOWAS) in May 1975. Contrary to this assumption, the formation of pan-regional identities in fact predates the ECOWAS formation (Iheduru 2015b, Obadare 2015). The pre-colonial struggle based on the pan-Africanist movement was a source of inspiration reinforced by regional ties and identities shared by those active citizens of West Africa. They included the West Africans both at home and in the diaspora, who were demanding an end to colonial rule in the countries that would now be known as member states of ECOWAS (Adedeji 1970, 2004, Obadare 2015, Asante 2019).

Historically, we can make a sense of the evolution of the regional civic movement through what Mazrui (1995) calls the duality of pan-Africanism. Mazrui looks at the agency of pan-Africanism in both its colonial and post-colonial

DOI: 10.4324/9781003257288-4

contexts. He divides the duality of pan-Africanism into two related phases that connects the decolonial struggle for the self-government of the African people as a historical phase, while the other phase focuses on the process of post-colonial unity and integration of Africa. Conceptually, these are referred to as the pan-Africanism of liberation, referring to the former that has produced independent African states, whereas the latter is known as the pan-Africanism of integration, which is associated with the whole idea of regionalism or regional integration in social, economic and political matters in Africa (Mazrui 1995).

In looking at the history of the pan-regional solidarity, it would be important to acknowledge the historical agency of those West African citizens in the decolonisation struggle. These may be seen as the idea of meta-agency. The meta-regional agency in the context of West Africa could be seen as the pan-Africanist activities undertaken by the people of West Africa as part of the struggle against colonialism and attainment of political independence (Kete Asante 2019). Molefi Kete Asante (2019) draws attention to the West African Students Union of London as 'one of the principal groups backing a call for the [Fifth Pan-African] Congress' (2019:275). At the time, the identity of the West African Students Union (WASU) did not represent a single colony. It was believed to be regional in outlook even though, geographically, it implied the then British West African space that comprised the subjects of the former colonies under the British colonial administration (Bach 2016). The era is considered a significant historical phase in the anti-colonial struggle which would later have a considerable impact in achieving political independence in the region and in other parts of Africa (Kete Asante 2019).

Another important phase in this evolution is the post-colonial era, especially in the late 1980s and the 1990s onward when the idea of civil society became widespread in Africa as champions of democratisation across the continent (Shaw 2000). The regional dimension of the post-colonial phase of these civil society organisations in West Africa was not only motivated by democratisation struggle, but also largely influenced by the violent conflicts in the 1990s shortly after the end of the Cold War (Karbo 2018, Lederach 2016, Ismail 2011, Olonisakin 2009). For a better understanding of both colonial and post-colonial phases of these societal actors, the next section provides an account to make sense of the post-colonial regional civil society organisations in West Africa.

Regional CSOs in a Colonial and Post-colonial Historical Reflection

According to Ebenezer Obadare (2015), a prominent authority on civil society in Africa, a form of pan-regional civil society in West Africa cannot be considered in isolation, without reflecting on the pre-independence history of countries that comprise the West African region today. Obadare (2015) posits that the idea of regional civic movement historically predates the independence of many of the present-day West African states. From this view, a number of civil society groups that existed towards the end of colonialism in West Africa were founded as part of the collective political goal of pan-Africanism (Iheduru 2015b, Obadare 2015,

Kete Asante 2019). For Obadare, these organisations had a 'pan-regional focus' and developed 'a sub-regional identity' on the basis of 'African political self-determination' (Obadare 2015:13–14). The examples included the West African Student Union (WASU), which was established in Britain on 7 August 1925. The West African Youth League was another example, founded in 1935, as well as the *West African Pilot* newspaper, established in 1937. The common interest of these movements was to work for the political independence of the West African states. In addition, Obadare argues that the formation of ECOWAS in 1975 may have been partly inspired by these pan-regional organisations (2015:13–14).

In a similar vein, Okechukwu Iheduru acknowledges the role of the pre-independence conglomeration of citizens groups that 'provided the anti-colonial movement leaders with robust platforms to forge new regional identities critical to the mobilisation of rural and urban dwellers against colonial rule' in West Africa (Iheduru 2015b:141). While emphasising the socio-political and cultural significance of the colonial civil society of West Africa, Obadare further calls our attention to the rationale of these organisations, which according to him was to 'expose the falsity of colonialists' claims and assumptions about Africans and African history; organise Africans against the brutal assault on their culture by the colonial order; and prepare Africans for self-rule' (Obadare 2015:14). Adedeji (2004) also draws our attention to the agency of people in the pan-Africanist struggle in the colonial West Africa. Adedeji asserts:

> In discussing the origins of West African integration, due recognition must be accorded to the great foresight of the fifth pan-African congress, held in Manchester, England, in October 1945. The congress recommended the establishment of a West African economic union 'as a means of combating the exploitation of the economic resources of the West African territory and for ensuring the participation of the indigenous people in the industrial development of West Africa'.
>
> (Adedeji 2004:22)

Although the above refers to the British West Africa (Adedeji 2004), nonetheless, it is a pointer to the regional consciousness of the people irrespective of their individual colonies at the time. From a pan-Africanist perspective, the independence and integration are closely linked together (Ola 1979:88). It is through this linkage that the agency of the people themselves is often acknowledged in the struggle towards the independence of the post-colonial states in Africa (Adi and Sherwood 2003). The independence is seen as a phase in the pan-Africanist movement. However, the subaltern realist, focusing on the Third World Countries, sees the independence of these states differently through the juridical sovereignties and recognition by the United Nations (Ayoob 2002). This perspective posits that the creation of these states was a result of the external forces. According to Ayoob, 'In Europe sovereignty followed the establishment of effective state control. In the third world, juridical sovereignty preceded the establishment of state control' (2002:44–45). Legitimacy relating to the sovereignties became a problem coupled with the task of state-building. The post-colonial state-building became burden-some on the part of the state elites who needed to 'mobilise human and material resources to effectively administer territories encompassed by colonially crafted boundaries' (Ayoob 2002:44). In the 1960s, pan-Africanism remained the uni-fying ideology for the unity of African people. At the same time, the attendant challenges faced by the political leaders in safeguarding their juridical sovereign-ties and 'consolidating state authority' resulted into violence and repression. It is posited that in an attempt to maintain state control 'the security of the state and the regime become closely intertwined' (Ayoob 2002:46) in the newly independent post-colonial states. This has also given rise to what is now known as the neopat-rimonial system of rule based on regime protection in West Africa (Taylor and Williams 2008, Ezeokafor 2015).

The Post-colonial West Africa: States, the Regime and Civil Society

As Claude Ake articulated, at independence, the independent nations of Africa remained 'highly statist' and embraced 'the legacy of colonial regimes which rested on the determined and sometimes brutal use of force' (1976:10–11). What is interesting about this is that those who assumed the political administration of the newly independent states were among the elites previously at the forefront of anti-colonial struggle. Obadare described it as 'the first ever mass defection from civil society to the state in the sub-region's history' (2015:14). These new political actors greatly treasured and determined to preserve their newfound post-colonial states and sovereignties (Interviewee 5, Madueke 2015). The states' sovereign-ties became sacrosanct and provided opportunities for the leaders to associate the security of the regime with the security of the states (Ayoob 2002:46). It would be observed that such an elitist political culture was not only embedded in the national politics during this epoch, it later found its way into the regional integra-tion architecture of ECOWAS (Taylor and William 2008, Ezeokafor 2015). The West African economic integration led by ECOWAS apparently became 'a club of dictators', driven mainly by state actors (Madueke 2015, Fayemi in WPForum 2016, Interviewee 5). *The ECOWAS of states* either ignored or failed to realise the role of civil society actors prior to political independence in the region, and the subsequent establishment of ECOWAS in 1975 (Iheduru 2015b:137).

According to an interviewee, the preoccupation of the 'old' ECOWAS (known as state-centric ECOWAS) was principally concerned with regime secu-rity, rather than the security of the West African citizens (Interviewee 5). It has also been argued that the trends of security in West Africa are designed to pro-tect the neo-patrimonial political culture that shields the West African political leaders and warlords from any existential threat to the survival of their regimes (Taylor and Williams 2008, Ezeokafor 2015). In 2015, during a special meeting on ECOWAS's 40th anniversary, this state-centric inclination was also reiterated by former WACSOF president, Jubrin Ibrahim. According to him, although West African leaders may have initiated the project of regional economic integration, a critical look at the old ECOWAS at the beginning shows that it was a replica of 'a club of dictators' primarily aimed at shielding West African leaders against agitations from the citizens (Madueke 2015). One can say the neo-patrimonial system of rule/political patronage would later result in incessant political breakdowns serving as an excuse for the military juntas to seize political power (Taylor and Williams 2008). While such an interregnum has a special meaning in the political evolution of modern West Africa, the post-colonial civil society movement in the region would later constitute one of the formidable civic voices that challenged the military incursions into the national politics in the early years of independence (Kandeh 2004).

Consequently, the West African national political interregna began in the republics of Togo and Benin in 1963. The Republic of Ghana had its first military coup in 1966, Nigeria in 1966, Sierra Leone in 1967, before it subsequently spread to other states in the region. The reign of the dictatorial regime was incessant in the region until the 1990s (Kandeh 2004:147–149). In addition, the region has experienced military coups in Mali in 2012 (and 2020) and Burkina Faso in 2015 (Nossiter 2012, BBC 2017b, 2018). However, ECOWAS has proactively sustained its post-Cold War democratic norm in the region by ensuring that coup d'états under whatever guise have no place in West Africa (Iwilabe and Agbo 2012, Bappah 2018).

As a result of the factors mentioned above, the first decade of political independence in the region produced a post-colonial civil society movement in West Africa to speak out against political maladministration and the incessant incursions of military juntas into national politics (Obadare 2015, Adejumobi 2004). While the West African national civil society movements were active in resisting these authoritarian regimes (Jusu-Sheriff 2004), they also played a role in condemning and protesting against the unpopular macro-economic policies, dictated by the liberal international financial regime of the Structural Adjustment Programme (SAP) of the 1980s (Obadare 2004, 2014, Akinrinade 2004, Iheduru 2015, Adejumobi 2004). Subsequently, the outbreak of civil wars in Liberia, Sierra Leone and Guinea Bissau in the early 1990s expanded the role of civil society in West Africa, especially those CSOs in the states experiencing civil wars. In that epoch associated with the aftermath of the Cold War, the main activities of CSOs were targeted at democratisation and conflict prevention in the region, started first from their respective national levels (Jusu-Sheriff 2004, Opoku 2007, Ismail 2011). According to Jusu-Sheriff (2004), some of these civic groups may not be organised in the classical sense of civil society, but they remained active in their democratisation struggle and developmental activities across the West African states. Yasmin Jusu-Sheriff observes that

> the classical conception of civil society may not be present in the West African experience, the actual character of civil society in the subregion is far more complex and variegated. Many civil society actors involving women, professional, workers, students, religious leaders, and rural inhabitants have disputably acted in recent times to challenge state authoritarianism, expand

democratic spaces, and defend issues of public interest in many West African
countries.

(Jusu-Sheriff 2004:266–267)

Jusu-Sherif's observation above refers to the impact of the national civil society
groups in the region, specifically in Liberia and Sierra Leone. Examples of these
are the Movement for Justice in Africa (MOJA) and the Progressive Alliance of
Liberia that worked as a civil society movement against the autocracy in Liberia
before they developed into political parties in 1985 (Jusu-Sheriff 2004:270). Also,
when the civil war broke out in Liberia in 1989, civil society groups, especially
the faith-based organisations and women groups, refocused their activities and
swung into conflict prevention and mediation diplomacy between the warring parties (Adejumobi 2004, Aning 2004). The Inter-faith Mediation Committee, which
consisted of the Liberian Council of Churches (LCC) and the National Muslim
Council of Liberia (NMCL), participated actively in mediating for peace in the
war-torn Liberian state (Jusu-Sheriff 2004:270–271). Other civil society groups
included the Catholic Justice and Peace Commission, the Centre for Law and
Human Rights Education (CLHRE), the Liberian Women Initiative (LWI) and
the Mano River Women Peace Network of Liberia. The truce reached in Liberia
after nearly seven years of civil war was in part attributed to the active role of civil
society organisations in the country (Jusus-Sheriff 2004).

The Liberia political malady spilled over like a contagious disease to the sister country of Sierra Leone. Just like in Liberia, Sierra Leone had its own share
of authoritarian regimes under the rule of the All People's Congress of Siaka
Stevens, which operated from 1968 to 1985 (Jusu-Sheriff 2004:272). Some of the
Sierra Leonean civil society organisations played a very active role in responding to the outbreak of civil war in the country, starting from 1991 (Ibrahim and
Majeks-Walker 2015). In the Republic of Benin, the resurgence of civil society
groups in the 1989/1990s marked a significant milestone in the region. These
groups included students' associations, trade unions, women associations and
sundry political groups (Bierschenk 2009, Obadare 2015). The pressure from
these groups led to abandoning of a single-party system. The Beninese National
Conference, comprising 493 participants, was convened from 19 to 28 February
1990 to fashion out the new political order in the country (Bierschenk 2009:340).
Obadare described it as 'a civilian coup of February 1990' (2015:14). According
to Biershenk (2009), regime change was not on the agenda of the conference.
However, the momentum of deliberations and debates resulted in the declaration of sovereign national conference on 25 February 1990. Despite President
Matthew Kerekou's initial resistance, he could not reverse the declaration due to
considerations such as the pressure from the trade unions with the threat of strike
and to avoid showdown and anarchy in the country. This particular political experience in Benin became a source of inspiration for civil society activism in other
parts of the region (Obadare 2015, Bierschenk 2009).

In Burkina Faso, post-colonial civil society activism played a different role in
the political evolution of the country (Saidou 2018). According to Saidou, it is

always difficult to discern the boundary between civil society and political parties as some of these organisations sometimes have dealings with political actors (2018:40). However, civil society in Burkina Faso has been a dynamic and counterforce against authoritarian regime in the country's history (Saidou 2018:40). Isiaka Coulibaly, a Burkinabe civil society practitioner, situated civil society in four temporal periods. From the 1960s to 1970s, 'it was an active and committed civil society whose main achievement was the fall of the government of the First Republic of President Maurice Yarmeogo on 3 January 1966 after popular protests led by labour unions and military intervention' (Coulibaly 2015:31). Derrick had also given a comprehensive account of the devastating effects of droughts in West African Sahel from 1972 to 1974, which resulted in a great humanitarian crisis of famine in the region (Derrick 1977, 1984). The northern parts of the Burkina Faso had its share from the perilous droughts. From 1974 to 1990, the attention of civil society was focused on 'humanitarian and development interventions that were less political' (Coulibaly 2015:31). The 1990s to 2000s was an era sparked by the struggle for democratisation. Another crucial point was the popular uprising of 30 October 2014 staged by the national civil society activists to oppose the revision of Article 37 of the country's constitution. The revision of the Article would have allowed the removal of the limitation on the president's mandate (Coulibaly 2015, Saidou 2018).

Gained its independence in 1975, Cape Verde is a small island country with less than one million population. The country is reputed for its multiparty system and political stability. Due to its geographical location, the country's economy is based on tourism, and its civil society activities are often linked with the Cape Verdean diaspora organisations in America and Europe (Baker 2006, Evora and Costa 2015). Like in other West African states, the Cape Verdean civil society groups such as NGOs also emerged in the 1990s. Their activities depended on the remittances and support the organisations were able to get from their people in the diaspora and foreign donors (Baker 2006, African Development Bank 2012). The coalition of NGOs known as Cape Verde NGO Platform was established in 1996 (Evora and Costa 2015). The general perspective about Cape Verde underscores its political stability, democratic culture and civil society participation in the national development issues (African Development Bank 2012, Baker 2006). The country has been a multiparty democracy since the 1990s.

The creation of the African Agricultural Union in 1944 by the late President Houphouet Boigny had a significant impact on the evolution of civil society movements in Côte d'Ivoire and more widely in the struggle for political independence in the erstwhile French West Africa (Dickovick 2012). Civil society groups (students' groups and Faculty's associations) were active in the 1980s, especially in response to the associated social and economic sufferings of the Structural Adjustment Programme in the country (Daddieh 1996). The era produced the first set of non-governmental organisations, such as the Association of Women Lawyers of the Ivory Coast (AFJCI) which was formed in 1986, and Ivorian Human Rights League (LIDHO), created in 1987, among others (Fini 2015). These organisations and other emerging networks would later synergise to lead the democratisation struggle of the 1990s. They culminated in part into National Elections Observatory (ONE), formed in 1995 with the objective of creating awareness for the populace about elections to the offices of the president, the legislative assembly and the municipalities (Fini 2015:54). Modifications to the thematic focus of civil society movements became a necessity. This was due to the 2002 political crisis with a score of human sufferings in the country (Aning 2004, Adejumobi 2004). As a result, these organisations are deemed so important in promoting peace to avert the reoccurrence of politically motivated violent conflicts in the country. With the new networks such as WANEP, the Civil Society Coalition for Peace and Democratic Development (COSOPCI) and the Ivorian Civil Society Convention (CSCI) (see Fini 2015:53–63), civil society remained an active part of the Ivorian political landscape. Some of their leaders were given political appointment by the Ivorian government. An example was Professor Bleou Martin of the Ivorian Human Rights League who was appointed the Minister of Interior in 2003 during Seydou Diarra's administration. In the post-2010 election, according to Fini (2015:54), 'Many of their leaders became members of independent state institutions in charge of issues on Human Rights, democracy, information, and communication'.

Looking at the civil society's early stride in the Gambia, the significant role of the Gambia Family Planning Association, set up in 1968, the Freedom from Hunger Campaign (FFHC) in 1969, Action Aid International in the Gambia in 1979, and the Young Men Christian Association in 1979, cannot be overemphasised (Jaborteh 2015). Today, The Gambia hosts the African Centre for Democracy and Human Studies (ACDHRS), a regional human rights NGO established by an Act of Parliament in 1989 that has been working in promoting human rights in the Gambia and across the continent of Africa. It gained full independence in 1995.[1] ACDHRS has been an African civil society hub for capacity building and regional advocacy on the African Commission on Human and People's Rights and the African Charter on Human and People's Rights (Saha 1999). The 22 years reign of Yahyah Jammeh was a tough time for civil society organisations. In Jabarteh's view, the primordial spirit of the Gambians themselves to civic associations for self-help and communal solidarity has been a source of strength for the local civil society in the country (2015:72). In addition, the aid of multiple networks of civil society organisations in Africa and outside of Africa that regularly converges in Banjul for human rights meetings has also made the small country of West Africa an important centre for the civil society activities in the region.

According to Ibrahim (2015), there is a historical link to the associational life in modern Ghana which can be traced to the colonial era around 1850s among the urban dwellers. At the time, a form of associational lives flourished through the formation of social groups including Gold Coast Debating Society, and formation of then called the Aborigines Rights Protection Society (ARPS) in 1897 (Ibrahim 2012, Atuguba 2015). The Ghanaian post-independence civil society activities faced stiff restrictions, especially during the prolonged military rule from 1966 to 1993 with the exception of the interregnums in between those periods (Atuguba 2015). Like in other sister countries, there was a significant boom in the activities of civil society from the 1990s. The significant part of this era underscored the 1997 National Conference on Civil Society (NCCS). This national conference led to the formation of the Civil Society Coordinating Council (CivisoC) in relation to the review of the Structural Adjustment Programme in the country (Atuguba 2015:86). Civil society has remained active in the country. It was in Accra that the Charter of WACSOF was signed in 2003. The country also plays a host to active regional civil society organisations and think tanks such as the Kofi Annan International Peacekeeping Training Centre (KAIPTC), WACSI, WANEP, West African Action Network on Small Arms (WAANSA) and Foundation for Security and Development in Africa (FOSDA).

According to Baldet (2015), from 1958 to 1984, the First Republic of Guinea was based on 'the socialist model of a Party-State'. The sociopolitical and economic directions of the country were under the control of the Democratic Party of Guinea (PDG). Although civil society became open in Guinea in the 1990s, groups such as trade unions, women's groups and/or youth organisations constituted the significant forces for civil society and 'played a major in the struggle for independence' (Civicus 2011:17–18). Apart from the struggle for democratisation in the 1990s, Guinean civil society NGOs also engaged in development activities, filling the vacuum in co-provision of basic necessities due to the dwindling capacity of the state (Baldet 2015, Corre 2003, Civicus 2011). Corre (2003) adds that the liberal policies of Guinean government of 1984 and the limited capacity of the state to provide the essential public goods to its citizenry greatly contributed to the proliferation of civil society groups and non-governmental organisations. The civil society boom at the time was noteworthy, reaching '3,500 grass-roots organisations, 700 NGOs and a number of joint chambers' by the year 2000 (Corre 2003:2). Corre further explains that the motivation for many individual involvements in civil society and NGOs in Guinea may not be only because they needed to contribute meaningfully to development but rather as 'survival strategies' amidst dwindling public service and loss of jobs (Corre 2003:2). The contextual relevance of this is to underscore the awareness of civil society movement in some of these countries before resulting into new regional networks in post-Cold War West Africa.

As in Liberia and Sierra Leone, civil society actors in Guinea Bissau played an important part in conflict management during the 1990s civil conflict (Adebajo 2002:142). Miguel De Barros explains that 'the political-military conflict in 1998/99 put an end to 18 years of absolute power under the regime of General Joao Bernardo Nino Vieira' (2015:106). According to Adebajo (2002:142), during this time civil society's role was strengthened in conflict prevention as evidenced by the role played by the Bishop of Bissau for his mediating activities between the two warring sides at the time, as well as the activities of civil society groups and organisations in the post-election peacebuilding.

For Mali,[2] the winds of democratisation of the 1990s did not leave it behind. The era was marked by the citizens' revolution of March 1991. The popular protests by the citizens paved the way for multiparty governments, after the prolonged dictatorial rule of President Moussa Traore (*The New York Times* 1991), who overthrew the first President of Mali, Modibo Keita, in 1968 (Togola 2015:129). According to Alou, the 1990s also saw the birth of civil society in Niger as part of the wave of democratisation in Africa (2015:139). In Nigeria, civil society had a great influence prior to and after the political independence of the country (Obono 2015:147). The country had its unfortunate share of prolonged military rule, but the quest for freedom was the hallmark of the civil rights' activism in the largest country of West Africa (Akinrinde 2004). Obono notes that 'The formation of Civil Liberties Organisation (CLO) by Olisa Agbakoba, Clement Nwankwo, other lawyers and journalists, in October 1998 was a momentous turning point in the history of (post-independence) Nigerian civil society' (Obono 2015:151). The 1990s saw the height of the pro-democracy civil society movement in Nigeria. The annulment of the 12 June 1993 presidential election result by the military head of state, General Ibrahim Babangida, was partly responsible for the mass movement of those civil society activists (Obadare 2016, Akinrinde 2004). Many of the opposition activists lost their lives in the struggle, and some were arbitrarily arrested and detained by the military government (Obadare 2016). Notable groups such as Campaign for Democracy and the National Democratic Coalition (NADECO) and other similar groups vehemently resisted the dictatorial rule of the military juntas, in their determination to show red cards to the military to hand over power to democratically elected civilians (Obono 2015:151, Momoh 2013:204, Lansford 2014:1073).

The Senegalese case of civil society has often been considered as vibrant and the country has enjoyed political stability in the region since its political independence (Villalon 1994, Lo 2006, 2010, Aidara 2015). Lo (2006, 2010) emphasised that the case of Senegalese civil society is better understood through its African contexts rather than through prescriptive conditions of neoliberal view of what a civil society entails. According to Aidara, in the tail end of the 1970s and the early period of 1980s, civil society experienced 'a strong growth' in size and its ability to influence the policies of the government (Aidara 2015:159). The period between the 1990s and the 2000s was regarded as another important epoch during which these organisations began to refocus their activities in the country. The time saw the consortium of non-governmental societies become active in the development activities (2015:161). The platform gave them the opportunity to promote dialogue with governments including with the donors and development partners (2015:161). This also shows that the 1990s was an important time for civil society in the country.

According to Civicus (2006), interest groups, comprising trade unions, youth associations and women have constituted civil society movement in Togo during the colonial period. Their activities were also manifested in the referendum of 26 April 1956 that led to the independence of the country in 1960 (Civicus 2006). In the 1990s civil society groups demanded reforms and democratic pluralism in the country (Mbrou 2015, Civicus 2006). Heilbrunn (1993) compared Benin and Togo and concluded that the successful transition to democracy was a result of the existence of civil society in Benin unlike Togo. Nwajiaku (1994) on the other hand made a suspect of Heilbrum's conclusion for ignoring the vulnerability of President

Matthieu Kerekou, the state's economic incapacitation, and loss of support. Unlike the experience in Benin, the democratisation struggle in Togo was manipulated by Gnassingbe Eyadema and militarily repressed his oppositions including the tacit support from France (Nwajiaku 1994). The contextual relevance of this is to emphasise the awareness of civil society movement across the region in this historic period.

Before WANEP, WADNET, WACSOF and the likes were formed, the historical examples discussed above provided the context for the responses of civil society movements in their respective countries in West Africa. One can notice that the widespread awareness of civil society activism was triggered by the post-Cold War democratisation struggle at the national levels. The post-Cold War awareness of civil society groups and their regionalisation in West Africa can be located in this period. It was the collective groups of civil society activists in Nigeria, Liberia, Sierra Leone, Senegal, Togo and Ghana, among others, that formed a regional alliance that later translated into some of the notable regional civil society organisations that we see in the region today (WPForum 2016).

The appreciation of this historical trajectory is necessary to understand the aspiration of these civil society groups. While the post-Cold War phase marked a significant drive in the political economy of Africa focusing on regionalisms as projects in promoting economic cooperation, development, and management of peace and security, it was also the era of democratisation across Africa (Ball and Fayemi 2004, Adejumobi 2010). Because regional organisations especially in West Africa had started to assume importance in the regional governance of security and other development matters, there was no longer any other justification for civil society activists in the region to close their eyes, without extending their coverage through a new network to engage with ECOWAS at the regional levels. The rationale driving the regionalisation of CSOs in West Africa will be briefly discussed in the next section.

Inspirations/Rationale for Regional CSOs in West Africa:

From an empirical point of view, West African CSOs actively began to regionalise from the 1990s onward. While these regional moves cannot be looked at in isolation, the era coincided with the advent of new regionalism which also witnessed what is called 'the Red Card Campaign' undertaken by interest groups in Europe in 1998 (Bello 2011, Garcia 2015). It was also part of the regional awareness of civil society movement to influence regional policymaking at the EU level (Kohler-Koch 2009). Referring to the civil society at the EU level, Garcia explains that

> The 1998 'red card' campaign (refers to) when social and citizens' interest organisations showed red cards to the president of the [European] Commission at a public hearing to demonstrate against legal and financial challenges against mechanisms of financial support for EU civil society platforms.

(2015:15)

For West Africa, it can be posited that the rationale behind civil society groups to go regional was broadly necessitated by the need to contribute to conflict prevention in the region (Interviewee 9, Interviewee 10, WPForum 2016). The pre-1990 regional governance of ECOWAS was based on the protection of political regimes of West African leaders on the pretext for the respect of the sovereignties of member states (Taylor and Williams 2008, Ezeokafor 2015, Madueke 2015). Thus, the regionalisation of the West African civil society in the 1990s/2000s was sought to open up opportunities first to create an interface between ECOWAS leaders and civil society groups (WACSOF 2014, 2008, Iheduru 2015b). The establishment of some of these regional civil society networks operating in West Africa today could be traced to this period. The empirical data from the field affirms that some of these regional civil society networks and platforms sprang up with the aim of democratising West African regionalism and contributing to regional conflict prevention/human security (Interviewee 1, Interviewee 20, Interviewee 13, WPForum 2016). For instance, WANEP was established in 1998 for the purpose of conflict prevention. Established in 2000, the 'MARWOPNET of Guinea, Sierra Leone, and Liberia is a regional organization that came into as a result of the civil wars in Liberia and Sierra Leone' (Steady 2011:41).

It was also due to the realisation that the military approach as practised by ECOMOG in Liberia and Sierra Leone was not an effective way of ensuring sustainable peace and political stability in the troubled parts of the region (Adejumobi 2004, 2016, Ebo 2004, WANEP 2016c, Lederach 2016, Interviewee 13). The ECOWAS policymakers looked inward and underscored the need for CSOs to fill the gaps in their efforts to build peace and ensure the stability and development of West Africa (Interviewee 13, Interviewee 20, Interviewee 24). This was partly responsible for the move by civil society organisations and networks to assume a transnational conflict prevention role, complimentary to the ones performed by the states and ECOWAS (WPForum 2016, Interviewee 7).

Another empirical fact that affirmed the need for a regional network of civic organisations and NGOs in West Africa and other African regions can be traced to Article 2, paragraph 13 of the African Charter on Popular Participations in Development, otherwise known as the Arusha Charter. The Charter emanated from the International Conference from 12 to 16 February 1990, under the coordination of the United Nations Economic Commission for Africa (UNECA). Article 2(13) of the Arusha Charter asserts as follows:

> We want to emphasise the basic fact that the role of the people and their popular organisations is central to the realisation of popular participation. They have to be fully involved, committed and indeed, seize the initiative. In this regard, it is essential that they establish independent people's organisations at various levels that are genuinely grass-root, voluntary, democratically administered and self-reliant and that are rooted in the tradition and culture of the society so as to ensure community empowerment and self-development [...] It is crucial that the people and their popular organisations should develop

links across national borders to promote cooperation and inter-relationships on sub-regional, regional, south-south and south-north bases.

(1990:20)

The general understanding of the Charter was mainly to promote the agency of Africa in its own transformation for a peaceful and inclusive development. The Charter emphasises the need for an inclusive collaboration in which the states, the regional organisations, civil society/NGOs and African people themselves are awakened to see the benefits of working together across national borders, in a variety of sectors. We may intend to look at the Arusha Charter as a response to the economic decline which emanated from the neoliberal Structural Adjustment Programme (SAP), and the waves of economic globalisation. However, the emphasis on the popular role of the African people and their organisations at the time could be partly considered as one of the triggers for the role that civil society organisations would play in the years to come (UNECA 1990). What also adduced to this fact was the revision of the ECOWAS treaty in 1993. The ECOWAS revised treaty remedied the defects of the principles of the founding ECOWAS treaty of 1975, by recognising and making a provision for the role of the ECOWAS citizens and their organisations in regional integration in West Africa (ECOWAS 1993). According to Article 81 of the Revised Treaty of ECOWAS:

The Community (meaning the ECOWAS), with a view to mobilise the human and material resources for the economic integration of the region, shall co-operate with regional nongovernmental organisations and voluntary development organisations in order to encourage the involvement of the peoples of the region in the process of economic integration and mobilise their technical, material and financial support.

(ECOWAS 1993:45)

When considering the evolution of modern regional civil society activities in West Africa, the revision of the ECOWAS Treaty played a significant role (Interviewee 1, WPForum 2016). One year after the revised treaty, in 1994, ECOWAS granted observer status to civil society organisations (ECOWAS 1996). Subsequently, in 1996, ECOWAS established the Forum of Associations Recognised by ECOWAS, based on the ECOWAS Decision A/Dec 9/8/94 (ECOWAS 1996). The main responsibility of the Forum was to coordinate the activities of the non-governmental organisations holding the ECOWAS observer statuses in their relationship with the ECOWAS institutions (Interviewee 20), especially the ECOWAS Commission (Iheduru 2015:142). According to Iheduru, FARE was to 'act as a liaison between the CSOs and the ECOWAS Secretariat' (Iheduru 2015b:142). In 2003, WACSOF was jointly created by the ECOWAS and CSOs to serve as the regional umbrella body for civil society organisations in West Africa.

The scope of WACSOF was to cover a range of thematic areas covering peace and security, democratic governance, human rights, gender, youth and the empowerment of women, among others (WACSOF 2003, Interview 20). The sharp difference between FARE and WACSOF was that FARE encompassed all conceivable non-governmental organisations and business groups, whereas WACSOF was meant to serve as the regional umbrella body for West African civil society organisations with interest in regional integration, and to assist ECOWAS in creating awareness at the grassroots and communities across the 15 member states (Interviewee 1, Interviewee 2, WPForum 2016). Through its thematic groups, WACSOF was also to serve as the mouthpiece of West African CSOs, especially in influencing regional policies and programmes of ECOWAS across spatial levels (WACSOF 2003, WPForum 2016).

The essence of this explanation is to broadly show that peace and security (regional conflict prevention) and participatory democracy (bringing ECOWAS to the grassroots) actually formed the basis of regional civil society engagement in West Africa. In the context of West Africa, to understand how regional civil society has evolved as a regional actor, the issue of security and democracy becomes cogent as it served as the *basis for the evolution* of these regional CSOs and their *sites of influence* on regional matters.

Regional Shades of Security and Democracy: Shifting from a Regime-focused Regional Governance

The notion of security that relates to the role of civil society in West Africa can be understood in the context of the post-Cold War and post-United Nations Development Report of 1994 relating to security, which focused on individuals rather than states (UNDP 1994, Arusha Charter 1990, Grant and Soderbaum 2003, Iheduru 2003, Olonisakin 2009, Ismail 2011). In the first treaty of ECOWAS, the notion of regional security was not explicit. The primacy of the treaty institutionally lies in economic and development cooperation among the member states. Although it appears to be state-centric, Article 58, paragraphs 1, 2 and 3 of the 1993 revised treaty draws attention to the complexity of regional security of West Africa (ECOWAS 1993), which was further developed into a participatory conflict prevention framework (ECOWAS Commission 2008). The above articles also underscored the need for subsequent protocols to articulate an idea of security that accounts for the context and complexities of the region (Ismail 2011, Olonisakin 2009, Hultin 2014).

Gradually, from the 1990s onwards, the referent objects of ECOWAS security architecture were transformed, at least in principle, from the state-centric protection of regime security into human protections (Aning 2004, Adejumobi 2004, Ismail 2011, Iwilade and Agbo 2012, Bappah 2018). Civil society involvement in this period received more visibility in the regional peace and security activities, especially in developing institutionalised relations with ECOWAS to respond to regional conflicts (Aning 2004). One illustrative example of this is the ECOWAS Mechanism for Conflict Prevention, Management, Resolution, Peacekeeping and Security, adopted on 10 December 1999 at the Heads of States Summit of ECOWAS held in Abuja, Nigeria (Olonisakin 2009, Adejumobi 2004). The cornerstone of the Mechanism includes the legal backing for ECOWAS to intervene when the need arises in the time of crises. This is clearly stated in Article 40 of the Mechanism which centres on alleviating the suffering of populations and restoring life to normalcy in the event of crises, conflict or disaster (ECOWAS 1999). The Article also recognises the role of women in peace and conflict prevention as it links to Article 41(a.b.c) which provides the need for cooperation with national, regional NGOs, including faith-based organisations, Organisational of African Unity (OAU), now the African Union (AU), the United Nations and agencies and other international organisations in humanitarian sectors (ECOWAS 1999).

Most of the civil society organisations which sprung up in the 1990s often framed the rationale behind their regionalisation in the context of responding to violent conflicts in the region. In articulating their aims, they frequently synonymise conflict prevention with human security (Ismail 2011, Olonisakin 2009, Iheduru 2003). Reflections on the evolution of these organisations could inform researchers that both democratic participation and human security have always remained their aim in principle. In practice, most of them engage in conflict prevention. Research by Opoku (2007) and Olonisakin (2009) partly reflect this reality. And the reason for this is that human security itself as a concept is broad and its conceptual broadness enables these actors to locate their activities within the security policy concerns of the post-Cold War challenges in the region. The most likely way to do this was to contextualise their aspirations in terms of promoting a kind of security that placed a premium on the protection of the people at the time. The notion of human security resonates well with the activities of civil society as it also invokes 'democratic participation', 'empowerment', and prioritises the 'individual security as the primary focus and as such it is much broader than "national security"' (Van Langenhove 2004:3–4). According to a participant, a general idea of democratic participation, human security or conflict prevention became a guiding principle of civil society's engagement because ECOWAS needed civil society at the time and development partners were also ready to make funds available to support civil society programmes in the region (Interviewee 20). With this, the participation of civil society networks was sought to serve as a form of legitimacy for regional governance to reinforce partnership in addressing the problems of violent conflicts facing the region at the time (WPForum 2016, Interviewee 20, Interviewee 13, Interviewee 24).

For instance, the 2003 WACSOF Charter states that WACSOF shall 'Promote democratic principles and institutions, popular participation and empowerment of the people, good governance, human rights and freedom, and social justice' (Article 3, para 4). The same Article 4 (9) also adds that it shall 'Promote peace, unity, human security and stability in the sub region and Africa' (WACSOF 2003:4). This is also applicable to some similar organisations in the region.

Drawing from the above, one can argue that the post-Cold War civil society regionalisation in West Africa was founded on the idea of conflict prevention/human security promotion in seeking access to contribute to regional governance in West Africa (Interview 20). In other words, the ECOWAS citizens through their formal associations, societies and informal networks have not only identified with the democratic deficits of the regional political space of West Africa. They have also claimed to be playing a complimentary role in regional management of peace and security. Consequently, ECOWAS would also realise and affirm this role in paragraph 4, Section 2 of the ECOWAS Conflict Prevention Framework:

ECOWAS Member States bear primary responsibility for peace and security. However, as steps are taken under the new ECOWAS Strategic Vision to transform the region from an 'ECOWAS of States' into an ECOWAS of the Peoples, the tensions between sovereignty and supranationality, and between regime security and human security, shall be progressively resolved in favour of supranationality and human security respectively. Consequently, civil society shall play an increasingly critical role alongside Member States in the maintenance and promotion of peace and security.

(ECOWAS Commission 2008:9)

Invariably, it can be arguably posited that there are two main roles often pursued by regional civil society actors in West Africa. They seek to democratise ECOWAS and promote human security in the region, implying a kind of popular participation in regional governance. These roles are reflected in the aspirations of major regional networks such as WACSOF, WANEP and WAWA.

How Civil Society Actors Regionalise to Contribute to Regional Governance

The main assumption of the political economy of the new regionalism about civil society's role is to bring back 'the political' to serve as the voice for the voiceless and represent the interest of the weak in how regions are governed (Hettne 1999, Soderbaum 2011, 2016a). Because regionalism as a project can either be positive or negative, the role of all actors in regionalism cannot therefore be taken as given without being problematised. As Taylor and William (2008) posit, the promoters of the political culture of neopatrimonialism in West Africa are not restricted to state actors alone. Some non-state actors also constitute a part of the cycle of personalising public offices for the purpose of promoting private interest. The role of civil society organisations in regional governance may either follow the logic of serving popular interest or otherwise. It is for this reason that the four analytical concepts introduced in Chapter 2 are important to assess or analyse the role and actorship of key organisations within civil society. Instead of taking a general look at civil society in the region, this study seeks to understand the regional identities, regional presence, the capacity and the impact of given regional civil society organisations in West African regionalism.

Conclusion

The purpose of this chapter is to establish the context to deepen the historical background for the two main case studies in this study. The emergence of regional civil society in West Africa in 1990s/2000s is closely related to participation in the problem-solving regional governance. Rather than being constrained by various political regimes at the national levels, there was enthusiasm on the part of the ECOWAS leaders in encouraging the participation of civil society in regional policy development as a problem-solving project. An example was the expressed support for youth (West African Youth Union) and women (WAWA) participation by the ECOWAS Authority at its 22nd Summit in Lome, Togo, from 9 to 10 December 1999 (ECOWAS 1999b:15). The Communique of its 25th Summit at Accra in 2005 also expressed the Authority's support for the creation of WACSOF as a regional body of civil society groups and encouraged the ECOWAS Secretariat to ensure 'that civil society organisations and non-governmental organisations serve as a positive force for the development and integration of West Africa' (ECOWAS 2005:7). The collective aspiration of civil society groups in the region may be understood in this context. Typical examples are West African Action Network on Small Arms (WAANSA) in peace and security, Foundation for Security and Development in Africa (FOSDA) in human security, West African Bar Associations (WABA) in human rights and promotion of the legal profession, West African Civil Society Institute (WACSI) in regional capacity building for civil society in governance, and Media Foundation for West Africa (MFWA) in human right and press freedom. The scope of this study does not cover the generality of these organisations in West Africa. However, reflecting on the agency of civil society groups in regional peacebuilding and democratic participation within the last two decades is a timely undertaking. It helps to fill the existing gaps in the literature and serves as an analytical guide for regional policymaking.

Notes

1 Source: the website of ACDHRS: http://www.acdhrs.org/about-acdhrs/ [accessed 4/09/2017].
2 Apart from the 2012 coup, Mali has also experienced another coup in 2020 following the popular protest of Malians that led to resignation of former president Boubacar Keita and eventual seizure of power by the military junta.

4 Civil Society and Democratic Participation in the West African Regionalism

Introduction

The West African Civil Society Forum (WACSOF) is one of the important regional organisations in West Africa by virtue of its relationship with the Economic Community of West African States (ECOWAS). This chapter therefore examines the extent to which it has evolved as an actor in the region, based on the available data from 2003 to 2019. I assess WACSOF as an organisation saddled with the role of promoting participation of civil society in regional integration in West Africa. It is important at this stage to clarify that my assessment of WACSOF is based on its mandate of coordinating civil society activities in regional integration. By regional integration I refer to ECOWAS programmes in the context of regional governance. I study the evolution of WACSOF as an organisation and the assessment of this chapter is based on its mandate in relation to ECOWAS. It should not be mistaken for the emergence or the evolution of the West African civil society as a political sphere based on the political dynamics of the West African states. The contextual understanding of this chapter should be seen from the perspective of the post-Cold War regionalism or civil society regionalisation in West Africa.

Therefore, this chapter deals with the following question: to what extent has WACSOF acted within the framework of its mandate in regional integration? This question will interrogate how WACSOF has been able to coordinate civil society activities across regional levels. It will also examine the opportunities and challenges as well as its notable impact in shaping regional policy preferences of ECOWAS between 2003 and 2019. Perspectives about civil society activities in regional integration in West Africa have been relatively positive. Such views posit that civil society groups in ECOWAS participate more in regional integration than their counterparts in SADC and the EAC (Reinold 2019). However, what is missing which is important is the holistic study of WACSOF as a regional coordinating actor and its contributions to regionalism in West Africa. The finding confirms the important role of WACSOF at its inception as a civil society arm of ECOWAS, working alongside ECOWAS Secretariat/Commission in promoting democratic norm in regional governance (Afadzinu 2015). It has actively engaged in regional election observation missions and provided critical reports

DOI: 10.4324/9781003257288-5

in some cases to draw attention of ECOWAS to take necessary actions (Iheduru 2015b). WACSOF also contributed to the development of ECOWAS gender policy (Wamai 2011). While this study finds that WACSOF has evolved as an actor, the findings also indicate that WACSOF's activities towards ECOWAS are largely dominated by the most influential or strong member organisations at the expenses of the weak or less influential members. This raises questions about the mandate of WACSOF itself as a rally point for civil society input in regional integration in West Africa.

The finding of this chapter tends to correlate another study in SADC that also asserts that there is tendency for civil society actors to make a claim to represent the interest of their members or the people in regional governance when in actual fact they either lack presence at the local levels or have no constituencies at all (Godsater 2015:131). The main aim of setting up WACSOF was to coordinate and promote regional integration at national and grassroots levels. These popular responsibilities placed an action-based regional identity on WACSOF but to manage it effectively has become difficult over the years. There is a perceived lack of proper coordination and weak micro presence. A consensus emerged in 2016 Biennial People's Forum in Abuja, calling for the review of the WACSOF's regional mandate to address its waning capacity to provide leadership for civil society participation in the ECOWAS programmes.

The chapter begins by introducing WACSOF. It provides the justification for it as a case study. The chapter discusses the background of WACSOF, its governance/organisational structure, and touches succinctly on regionalism/regionalisation discourses to reiterate the usefulness of this study's analytical framework. The chapter concludes by showing the strengths and weaknesses of WACSOF in terms of its regional social identity, regional presence, regional capacity and societal impact. Apart from WACSOF's relative weakness as a regional civil society actor, the chapter also posits that the inability of WACSOF to act effectively in West Africa is implicitly linked to the crisis of its regional identity.

WACSOF at a Glance

WACSOF sought to act as the umbrella body of civil society organisations in West Africa. According to some participants, WACSOF is considered as a joint initiative between civil society organisations in West Africa and ECOWAS (Interview 1, Interview 27, Interview 20, Interview 13). In the early 2000s, some active CSOs of the region were interested to engage with ECOWAS. The Centre for Democracy and Development (CDD), an NGO based in Nigeria, and International Alert, another NGO based in London, spearheaded the first proposal for a regional platform of civil society in West Africa (Opoku 2007, Interview 1, WPForum 2016). The former Executive Secretary of ECOWAS, Dr Muhammad Ibn Chambers also played a significant role in the process of forming WACSOF (Olonisakin 2009, WPForum 2016). The receptivity of the ECOWAS Executive Secretary at the time significantly contributed to the evolution of an institutionalised relationship between West African CSOs and ECOWAS (WPForum 2016).

One vital observation prior to establishing WACSOF was an initial platform known as the West African Democracy Network (WADNET) (Fayemi in WPForum 2016). WADNET was mainly conceived by West African civil society activists at the time. It was a regional network of CSOs interested in the democratisation struggle and the post-Cold War security challenges in the region. Revealing how WADNET metamorphosed into WACSOF at the Biennial Peoples Forum of the WACSOF held in Abuja in August 2016, Dr Kayode Fayemi, WACSOF's co-founder, explained in his keynote address that the desire to institutionalise the relationship between West African CSOs and ECOWAS was the main reason for transforming WADNET into WACSOF (WPForum 2016). Another significant reason he gave in his keynote address was that both West African CSOs and ECOWAS policymakers realised the need to adopt a collective regional approach in responding to conflict prevention/human security challenges in the region (WPForum 2016). It is from this understanding that this chapter interrogates the extent to which WACSOF has evolved as an actor in line with the interest that underpins its regional identity vis-à-vis promotion of democratic participation of civil society in regional integration in West Africa.

Why WACSOF as a Case Study?

In addition to the above, it is important to note that WACSOF is the official body of civil society organisations in West Africa. Since 2005, the Authority of the Heads of States of ECOWAS have recognised WACSOF as the umbrella body of civil society organisations in the region (ECOWAS 2005:7). The Authority also directed the ECOWAS Secretariat (now Commission) to work with WACSOF to promote ECOWAS integration (ECOWAS 2005:7). The aims and objectives of WACSOF transcend individual ECOWAS states. They represent key components of ECOWAS regional integration projects, and the aim is to open them up for wider civil society participation. It also has an interregional aspiration with other civil society bodies in African regions, such as SADC-CNGOs, EACSOF and the Centre for Citizens Participations on African Union (CCP-AU).[1]

WACSOF was conceived as a regional platform through which national and regional civil society organisations and networks can enter into dialogue and mobilise on regional matters in West Africa (Interviewee 1, WPForum 2016). The main goal of WACSOF is to ensure that civil society organisations have a say or contribute to regional governance that is being led by the ECOWAS Commission in West Africa, in the context of democratising ECOWAS (WPForum 2016). Unlike other active regional civil society organisations such as West African Network for Peacebuilding (WANEP), the Media Foundation for West Africa, the West African Civil Society Institute and West

African Women Association, WACSOF was jointly established by the civil society organisations and ECOWAS (Interview 1, Interview 27, Interview 20, Interview 13).

WACSOF and Its Governance Structure

WACSOF draws its membership from all the 15 member states of ECOWAS. As an organisation, WACSOF has a set of internal rules that guide how it conducts its activities in the region. It has a governing structure based on its institutional design. This structure comprises the People's Forum, the Executive Committee, the Regional Secretariat, 15 National Platforms, and Thematic Groups. Let us look briefly at the role of each of these organs.

The People's Forum

The People's Forum is 'the supreme organ of WACSOF' (WACSOF 2015:10). In line with Article 6, paragraph 3 of the WACSOF Charter (in conjunction with its rule of procedure), the People's Forum constitutes a democratic source of WACSOF's decision-making processes. Though WACSOF may portray itself as an organisation that represents the interest of the people of the region, the term 'People's Forum' does not necessarily imply a forum of common West African people or the citizens of ECOWAS. It is rather a forum of the aggregate number of registered civil society organisations that are members of WACSOF. These organisations are characterised by diverse interests from agriculture, trade, women empowerment, peace and security, human rights, governance to youth empowerment. They operate across the 15 member states of ECOWAS (Iheduru 2015b, WACSOF 2015, Interviewee 1, Interviewee 2).

Apart from these local CSOs, the Forum is also comprised of the observer organisations and individuals that are accredited from time to time by WACSOF, such as donor/development partners or agencies, regional and international organisations (WACSOF 2003:7). The meeting of the People's Forum is designed to take place before the meetings of the ECOWAS Council of Ministers. The same also applies to the annual summits of the Authority of the ECOWAS Heads of State and Government (WPForum 2016, Interviewee 1). The aim of these meetings is to enable these civil society organisations to use the platforms to influence regional policy or draw the attention of ECOWAS policymakers at the national and regional levels to matters relating to any of its thematic areas (WACSOF 2003, WPForum 2016, WACSOF 2016).

My observations at the 6th WACSOF People's Forum held in August 2016 in Abuja, Nigeria, provided an insight into the People's Forum's operational powers and how it exercises them. These powers are mainly electoral in nature, that is, the powers to elect members of the Executive Committee. The Forum also participated in the performance reviews of the WACSOF regional secretariat in line with the set targets of the organisation, but this was conducted in the context of revamping WACSOF to become an effective regional civil society actor.[2] The Forum underscored that WACSOF is faced with many challenges, which are not only limited to funding. Some of these challenges border on operational leadership, institutional capacity and divergent interests among the member organisations. Therefore, the major focus of the 2016 Forum was targeted at how to develop new strategies to make WACSOF work more effectively to actualise its mandate in the region. Further explanations on WACSOF's capacity will be provided later in the chapter.

The Executive Committee

The Executive Committee comprises all the elected officials from among the representatives of the member civil society organisations in the region. The allocation of executive positions is done based on the three official languages of ECOWAS (Anglophone, Francophone and Lusophone). There is one representative from the youth wing, and one representative from the Diaspora chapter. All these positions are equally allocated based on the gender (WACSOF 2003:8). Table 4.1 shows how WACSOF executive posts are allocated.

The Executive Committee coordinates WACSOF regional activities and networks with relevant organs and agencies of ECOWAS in line with the aspirations of the regional integration projects in West Africa. It has the power to appoint the administrative staff of regional secretariat including the General Secretary. Part of the committee's mandates is that it sees to the membership expansion of WACSOF and portrays a good image of the West African civil society by adhering to the core values and the code of conduct that govern general civil society activities in the region, among other functions.

Table 4.1 Distribution of WACSOF Executive Offices

Representation by Regions	Constituting Countries	Number of Executive Posts
Anglophone West Africa	The Gambia, Sierra Leone, Liberia, Ghana and Nigeria.	Four
Francophone West Africa	Senegal, Benin, Togo, Cote d'Ivoire, Guinea Conakry, Burkina Faso.	Four
Lusophone West Africa	Cape Verde and Guinea Bissau.	Two
Diaspora WACSOF Chapter	From a diaspora organisation that focused on issues in West Africa. It must have registered as a member organisation with WACSOF.	One

There are two ex-officios. A Youth Delegate is elected by the Forum to serve as an ex-officio. The second ex-officio is the serving General Secretary of WACSOF, who is the administrative head of the regional secretariat.

Source: author.

Thematic Groups

In the context of this study, WACSOF thematic groups can be looked at as sub-social groups or the working committees that cover the broad activities of WACSOF member organisations. These groups include the following thematic strands: agriculture and food security, democracy and good governance, human rights, peace and security, environment and climate change, women and gender, youth empowerment, migration and free movement, humanitarian and social affairs, health and HIV/AIDS, education, and economic development (WACSOF no date). The functionality of thematic groups is central to the regional image of WACSOF. According to a staff member of ECOWAS in the 2012 report of the workshop held in Abuja on WACSOF Thematic Group:

> ECOWAS remains committed to the agenda that the civil society defines for itself, and that they would like to see a demand driven WACSOF, where the civil society would be able to demand the change they would like to see happen at the Commission as well as [at] the member state level and regional level. This could not be possible […] if the thematic groups are not made strong enough to function properly.
>
> (WACSOF 2012:8)

Based on the statements made by the representative of the ECOWAS at the meeting, seven thematic groups are presently working with ECOWAS. They are Agriculture, Youth and Employment, Gender, Health, Peace and Security and Good Governance (WPForum 2016).[3] The importance of these thematic groups cannot be overemphasised in the sense that these are the groups that are supposed to cascade the regional policies and programmes down to the local and community levels. WACSOF also has national platforms that are supposed to produce these core thematic groups as enshrined in Article 9 of the 2003 WACSOF Charter (see WACSOF 2003:9).

WACSOF National Platforms

The National Platform is an important part of the WACSOF governance structure. The national platforms consist of registered civil society organisations and coalitions across the 15 member states of ECOWAS (WACSOF 2003, 2008, 2013, 2016, WPForum 2016). They are meant to extend WACSOF's regional presence at the national and community levels. It is important to note that at present, these national platforms are hosted by the member organisations. For an example, Nigeria's national platform is being hosted by Civil Society Legislative Advocacy Centre (CISLAC), a member organisation in Nigeria. The Ghana's National Platform is hosted by the Institute of Democratic Governance (IDEG) like other member states (see Appendix 1). The national platforms are overseen by WACSOF national coordinators who are elected by the representatives of member organisations at the national levels. In the WACSOF structure, these member organisations are grouped into relevant thematic groups based on their activities both at the national and regional level.

Having explained WACSOF's structure, I shall therefore discuss its role analytically in the context of regionalism/regionalisation in Africa.

WACSOF in the Context of Regionalism/Regionalisation in Africa

The establishment of WACSOF as a civil society arm of ECOWAS can be seen as a manifestation of the post-Cold War regionalism which is in line with the new regionalism perspective (Hettne 1999, Soderbaum 2002, 2003, Iheduru 2003). This is understood differently from the kind of regional integration models that prevailed after the Second World War which also manifested in ECOWAS's objectives when it began in 1975 (Iheduru 2003, 2013, Madueke 2015, WPForum 2016). ECOWAS maintained the prominence of states as the only drivers of integration (Bach 2004, Akinyeye 2010, Kirschner and Stapel 2011), whereas the role of civil society and other non-state actors attracted lesser attention in the period. The revision of the ECOWAS founding treaty in 1993 made some significant changes to its regional governance structure, even though the role of civil society was not explicitly detailed in it. Prior to the formation of WACSOF, ECOWAS had begun to realise the importance of involving its citizens' groups in its regional activities (Iheduru 2015b). Although Amitav Acharya suggests that democratisation is likely to engender 'regional socialisation by according space to civil society and accommodating its concerns' (2003:377), the emergence of WACSOF also coincided with the democratisation struggle within the region (WPforum 2016). In 1994, ECOWAS started to grant observer status to civic organisations/association (Iheduru 2015b). By 1996, the Forum of Associations Recognised by ECOWAS (FARE) was formed for the participation of CSOs in the ECOWAS programmes (ECOWAS 1996, Interviewee 20). The subsequent ECOWAS protocols, such as supplementary protocol for the establishment of ECOWAS Parliament, mechanism for management and conflict prevention, ECOWAS Protocol on Democracy and Good Governance embraced the civil society involvement in their operationalisations (Ismail 2011, Afadzinu 2015, Adejumobi 2016, Bappah 2018). The background given above is contingent to understand the context in which WACSOF emerged. In the New Regionalism Approach's postulation, a civil society network like WACSOF is an actor (see Hettne 1999, Soderbaum 2004a). It is therefore important to examine how WACSOF has evolved as an actor in West Africa. The next section employs the analytical framework of this study to make sense of WACSOF as an actor.

Analysing WACSOF as a Regional Civil Society Actor

The analytic concepts extensively discussed in Chapter 2 are thereby employed to analyse WACSOF as a regional civil society actor. These concepts are regional social identity, regional presence, regional capacity and societal impact.

WACSOF's Regional Social Identity

Over the years, the process of regional identity formation in Africa has been led by states and the regionalist bureaucrats (Shaw 2000, Checkel 2016, Iheduru 2019, Börzel and Risse 2020). The notion of WACSOF's identity here is action-based, implying a form of solidarity, and relates to the role civil society plays in regional governance in West Africa. Regional identities formation often focuses on states in regional building. Karl Deutsch's work on security community is a prominent example that links the emergence of community and shared identities through transactions and communications among states (Checkel 2016:560–561). However, the critical perspectives of the New Regionalism Approach also posit that civil society actors do construct regional identities as co-actors in regionalism and regional governance (Fioramonti 2015, Iheduru 2015b, Godsater 2016). The emergence of regional identity can be seen as an outcome of social interaction among these actors (Checkel 2016). In this sense, construction of shared collective identity becomes a regionalist project for civil society actors (See Godsater 2016). In other words, identity can also be interpreted as a basis for action that defines how civil society groups participate in regional governance (Bello 2011). In this sense, a social identity based on shared values (e.g. democracy, human rights etc.) becomes a driving force for civil society to engage in regional governance. The regional dimension of WACSOF's identity formation was based on the latter. Its main purpose was to create a regional platform that would constitute various civil society groups in West Africa to enable them to act together as an actor in the regionalism of ECOWAS (Interviewee 1, Interviewee 20). The direct account gathered during the fieldwork from the WACSOF founders and members indicates that the aim of WACSOF was to democratise peace and security governance of ECOWAS in West Africa (WPForum 2016, Interviewee 26). By its inherent understanding, identity could be intersubjective and interest-constitutive (Musschenga 2004:84). For Alexander Wendt, 'identities are the basis of interest' (Wendt 1992:398). The existing structure of ECOWAS implied a form of collective identity for its 15 member states in West Africa. The solidarity that led to the formation of WACSOF was in the context of changing political dynamics at the national levels. WACSOF emerged and supported by ECOWAS to create a 'space for effective CSO engagement with regionalism' (Iheduru 2015b:143). The attempt towards engaging regional institution (ECOWAS) by the civil society groups beyond their individual national levels suggests WACSOF's tendency towards what Valeria Bello (2011:44) describes as a 'regional social identity'. She explains that:

> By coming together, groups of different nationalities can find common interests and can interact in such a way as to create the tools for constructing a social identity. Of course, this regional social identity is limited and holds a particular meaning for each individual and each group.
>
> (Bello 2011:44)

The above description tends to underscore the basis of forming WACSOF. However, the main aim was not only to West-Africanise civil society groups but also to serve as a basis for collective actions in regional governance. Even though the individual interests of WACSOF member organisations may be hard to define, some of them still shared common interests in promoting civil society participation in the affairs of ECOWAS (WACSOF 2003, Interviewee 5, WPForum 2016). (Interviewee 1, WACSOF 2003). It was also reaffirmed publicly in 2016 that WACSOF was formed in order to 'democratise ECOWAS' (Fayemi in WPForum 2016). Democratising ECOWAS does not necessarily refer to the direct election of ECOWAS policymakers. What this implies is that democratising a global or regional organisation like ECOWAS may imply 'democratic accountability' (Scholte 2011:1, 36, Buckley 2013:73), or 'social accountability' (Brustz and Palestini 2016:389, Armstrong and Gilson 2011). In either way, the emphasis is predominantly placed on the participation of organised groups of citizens in ECOWAS programmes (Iheduru 2015b).

Moreover, the perception of civil society activists in the late 1990s was that the summits of the Authority of the ECOWAS Heads of State and Government were mere ceremonial (WACSOF 2003, Interview 1, WPForum 2016, Madueke 2015, Interviewee 5). The summitry of ECOWAS political leaders, as perceived by some of these civil society groups in the 1990s, was far from the needed forums that prioritised the welfare of the ordinary citizens on the top agenda (WPForum 2016). According to Kayode Fayemi (2016), civil society activists observed that the ECOWAS leaders would come together every year as a club of West African leaders without paying serious attention to the suffering of their countries' citizens (Fayemi in WPForum 2016). Realising this shortly after the Cold War, civil society activists decided that there was a need to establish a regional civil society network in order to open ECOWAS to a wider civil society participation (Fayemi in WPForum 2016).

Their social interactions in the period were tailored towards regional identity formation to respond to sociopolitical and security issues arising from the region. These organisations started to look beyond the internal sociopolitical issues in their individual countries. As explained at the 2016 People's Forum, it was WADNET that transformed into WACSOF (WPForum 2016). On 12 December 2003, WACSOF signed its Charter in Accra, Ghana. According to Iheduru, about 100 representatives of civil society groups participated in signing of WACSOF's Charter and the event marked the attempt towards institutionalising collaboration between CSOs and ECOWAS (2015b:142). The WACSOF's Charter draws attention to the social-economic challenges of the region and shares the belief in the regional integration of ECOWAS as a developmental approach for the region. These identified challenges within the ECOWAS member states are characterised by 'bad governance, human rights violations and conflicts and human insecurity' in general (WACSOF 2003:1). WACSOF's coming into being was therefore a manifestation of an attempt towards a regional approach 'to involve the representatives of the civil society organisations in the process of elaboration, implementation, monitoring and evaluation of political, security, economic, social and cultural programmes of ECOWAS' (WACSOF 2003:1).

One may posit in principle that WACSOF represents a popular intention of civil society to practically transform the ECOWAS framework from its state-centrism. According to interviewees, WACSOF was able to exploit the opportunities in the post-1993 treaty and the protocols relating to the establishment of the ECOWAS Parliament, and the ECOWAS Mechanism for the Conflict Prevention (Interviewee 1, Interviewee 5, Interviewee 22). The most significant instrument for WACSOF was in the operationalisation of the ECOWAS Protocol on Democracy and Good Governance. These are provided for in Article 8 and Article 23(2). There is also an implied reference to civil society in Article 39 in relation to the media. The protocol also provides for a right-based protection for women and children in the member states in Article 2(3), Article 14(2) and Article 30. Even though the omission of civil society's substantive role is obvious in the founding treaty, the relevant sections of the above protocols recognised the relevance of civil society in regional democratic governance in West Africa. This has formed the basis of activities of WACSOF and its member organisations in the region. According to Jibrin Ibrahim, a former president of WACSOF:

> My sense of a better engagement between WACSOF and ECOWAS is really to place on the table the importance of close collaboration, close engagement between those two sides of the equation and the equation is the people of West Africa. My sense is that today it is the question of survival of the people of this region that is at stake.
>
> (WPForum 2016)

Although the underlying perspective of the above tends to reinforce the importance of a collaborative relationship between ECOWAS and WACSOF, the remark of the representative of the President of the ECOWAS Commission at the 2016 WACSOF Peoples' Forum also acknowledged this importance and urged civil society organisations to work together to build and sustain the synergy between ECOWAS and civil society led by WACSOF (WPForum 2016). The remark added that 'ECOWAS cannot succeed on its own without formulating synergy with civil society organisations' (WPForum 2016).

The importance of civil society can only make more sense when it relates to the bottom-up role in African regionalisms (Godsater 2015). Because ECOWAS is based on a formal and top-down institutional structure, in theory, WACSOF becomes an important stakeholder because it is assumed that WACSOF possesses a bottom-up advantage as a civil society actor to popularise ECOWAS activities at the local levels (Interviewee 20). The new regionalism scholars have also underscored that civil society actors can also be co-opted in regional governance if their involvement serves the dominant interest in the region (Iheduru 2015b, Fioramonti 2015, Scholte 2015). It appears that the essence of the 2016 WACSOF Peoples' Forum was to rediscover the regional identity of WACSOF in order to fulfil its bottom-up role in the region. A commentator from the ECOWAS Parliament also looked at WACSOF's identity with its expected role in relation to the key ECOWAS Organs, the Commission, the ECOWAS Parliament and the ECOWAS Court of Justice, as follows:

> I see WACSOF as the mouthpiece of civil society in West Africa. It is like a third sector organisation which is different from what we are operating. It is like the watchdog on the activities of the institution we have – the executive, the judiciary and the legislative institutions which comprise the commission, the parliament and the community court of justice. If we are not following the rules, they should be able to draw our attentions to what we are supposed to do.
>
> (Interviewee 15)

The above statement should not be taken at its face value; however, it draws attention to the typical role of civil society in regional democratic governance. If we understood the identity of WACSOF based on its aspiration to democratise ECOWAS, it is as well important to see the extent to which WACSOF has been a champion of democratic participation across regional levels. As explained in Chapter 2, constructing or forming a regional social identity is not the sole criterion to determine a regional civil society actor. It can mainly help to draw observers' attention to the basis of action of a given civil society actor as clearly explained above. The next section focuses on regional presence. The rationale is to see the extent to which WACSOF is active at the regional levels. As stated in the analytical framework, this presence comprises regional, national and subnational levels otherwise termed as macro-, meso- and micro-regional levels.

WACSOF's Regional Presence

Analytically, the use of presence here is an adaptive application of three main regional levels that refers to the macro, meso and micro levels (see Soderbaum 2002, 2004a). Because of its intersubjective nuance, Andrew Grant posits that what is 'regional' is not always given as it could imply global, regional, national and subnational levels (2017:152). The analytical context of this chapter applies to three common levels in the regionalism literature (see Shaw 2000, Grant and Soderbaum 2003:5–6, Soderbaum 2002, 2004a). Vleuten and Eerdwyk also locate the role of civil society in regional governance on three levels: regional, national and subnational (2014:18). Therefore, this section attempts to look at the role that WACSOF plays at these regional levels. Chapter 2 has explained the analytic application of this concept. In the case of WACSOF, its presence tends to follow the three levels mentioned above. These levels can either be 'physical' in terms of durable activities, or 'operational', which relates to occasional activities of regional CSOs. Whether physical or operational, the scope of activities taking place at these levels is usually dependant on the mandate or aim of a given civil society actor. The subsequent discussion focuses on this presence, starting with the macro-regional presence.

WACSOF's Macro-regional Presence

I will begin by drawing on the new regionalism theoretical perspective about the levels of activities of an actor. According to Soderbaum and Shaw, an actor is 'regional' when he/she takes part – consciously or unconsciously – in activities in a regionally defined 'arena' (2003:221). The consideration of WACSOF as an actor is presumed on the understanding that it takes part in regional governance in West Africa as a coordinator of civil society groups in the ECOWAS region. It has a regional secretariat in Abuja, Nigeria. At this level, WACSOF activities are targeted at its focal regional organisation – ECOWAS. It is predominantly seen as 'the civil society arm of ECOWAS' (Interviewee 1, WACSOF 2008, WPForum 2016). One notable feature about WACSOF unlike other regional civil society bodies such as the West African Bar Association, Media Foundation for West Africa, West African Women Association, West African Network for Peacebuilding, is that WACSOF was mainly established to provide civil society input into ECOWAS programmes (WACSOF 2003, 2013, Interviewee 5, Interviewee 27, Interviewee 26, Ismail 2011, Iheduru 2015b). A participant close to the WACSOF regional office added that 'What we do is to coordinate and to ensure the effectiveness of the work of civil society at the national platform in each country' (Interviewee 1). In a 2016 interview, another participant also noted that 'WACSOF's principal mission is to help ECOWAS in the implementation of the Vision 2020 of the ECOWAS of the People and promote ECOWAS treaty and protocols in the different member states' (Interviewee 2). By design, WACSOF coordinates the participation of civil society in regional integration and makes policy recommendations to the meetings of the ECOWAS leaders on various regional policy issues affecting the people in West Africa (Ismail 2011, Iheduru 2015b, WACSOF 2003).

Apart from routine activities of the regional secretariat in Abuja, the affirmation of WACSOF at the regional level is evidenced through the People's Forum which is to be 'convened on annual basis, prior to the statutory meetings of the ECOWAS Authority of Heads of States and Government' (WACSOF 2016:1). From 2003 to 2019, WACSOF convened a total of six People's Forums and used the occasions to issue communiques and recommendations to the ECOWAS leaders. So far, these Forums have taken place in Ghana (2003, 2005, 2010), Niger (January 2006), Burkina Faso (December 2006), Nigeria (2016) including a mini one held in Ghana (in 2007) (WACSOF 2016). The People's Forum is an annual flagship platform in the WACSOF's Charter. It has since been amended to be held every two years, due to the paucity of funding (WACSOF 2016). WACSOF has also coordinated citizens-led election observation in the region as a means 'to contribute to regional integration efforts through the promotion of democracy and good governance' (Iheduru (2015b:145). According to the West African Civil Society Institute (WACSI) (2009:9), the emergence of WACSOF has led to an 'institutionalised indigenous citizen-led election observation in the sub-region'. This is one of the key activities that WACSOF had undertaken in the context of conflict prevention, 'to contribute to regional integration efforts through promotion of democracy and good governance' (WACSI 2009:9). Within the first three years of signing its founding charter, WACSOF was able to mobilise civil society across the region and successfully observed the following elections in the table below (see Table 4.2).

Table 4.2 WACSOF's Election Observation from 2004 to 2006

Country	Elections	Years
Ghana	Presidential and Parliamentary Elections	December 2004
Togo	Presidential Election	April 2005
Guinea Bissau	Presidential Elections	June and July 2005
Liberia	General Elections	October and Nov. 2005
Burkina Faso	Presidential Election	November 2005
Cape Verde	Parliamentary and Presidential Elections	Jan and Feb. 2006
Benin	Presidential Election	March 2006
Nigeria	Bye-elections in Ekiti State	April 2006
The Gambia	Presidential Election	September 2006

Sources: WACSOF's 2006 Annual Report and West African Civil Society Institute (2009:9).

Apart from the above specific elections, WACSOF has subsequently observed elections in other member states of ECOWAS, including contributing to the formation of the ECOWAS Network of Electoral Commissions (WACSI 2009, WACSOF 2015, Iheduru 2015b). The first meeting of WACSOF with ECONET took place in Abidjan, Cote d'Ivoire from 8 to 9 May 2008, with the aim of promoting dialogue and collaboration between civil society organisations and the national electoral bodies 'at all stages of electoral processes in ECOWAS member states' (WACSOF 2008:22). Overall, WACSOF is known for its regional activities in working alongside the ECOWAS Commission in promoting regional democratic norm in West Africa (Afadzinu 2015). The available records of the organisation's activities as documented in its annual reports from 2006, 2008, 2009, 2012, 2013 and 2015 indicated a series of activities from election observations, gender mainstreaming in ECOWAS activities, organising a regional contact meeting in curbing early marriage practices in West Africa and development of a strategic plan 2012–2015 (WACSOF 2013). The main aim of the plan was to activate WACSOF thematic groups, and revamp the national platforms which also remained a crucial issue (see WACSOF 2013:10, WACSOF 2014:8–9). WACSOF also engaged in other projects such as conducting studies on civil society's role in prevention and control of Malaria, youth unemployment, developing measures to curb statelessness, civil society's role in promoting transparency in extractive industries among others (WACSOF 2013, 2015). At the regional level, the available reports show that there is a series of regional activities being undertaken by WACSOF. However, most of these programmes are top-down. What seems to be missing is the coordination of participation of civil society at the national and local levels.

The dominant perspectives that emerged from the fieldwork (2016–2018) indicated concerns about the dwindling status of WACSOF especially with regard to regional coordination. These views were not only expressed by civil society actors interviewed. The views were also shared by some ECOWAS staff and a staff of an external organisation who also undertook a field study on the activities of WACSOF between 2015 and 2016. The deliberations at the 2016 edition of the People's Forum also acknowledged those concerns that WACSOF needed to be reawakened (WPForum 2016). There have also been instances where the officials of ECOWAS have urged WACSOF to demand the change the civil society wants to see happen in regional policy and programmes of ECOWAS (WPForum 2016, Interview 19). This happened at the 2012 WACSOF Thematic Workshop in Abuja and during the proceedings of the Peoples' Forum held in August 2016 in Abuja, Nigeria.

At the ECOWAS Parliament, the regional civil society participation is also very limited. Although the parliament did not yet have a legislative power (Kizito and Patrick 2012), it has only been engaging in parliamentary diplomacy within the region (Salih 2013). According to the interviews with the parliamentary staff and WACSOF, the ECOWAS Parliament only initiated a formal relationship with WACSOF in 2016 by signing a memorandum of understanding (MOU) (Interviewee 16, Interviewee 18, Interviewee 1, Interviewee 19). Prior to the signing of the MOU, one of the commentators admitted:

> We have not been engaging with the CSOs. Our engagement is very limited. In the current plan, part of the structures we have identified is to use CSOs. We have difficulties. We are a regional organisation. Most CSOs are nationally based.
>
> (Interviewee 19)

Reflecting on the comment, it is important to put it into a proper context to avoid misrepresenting the regional dynamics of civil society in West Africa. The claim that there are a limited number of regional CSOs in West Africa may be true to some extent. Perhaps, what the commentator had in mind was the waning presence of WACSOF at the national levels. The limited activities of the parliament itself, because of its advisory status in the region, may also be a factor for the lack of a robust relationship.[4] Irrespective of the challenges WACSOF may have been facing in consolidating its regional presence, one cannot rule out the fact that the organisation had also contributed to regional election observations since 2004 (WACSI 2009, Iheduru 2015b). The shortage of empirical knowledge on how some of the existing regional civil society organisations work in West Africa is also a problem. As observed from the field, most CSOs with interest on regional issues are largely working as networks. Some of them may not have physical presence but they tend to be active on the regional matters. Because it is believed that WACSOF 'coordinates civil society activities in regional integration at local and national levels' (Interviewee 2), emphasis on its regional presence matters a lot to its role in the region.

For now, most of the WACSOF national platforms are hosted by its member organisations (see Appendix 1). The concerns documented in the various annual reports of WACSOF also show that some of these national platforms are not active on one hand. According to 2014 Annual Report, 'the National Platforms is very crucial, it is clear that these National Platforms are yet to function as effectively as expected as a result of several inadequacies and bottlenecks' (WACSOF 2014:10). On the other hand, there are also challenges in terms of rivalry between its member organisations (Interviewee 8). A civil society actor like WACSOF tends to represent what the new regionalism scholars describe as a 'legitimiser of the status quo' (Fioramonti et al. 2015, Iheduru 2015b, Godsater and Soderbaum 2011). Civil society plays a legitimating role 'through formal participation in the existing top-down controlled institutional mechanisms that afford some civil society groups voice and influence, in return for legitimisation of otherwise technocratic policy making processes' (Fioramont,2015:6). This tends to explain WACSOF's activities at the regional level. As explained by one of its founders at the 2016 People's Forum, WACSOF was designed to democratise the West African regionalism which implies a form of legitimacy for the ECOWAS programmes (WPForum 2016). At the same time, WACSOF tended to exhibit what scholars of regionalism describe as counter-hegemonic or contesting the status quo (Godsater and Soderbaum 2011, Fioramonti 2015, Iheduru 2015b). Iheduru also adds that:

> While WACSOF has provided legitimacy to many ECOWAS election monitoring assignments under the 2000 Protocol on Democracy and Good Governance in the region since 2005, it has also often contested some ECOWAS approaches to electoral processes.
>
> (2015b:145)

Some of those contestations often came in form of press releases to either condemn or challenge certain positions of ECOWAS or a person acting on behalf of ECOWAS. Through a press statement WACSOF challenged the 'undemocratic' statement about the integrity of the elections made by the former president of Nigeria, Chief Olusegun Obasanjo, the appointed leader of the ECOWAS election monitoring in Ghana and Senegal in 2011 (Iheduru 2015b:145). WACSOF expressed concerns and went further to advise ECOWAS to only appoint past leaders with democratic records to head its election monitoring (Ibekwe 2012). Also in 2015, during a special event, marking the 40th anniversary of ECOWAS in Abuja, Ibrahim Jubrin (the WACSOF leader) publicly criticised ECOWAS that in the history of the organisation, violent conflicts and political instability perpetuated by the West African leaders has not enabled ECOWAS to focus on the primary goal of regional integration. In his view, WACSOF needed to be more critical of ECOWAS so that it can be taken more seriously. According to him:

> [as WACSOF] if we begin to do effective petitioning against this august institution [referring to ECOWAS], I think two things would happen. First, they will stop coming to WACSOF's meetings which is fine. The second is that they will begin to take civil society seriously.
>
> (Madueke 2015 [YouTube])

This type of contestation tends to reflect part of the attributes of WACSOF as a critical civil society actor in the region. For Fioramonti such a contestation is likely to help in reshaping how regions are governed (2015:7). Critical scholarship of the new regionalism tends to see the civil society participation in regionalist schemes as one possible way to protect the societal interest by setting a transformative agenda for regionalism (Mitlleman 1999, Fioramonti 2015, Scholte 2015).

The understanding of 'the possibilities and limitations of transformative regionalism' according to Mittleman is based on 'the strength of its links to civil society' (1999:48). The possibilities of such transformation in West Africa tend to rest more on WACSOF's status and leadership in the region. WACSOF, as it is presently constituted, will need to reposition itself to be able to inspire that transformation (Interviewee 13, WPForum 2016). One of the key observations about WACSOF is that it emerged regionally from the top. As a member organisation noted in 2017, 'WACSOF is desirable, but we want more than what we are seeing at the moment' (Interviewee 31). Another commentator expressed concerns on how the Nigerian national platform is being run: 'We only have the coordinator. No other office exists, and it is not supposed to be so. That is the issue' (Interviewee 6). According to civil society workers from Ghana, some of the problems that WACSOF is facing included the competing interests of its member organisations across the 15 ECOWAS member states (Interviewee 8, Interviewee 9). Most CSOs in the region 'compete for funding from the same donors' (Interviewee 8), thereby making them wary of becoming subservient to their competitors.

Many scholars in the new regionalism literature such as Mittleman (1999), Fioramonti et al. (2015), Godsater and Soderbaum (2011), Soderbaum (2016a), Godsater (2016) and others argue that a counter-hegemonic/resisting civil society tends to produce a transformative regionalism (Mittleman 1999, Soderbaum 2007). In the case of WACSOF, apart from the examples cited above, WACSOF has often been critical of ECOWAS even though it is top-down in its approach. According to Mittleman, such transformative regionalism is rooted in 'popular support and a sense of involvement of multiple strata of the population' (1999:48). If the assumption about transformative regionalism is predicated on popular support and wider citizens' participation, then effective functioning of WACSOF's national platforms becomes important.

This is not to overlook that WACSOF has lobbied, advocated and commissioned studies on many issues covering some of its thematic areas to educate its over 500 member organisations. WACSOF has commissioned studies on domestication of international and regional protocols/instruments on human rights, democracy and good governance, gender, health and security. In 2016, it released its study report on statelessness in the North Eastern part of Nigeria where it established statelessness as one of the sources of insecurity to the stateless persons and to the society in general due to the vulnerability of the stateless people as potential recruits for insurgent groups (The Tide 2017, Interviewee 3). It participated in the regional meeting that led to the adoption of an Action Plan towards addressing the menace of drug trafficking and related organised crime in West Africa (ECOWAS 2016). The meeting included ECOWAS, the United Nations Office for West Africa and the Sahel (UNOWAS) and other partners. In addition, WACSOF has worked collaboratively with the ECOWAS Commission on Gender and Social Affairs to establish some of the regional level thematic groups reflecting the activities of civil society organisations in the areas such as democracy and good governance, peace and security, food security, gender equality, youth and employment (WPForum 2016).

Importantly, WACSOF members have championed the cause of human rights through the ECOWAS Community Court of Justice. These organisations include the Media Foundation for West Africa (MFWA) defending the rights of journalists in the region (MFWA 2014). MFWA has effectively filed cases before the ECOWAS Community Court of Justice to seek justice in response to the violation of the human rights of journalists in West Africa, especially against the Jammeh-led government of the Republic of the Gambia (US Department of State 2008:249). Like WANEP that collects open source data for the early warning programme in West Africa, MFWA also documents and publishes incidents on the violations of the rights of freedom of expression in West African states in its periodic report, *The Monitor*, covering the incidents of the right to the freedom of expression, policy or law or reforms that affect the freedom of expression among others (MFWA 2016). The Social-Economic Right and Accountability Project (SERAP) based in Nigeria is a member of WACSOF that has filed cases before the ECOWAS Court of Justice against the Federal Republic of Nigeria on children's right to education (Global Legal Monitor 2010).[5]

WACSOF's regional response to the presidential electoral log-jam in Gambia deserves acknowledgement. In collaboration with member organisations, WACSOF placed the Gambia under a civil society watch to ensure a smooth transition during the last presidential election in the country. According to the *Freedom* newspaper on 6 June 2016:

> the Coalition for Change in The Gambia (CCG) and the West African Civil Society Forum (WACSOF) that gathered on June 1-2 in Dakar called on ECOWAS to act on Gambia. The group raised the alarm over rapid deterioration of rule of law, further erosion of human rights, enforced disappearances, arrests of opposition party members, torture, illegal detention and extrajudicial executions, rape and sexual violence against women, as well as wanton abuse of executive power in The Gambia, civil society groups said in a statement issued on Sunday.
>
> (*Freedom Newspaper*, 2016)

Yahya Jammeh was initially reluctant to hand over power after losing the 2016 presidential election. Through consistent pressures from a civil society coalition, the Authority of ECOWAS Heads of States, the AU and support of the EU, he subsequently accepted the results. Mr Barrow who won the election was later sworn in (Saharan Reporter 2016, *BBC* 2017a). That election created political tension in the Gambia and what appeared as imminent humanitarian crises in the region at the time (*EuroNews* 2017). The deployment of the ECOWAS Mission in The Gambia (ECOMIG) became an option when Yahya Jammeh was not ready to leave the office in peace (*Al Jazeera* 2017). ECOMIG was probably a reassurance of the ECOWAS' commitment to its regional democratic norm as enshrined in the ECOWAS Protocol on Democracy and Good Governance (Akwei 2017, Maclean 2017). However, allowing Yahya Jammeh to leave the country without a trial for the alleged atrocities he had committed was met with criticisms that it could potentially set a bad precedence in the region (Human Rights Watch 2017).

There is no doubt that WACSOF has presence at the macro level. This is not only due to its recognition by the ECOWAS Commission to serve as a body to coordinate the input of civil society in regional integration in West Africa. We should also underscore that WACSOF in fact started from above instead of evolving from below. Looking at its mandate, the role of WACSOF as an actor has much to do with the national and local levels. One presupposes that the effectiveness of this macro level is intrinsically linked to what happens at the national levels and vice versa. The next section provides a detailed account of the extent to which WACSOF has acted at the national levels.

WACSOF's Meso-regional Presence

According to Godsater and Soderbuam, 'civil society activities at different levels tend to be closely connected' (2011:150). This is another level that is recognised in the New Regionalism Approach as integrated in the analytical framework. Contextually, the WACSOF's meso-regional level refers to its national platforms. In principle, the essence of WACSOF national platforms is to coalesce the national civil society groups from their diverse thematic areas in each of the 15 member states of ECOWAS. Ideally, the national platforms constitute the vital core of WACSOF activities in the region. Unlike what is happening at the macro level, the impressions of WACSOF at the national levels indicate that the organisation needs to connect more with its supposed constituencies in the region. According to a commentator:

> What I can say is WACSOF is supposed to have national chapters in all the ECOWAS countries [but they] are not working. That tells the complexity around civil society work. For the chapters to work, it means, nationally, the civil society presence must also be strong. There is a need to have a united civil society front in all the countries before the national WACSOF chapters can work.
>
> (Interviewee 9)

The above excerpt appears plausible based on the evidence that emerged at the WACSOF People's Forum in 2016. However, one can also observe that the comment did not take cognisance of how WACSOF emerged in the first instance as a top-down organisation. In its 2008 report, it was acknowledged as 'defects' in the formation of WACSOF (WACSOF 2008:7). In West Africa, Ghana is one of the democratic ECOWAS member states where there has been active civil society in governance. How do we explain that the WACSOF National Platform in Ghana has not been effectively functional? The challenges relating to the functioning of national platforms formed a key part of the deliberation at the 2016 WACSOF People's Forum in Abuja with about 100 delegates across the region. The general expectation as evidenced in the Forum's communique was to see revived national chapters of WACSOF working towards participatory regional integration or what ECOWAS termed 'ECOWAS of the People' (ECOWAS Commission 2008, WACSOF 2016, WPForum 2016). A similar attempt was made in 2009. WACSI conducted the Needs Assessment focusing on WACSOF Liberia, WACSOF Senegal and WACSOF Sierra Leone. The study touched on the weaknesses, such as lack of national secretariat, the funding challenges, management and leadership in these countries. Despite the study's recommendations to address some of these weaknesses at the national and regional levels, these issues still featured again as parts of the challenges deliberated upon at the 6th Biennial People's Forum held in Abuja in August 2016. I also made further efforts until 2019 to find out any positive progress on revitalisation of the national platforms as recommended by the People's Forum. Unfortunately, there was no concrete evidence of the change in the status quo except the replacement of the regional secretariat team in Abuja.

Talking about weak national or meso-regional presence of WACSOF does not necessarily imply that the national platforms have not worked at all. Understandably, they are hosted by member organisations but some of them have acted either with the support of the WACSOF regional secretariat or through the assistance of the development partners. An example was the civil society's response to Ebola in Liberia. One respondent explained that WACSOF Liberia sought support from the WACSOF Regional Secretariat to aid the members' activities on the sensitising projects on Ebola in Liberia (2014–2016). Although WACSOF was not in a position to provide support in terms of funding or logistics, the regional secretariat published a press release on the outbreak of Ebola, urging ECOWAS to act swiftly to respond to the deadly virus (Interviewee 1, Interviewee 2, Interviewee 3, Interviewee 31). A commentator from WACSOF Nigeria commented on how WACSOF has been contributing in shifting the conversation from regime security to underscore the importance of human security in line with the evolving regional norms in West Africa:

> If you look at the antecedent of ECOWAS countries, you will find out that what they've done mostly is focusing on regime security, but what we are doing is to shift that paradigm and begin to look at possibilities of increasing and entrenching human security across the region.
>
> (Interviewee 5)

In principle, the understanding of human security in the context of West Africa is synonymous with conflict prevention which has served as the basis of collective action of civil society groups in the region (Ismail 2011, Iheduru 2015b). The resonance of the regional human security perspective of the New Regionalism

Approach can be situated contextually but the evidence of it may be hard to relate in practice. The inherent understanding of this claim is often based on prioritising the people's protection from violence as encapsulated in the ECOWAS Conflict Prevention Framework (ECPF). According to ECOWAS Commission (2008:72), '[t]he core value of ECPF is human security'. Democratic participation of WACSOF from the regional to local was expected by its founding charter to reflect this reality (WACSOF 2003). One should not be surprised if some of these civil society organisations had chosen to link their aspirations with the promotion of human security or conflict prevention in their regions. Inspirations for these are also evident in the Arusha Charter (UNECA 1990), and the new regionalism literature, particularly Iheduru (2003) and Shaw et al. (2003). The 1994 UNDP report's call for solidarity to promote a people-centred approach to security over national security or regime security resonates well with the role regional civil society actors like WACSOF sought for themselves in West Africa. These organisations sometimes claim to promote popular participation in regional governance to engender regional security that is popular or people-centred over regime protections. They may as well engage in rhetoric, especially when they are constrained by some structural factors at the national levels.

Reflecting on the interviews, WACSOF Nigeria tends to show a clear understanding of its expected role at the national level, including the six geopolitical (subnational) zones of the Federal Republic of Nigeria (Interviewee 5). These geopolitical zones can otherwise be considered as micro-regions in themselves with peculiar issues of peace and security. Even though it is the primary responsibility of the Nigerian state to protect the lives and properties of its citizens, civil society organisations (and other NGOs and private sectors) have lent their support to the government in conflict resolution, responding to the humanitarian crises within Nigeria (Interviewee 5, Interviewee 4). The Boko Haram's case is an example. The Centre for Democracy and Development (CDD-West Africa), a member of WACSOF Nigeria, has been active in responding to the human insecurity arising from the Boko Haram insurgency in the North Eastern region (Interviewee 4, Interviewee 5). CDD-West Africa has continuously adopted a dialogue approach to bring the concerned stakeholders, such as the government of Nigeria, community leaders, the Civilian Joint Task Force and the renounced members of Boko Haram insurgent groups in the North East to round table discussions in search for peace and security in the region. According to a participant, 'a lot of the roles you will waive for states to play are gradually being played by civil society organisations' (Interviewee 4). The commentator was trying to emphasise the supporting role of civil society organisations in the area of peace and security. One of the examples cited was the use of dialogue to promote peace and the stability of the communities in the North East of Nigeria through 'conducting dialogue between community stakeholders and the Safe Corridor Initiative' (Interviewee 4). The idea of the Safe Corridor initiative was borne out of ECOWAS's Counterterrorism Strategy in which civil society actors play an important role. The participant expounded further:

Between April 4ᵗʰ and 5ᵗʰ (2016) we trained people that came from different countries of West Africa and the Sahel. We had regular conversations with statutory institutions and civil society. From the conversation, we felt that the Civilian Joint Task Force (in the North East) has become a regional player in the security discourse in the North at the micro-level. So, we brought them to Abuja. We had a conversation with them. In the course of the conversations, something came up called 'operation safe corridor'.

(Interviewee 4)

The participant also reiterated that they have looked beyond linking the Civilian Joint Task Force and government together, because they felt that 'the whole conversation should be larger than just ordinary Civilian Joint Task Force. It should involve a whole community of people that are affected by the insurgency' (Interviewee 4). There were additional corresponding views from other partici- pants such as Interviewee 3 and Interviewee 5. The interviewees underscored that civil society input was part of the idea of integrating the members of the Civilian Joint Force (CJT) into the Nigerian security structure. CJT consisted of youth vol- unteers that rose in 2014 to defend their people and communities from the Boko Haram attacks (Premium Times 2013, Interviewee 3, Interviewee 4, Interviewee 5). The response of CJT was not only to counter Boko Haram but also to protect themselves against the massive arrests of innocent youths and occasional extra judicial killings by the Nigerian special task force deployed to the North East (Interviewee 34). As one participant adds:

Civilian JTF were never vigilante before they rose to the threats of Boko Haram. There have been more kidnappings by Boko Haram after the Chibok girls. What about 60 boys kidnapped by Boko Haram in Bunio-yadi Federal Government College, Yobe State? Nobody hears about them. They, youths, rose to police Boko Haram because they said if we did not stand, they will kill our mothers, our fathers and us.

(Interviewee 34)

Based on Interviewee 34 with corresponding views from other participants, the Civilian Joint Task Force (CJTF) rose as a response to double threats: the threat of attacks or forceful recruitment or killing by Boko Haram and the threat of being mistaken for Boko Haram members by the Federal Government Task Force. Agbiboa's (2018) study also adds that:

In May 2013, victimized local youth in the Hausari part of Maiduguri organ- ized themselves into a vigilante group (that became known as the Civilian JTF) with the goal of rooting out Boko Haram members from their midst. In a matter of months, the group succeeded in chasing Boko Haram members out of Maiduguri forcing the jihadi group to decamp to the surrounding country- side and bush. The Civilian JTF emerged in response to the violent campaign of Boko Haram and, especially, the retaliatory arrests and killings of locals by the Nigerian military.

(2018:1028)

The response above expressed sentiments of vulnerability and victims of terror. The vulnerable condition of youths resulted in them standing against insurgency in their region. They became agents of necessities to support the government in policing suspected Boko Haram members in order to free their people and communities from terrorist attacks. A Nigerian newspaper once reported that 'The Civilian JTF recognised the danger and damage to economic and social livelihood of the people wrought by Al-Qaeda-inspired terrorists and decided to assist our men and women under arms to bring insurgency to an end' (*Vanguard* 2013). The activities of the Civilian JTF have received commendations from the public, as Civilian JTF has provided the local support for the Nigerian soldiers' operation in the North East (Agbiboa 2018, Bamidele 2016, Vanguard 2013, *Premium Times* 2013). Agbiboa (2018:1032) acknowledged that the role of the Civilian JTF is that of 'knowledge broker' in collective fights against Boko Haram. Civilian JTF has contributed significantly to counterinsurgency in the North East (Agbiboa 2018) and complemented the role of the Military JTF in rescuing captives of Boko Haram including the first Chibok schoolgirl (one of over 200 girls kidnapped by Boko Haram in 2014) (Bamidele 2016). While these are noted, there are also some critical reports that members of the Civilian JTF have a tendency of taking laws into their own hands (*Premium Times*, 13 October 2013). The role of civil society appeared imminent when public opinions via the print media started drawing attention to the rising profile of the Civilian JTF. This observation stemmed out of the perceived danger that there was a need to restrict the activities of Civilian JTF members to civilian policing as a complimentary role in the counterinsurgency. This fear was captured by the *Vanguard* newspaper in 2013 that:

> Apart from risking their lives unnecessarily, a greater danger of exposing civilians to battle situations includes the possibility of some of these Civilian turning into warlords. In the North, such warlords inevitably put on the religious garb. Before we know it, civilians helping to fight terrorists may fall under the influence of politicians and other foreign sponsors to float their own terror outfit. We must avoid this at all costs. We call on Civilian JTF not to lose heart but to intensify their efforts to assist the military to victory.

(2013)

The essence of the above examples is to show the stake of the members of WACSOF Nigerian national platform in the critical issues bordering on the security of the citizens as well as the communities where they live. In a comment from one of the leaders of WACSOF Nigeria, it was also claimed that Boko Haram's onrush in the North Eastern region has been one of the many challenges that are of concerns to them. However, the person adds that beyond the North East, we have taken very costly look at all of the issues that border around human security, and we have not only engaged with the regional secretariat, of course, we also called civil society organisations to respond.

(Interviewee 5)

The comment tends to suggest that the WACSOF Nigerian national platform has a well-coordinated platform as a meso-level between the macro and the micro due to the proximity to the regional secretariat. However, based on the empirical data (2016–2019), WACSOF still requires to constitute an active national executive committee that serves as a meso-link as against the provision of the WACSOF Charter. Of course, there are cases where the WACSOF National Platform used a policy dialogue approach to bring both the state and the non-state actors together to discuss how they could shape certain policies that relate to human security in the region (Interviewee 5, Interviewee 4, Interviewee 3, Interviewee 2). Yet, the effectiveness of the national platform as a meso-link is hampered by the lack of coordination and leadership on the part of WACSOF on the national levels.

For example, in 2016, Ghana's Ministry of Foreign Affairs and Regional Integration collaborated with 24 Ghanaian organisations to establish Ghana's Chapter of the African Union's Economic, Social and Cultural Council (African Union 2016). However, Ghana's Chapter of WACSOF, since it was re-activated in January 2015 after a prolonged lull, has only been surviving on the reputation of the host organisation

(Interviewee 32). According to one commentator, the Institute for Democratic Governance (IDEG) serves as the secretariat for WACSOF Ghana not because IDEG was mandated by member organisations in Ghana to do so. Rather, IDEG decided to provide a secretariat for WACSOF activities in Ghana when the Executive Director of IDEG was elected as the vice president of WACSOF in 2014 (Interviewee 32).[6] Quoting from the interview:

WACSOF Ghana does not have an office. It is hosted by a member organisation which is IDEG. There has not come up a letter or information informing the member organisations that IDEG will be the official host organisation. Officially, we do not have a host organisation.

(Interviewee 32)

In addition to the revelation at the WACSOF People's Forum in 2016, the statement above indicates a lack of formidable meso-presence of WACSOF in a member state where WACSOF was officially launched in 2003. The lesson from this can also be linked to the significance of the analytical framework of this study that assumes the need to problematise the presence of regional civil society organisations across multiple levels.

According to Godsater (2015), many regionally active CSOs often get criticised for not having local constituency which is supposed to be a source of local legitimacy for them. Understanding how organisations such as WACSOF have been able to coordinate and effectively manage their regional presence is vital in framing the extent to which they can act in the region. This framework helps researchers to find out whether there is both physical and non-physical presence of these civil society actors as indicated above. It is reflectively vital to look at the micro presence of WACSOF. What therefore goes on at subnational or community levels?

WACSOF's Micro-regional Presence

One of the theoretical perspectives of the new regionalism borders on 'how the regional arena manifests itself and how various types of civil society actors use it to further their (regional, national and local) interest' (Godsater and Soderbaaum 2011:151, emphasis in the original). As explained in the analytical framework, micro-regional presence is assumed as an integral attribute of a typical regional civil society actor. Godsater also argues that it is important to examine the extent to which regionally active CSOs connect from below (2015:132). The WACSOF's democratic mandate relating to civil society participation in regional integration in West Africa makes the importance of this micro presence more relevant to its analysis. This study takes the micro level to depict WACSOF presence at the local level. The information received through my interaction and interviews at the WACSOF regional secretariat affirmed that local presence is very vital to WACSOF. Drawing from one of such interviews:

> We are not just at the regional or at the national level. We go also to the grassroots level. Our mandate is to just ensure that ECOWAS actions and the decisions are understood and have an impact on the population. But this cannot stay at the regional and the national level. It has to go to the population at the grassroots. We don't just stay at the national level and regional level. We go deep at the grassroots level in the rural communities.

Analytically, the subnational/micro presence of WACSOF resonates with its thematic groups. As aforementioned above, these thematic groups are constellations of civil society organisations that are expected to hold the base for WACSOF at the subnational and local levels across the 15 member states of ECOWAS. However, activities of these thematic groups are often dominated by the influential member organisations, including those that host the WACSOF national secretariats at the respective ECOWAS member states. In 2017, a member of the Ghanaian National Platform belonging to the Youth Thematic Group was asked how the Youth Thematic Group of Ghana has been able to engage with the ECOWAS Youth and Sports Development Centre (EYSDC). The response showed that there has not been an existing relationship with EYSDC. However, the interviewee mentioned the existing plan to decentralise the activities of the WACSOF Ghana to the subregions with each subregional zone having its own coordinator so that WACSOF can truly be accessible to the ECOWAS citizens in Ghana.[7] Yet, from

January 2015 to June 2017, no programme had been organised, no meeting of members conveyed; nothing was happening at the WACSOF national secretariat in Ghana (Interviewee 32). In the words of the interviewee:

> There is a national workplan. WACSOF Secretariat is aware of it. The only thing that is hindering and blocking the implementation of it is the funding. That is it. So, to execute these plans, to basically conduct activities nationally, even if it means to publicise, to put WACSOF Ghana national platform into the limelight, it requires money: even to convene a single meeting of national platform members, it requires money. That is the only thing hindering the operationalisation of the national platform.
>
> (Interviewee 32)

Reflecting on the above statement, the implied message tends to point to the existing institutional weakness at the national level. It also draws attention to the needed capacity in terms of funding to be able to implement necessary projects. However, one commentator seems to underscore that WACSOF is weak nationally because it did not start from below, 'it is as if ECOWAS asked for it' (Interviewee 13). The case of inactivity at the national level is not limited to the case of Ghana. In Nigeria, where the regional secretariat is even located, the national platform does not seem to fare well in terms of working closely with member organisations. Even though the CISLAC hosts the national secretariat of WACSOF in Nigeria, one of the representatives of a member organisation believed that WACSOF Nigeria's National Platform is not yet constituted due to the fact that only the office of the coordinator is apparently existing at the moment: 'The structure in Nigeria, honestly, they have not been able to put it as it supposed to be' (Interviewee 6). However, the comment from the host organisation gave a positive impression of a functioning WACSOF Nigeria with coordinators across the six geopolitical zones of Nigeria. At the People's Forum in 2016, one may also observe some members who had the sentiments relating to lack of inclusion and marginalisation of smaller civil society groups and the urgent need to revitalise the national platforms of WACSOF across the member states (WPForum 2016, Interviewee 31, Interviewee 33).

The question of subnational/grassroots/community levels is important as potential sources of influence and consolidation of the civil society legitimacy on particular regional issues that affect the people of the region (Godsater 2015). As at the time of writing this report, the observations and available evidence tend to suggest that WACSOF needs to build a strong base locally in the 15 ECOWAS countries in terms of actively connecting with its thematic group members (WPForum 2016, Interviewee 8). One wonders whether the responsible factors for the weak or non-functioning national platforms of WACSOF are a result of the lack of necessary capacity or constrained by other factors such as the types of political regimes operated at the ECOWAS member states. The next section will focus on the regional capacity of WACSOF.

WACSOF's Regional Capacity

In the previous sections, I discussed the formation of WACSOF's identity and the dynamics of its presence. This section focuses on regional capacity as developed in the analytical framework. As explained earlier, capacity is mostly used in the context of governance and the effective implementation of a given project (Olowu 2003, Armstrong and Gilson 2011, LindVall 2017). Regional capacity of WACSOF is contextualised here based on its ability to effectively manage its mandate in the region. It is also assumed that WACSOF's institutional and operational capacities as a relevant actor in the region will depend on the support it is able to get internally from the existing organisations. As noted in a report:

> WACSOF cannot be strong if it receives no support from already established networks of organisations such as WANEP, CDD, GERDES, RADDHO, ROPPA, WAWA, etc. Its success will depend to a very large extent on its capacity to be the rally point of non-state actor's organisations in West Africa.
>
> (WACSOF 2008:8)

The above does seem to suggest that the strength of WACSOF lies in the vibrancy of its member organisations in the 15 ECOWAS member states. However, the concern is whether these member organisations, especially the active regional networks among them, really accept a collective ownership of WACSOF. For instance, a participant noted that 'WANEP was a strong member of WACSOF but at a point they parted way' (Interviewee 20). There are assumptions that WACSOF does not seem to have its own mandate as its mandate is given or modified by ECOWAS. That is probably why one of the participants said, 'They (WACSOF) have not been able to prove to civil society organisations that they have the capacity to do what ECOWAS would want them to do' (Interviewee 13). Another concern that seemed to have negatively impacted WACSOF's capacity is the assumption that it was not inspired from below. WACSOF had once reported this as an institutional defect: 'Priority is now given to national platforms to correct the defects of our previous history of being a top-down institution' (WACSOF 2008:7). Eight years later, at the 2016 gathering in Abuja, addressing its top-down defects was also central to the deliberation. The issues of how to reposition the national platforms and making the thematic groups functional at local, national and regional levels dominated the major parts of the debates. Prior to that, in 2015, the first civil society conference in West Africa was jointly organised in Ghana by WACSI and WACSOF. The conference deliberated on WACSOF's inability to act effectively. The conference observed that:

> Despite WACSOF's thematic areas of focus that serve as a good plan to have civil society input on governance and other development policies, several challenges have prevented the forum from achieving its set mandate. WACSOF continues to face a serious lack of recognition by West African

governments. Secondly, there is a serious lack of funds to support activities of WACSOF and this has grossly undermined the scope of its work.

(WACSI and WACSOF 2014)

As gathered during the fieldwork, Nigeria, which is one of the oldest WACSOF national platforms, does not have an executive committee that decides on WACSOF matters in the country. According to a WACSOF member, 'Only the office of the national coordinator exists. It is not supposed to be the case but unfortunately that is what is happening' (Interviewee 6). What the above tends to suggest is an institutional defect with a potential impact on WACSOF's capacity. Operationally, there is also a concern about the capacity of the programme staff, coupled with weak presence at the national levels. Perennial challenges of capacity especially in relation to funding have been impacting negatively on WACSOF. It was admitted in its 2016 Concept Paper that WACSOF has been 'confronted with funding challenges and the many attempts to address this has been ineffective' (WACSOF 2016:2). The report stated further that Article 6.3 of WACSOF Charter makes provision for the People's Forum to meet on an annual basis to review the activities of the Regional Secretariat, induct new members, appoint new leadership, review activities of ECOWAS member states and make recommendations to the annual ECOWAS Heads of States and Government summit. However, due to inadequate funding, the organisation amended it and the Forum now meets every two years (WACSOF 2016:2). The 7th edition of the People Forum was expected to meet in 2018 but the organisation was not able to convene the Forum. Many of those interviewed about WACSOF tended to draw attention to the issues of capacity that WACSOF has been struggling to address so that the organisation can operate effectively. An excerpt from one of the interviews conducted in 2016 is quoted below:

WACSOF is supposed to work as a secretariat for civil society organisations but over the years it has struggled to survive for the past few years. I can say, it is only in the last three years that it is beginning to come back and forcefully make some impact [...] It is very difficult to pool all these organisations in the region together. It is not an easy thing.

(Interviewee 9)

As noted earlier, WACSOF depends on its member organisations for capacity support. These include WACSI, WANEP, Centre for Democracy and Development, CISLAC, West African Women's Association (WAWA) and REPAOC otherwise known as the Network of West African NGOs. Unfortunately, there appears to be competing interest among these organisations even though the regional mandate of WACSOF may be slightly different from some of these regional organisations. They seem to compete for visibility at the regional level. According to the interviewee:

Somebody was telling me that ECOWAS is creating a new civil society body. I don't know how true it is. For me, I know WACSOF was given that mandate. If WACSOF can put its hat together ... we would have a fantastic civil society presence in West Africa.

(Interviewee 8)

The participant explains that due to the position of WACSI in the region, many people tend to see it as the umbrella body for civil society organisations in West Africa. 'Sometimes people take WACSI to be the West African body for civil society organisations' (Interviewee 8). However, the participant clarifies that WACSI is not ready to take over from WACSOF as its mandate is different from the mandate of WACSOF in the region. As observed at the 6th WACSOF People's Forum in Abuja, the main issues that dominated the proceedings were how to transform WACSOF and position it to be as effective as possible. One representative of a donor agency who partook in the 2016 Biennial People's Forum, said 'there was a need for a reform'. He explained the essence of his participation was to observe WACSOF's new direction in order to inform what his organisation would do to support its programmes in the region. One of the external actors with a recent engagement with WACSOF is the Commonwealth Foundation. According to the Commonwealth Foundation:

> CSOs in West Africa are operating with serious challenges, some of which include, low capacity to carry out their mandate fully, the lack of recognition and respect from governments and the unavailability of financial resources to develop innovative approaches to regional development challenges.

(2013)

The Commonwealth Foundation had provided grants to enhance the capacity of both the staff of WACSOF Regional Secretariat and the national platform. A capacity-building workshop sponsored by the Commonwealth Foundation was organised for WACSOF regional staff from 4 to 5 September 2014 in Accra, Ghana, focusing on areas such as 'administrative procedure, financial management, communication and corporate governance' (WACSI and WACSOF 2014). During the fieldwork at WACSI Office in Ghana in August 2016, a WACSI staff confirmed that WACSI has been given a grant for capacity building for both WACSOF staff at the regional office and those who coordinate its activities at the national levels so that the impact of WACSOF could be felt in the region. Another interesting view also emerged from a participant in Abuja during the follow-up interview in 2018. According to the participant, WACSOF at the inception did not lack the necessary capacity to act in the region, but due to lack of leadership, the organisation missed the opportunity in managing its relationship with external partners that were ready to support its activities: 'In those days, partners were really coming to fund WACSOF. They were really funding WACSOF with a lot of money' (Interviewee 20). The participant explained that WACSOF was proactive in various activities of ECOWAS, especially in peace and security in the region mainly because funding was not a problem at the time. The time also coincided with the period when ECOWAS needed active participation of civil society in order to deal with the governance challenges in the region:

> Many partners were coming to work with ECOWAS on issues of civil society. So, when they came, they were referred to WACSOF. They were funded because WACSOF was involved in peacekeeping and peacebuilding activities and other aspects too, such as issues of gender, youth, migration and all the rest. I will say that was the heyday of WACSOF as it was everywhere.
>
> (Interviewee 20)

Inferring from the above seems to suggest that WACSOF's present capacity is not as strong as its previous capacity when there were funds from its partners. Although the above interview was conducted in 2018, the view tends to reinforce the discussions about the so-called weak capacity at the People's Forum in 2016. Despite the capacity constraints, this chapter has also touched on the key role WACSOF has played or attempted to play in promoting democratic participation of civil society in regional integration in West Africa. WACSOF still remains active at the macro level but the main area of weakness lies in its ability to effectively coordinate its national platforms in the region. This, on its own, is a very complex task as one of the participants mentioned (Interviewee 9). However, it is also important to consider the extent to which political dynamics and prevailing types of regimes in the ECOWAS member states have impacted on WACSOF's capacity at the national levels.

The Impact of Political Regime of ECOWAS Member States on WACSOF's Capacity

Since the end of the Cold War, majority of the member states of ECOWAS are more or less electoral democracies (Freedom House 2015). As detailed in Polity IV's 2014 report, the regime trends of the ECOWAS member states show that some of these countries have undergone different political regimes from being democratic, open anocracy, closed anocracy or autocracy (Centre for Syemic Peace 2014). The assumption is that if member states of ECOWAS are not democratic, there is tendency that it would constrain the capacity of WACSOF to act especially at the national levels as in EAC and SADC (see Reinold 2019 and Hulse et al. 2018). The table below shows the Freedom House's (2015) report on the level of Freedom in the ECOWAS member states for the period of ten years (see Table 4.3).

Only three member states: Benin, Cape Verde and Ghana were reported 'free' in terms of political rights and civil liberities which are an essential factor for civil society participation. Other member states are majorly 'partly free' except Mali and Senegal. Mali was ranked 'free' yearly from 2005 to 2011 but became 'not free' due to the coup of 2012. Since then, it has backslided to 'partly free' (before the 2020 crisis). Senegal on the other hand was ranked 'free' for the years 2012, 2013 and 2014. Despite the fact that ECOWAS members are majorly 'partly free',

Table 4.3 Freedom in the ECOWAS Member States from 2005 to 2014

ECOWAS Member States	2005	2006	2007	2008	2009	2010	2011	2012	2013	2014
Benin	Free	Free	Free	Free	Free	Free	Free	Free	Free	Free
Burkina Faso	Partly Free	Partly Free	Partly Free	Partly Free	Partly Free	Partly Free	Partly Free	Partly Free	Partly Free	Partly Free
Cape Verde	Free	Free	Free	Free	Free	Free	Free	Free	Free	Free
Cote d'Ivoire	Not Free	Not Free	Not Free	Not Free	Not Free	Not Free	Not Free	Partly Free	Partly Free	Partly Free
Gambia	Partly Free	Partly Free	Partly Free	Partly Free	Partly Free	Not Free	Not Free	Not Free	Not Free	Not Free
Ghana	Free	Free	Free	Free	Free	Free	Free	Free	Free	Free
Guinea	Not Free	Not Free	Not Free	Not Free	Not Free	Free	Free	Free	Free	Free
Guinea Bissau	Partly Free	Partly Free	Partly Free	Partly Free	Partly Free	Partly Free	Partly Free	Not Free	Not Free	Partly Free
Liberia	Partly Free	Partly Free	Partly Free	Partly Free	Partly Free	Partly Free	Partly Free	Partly Free	Partly Free	Partly Free
Mali	Free	Free	Free	Free	Free	Free	Free	Not Free	Partly Free	Partly Free
Niger	Partly Free	Partly Free	Partly Free	Partly Free	Partly Free	Partly Free	Partly Free	Partly Free	Partly Free	Partly Free
Nigeria	Partly Free	Partly Free	Partly Free	Partly Free	Partly Free	Partly Free	Partly Free	Partly Free	Partly Free	Partly Free
Senegal	Partly Free	Partly Free	Partly Free	Partly Free	Partly Free	Partly Free	Partly Free	Free	Free	Free
Sierra Leone	Partly Free	Partly Free	Partly Free	Partly Free	Partly Free	Partly Free	Partly Free	Partly Free	Partly Free	Partly Free
Togo	Not Free	Not Free	Not Free	Not Free	Partly Free	Partly Free	Partly Free	Partly Free	Partly Free	Partly Free

Source: developed by the author from various reports of Freedom House's Freedom in the World.

West African regionalism is regarded more open to civil society participation than any other regions in Africa (Reinold 2019). Although there has been a decline in the democratic gain in West Africa as shown in the BTI (2020) political transformation index where nine out of 15 member states of ECOWAS are regarded as 'defective democracies', four are 'highly defective democracies' and one (Togo) is described as 'moderate autocracy'. (Cape Verde not included.) (BTI 2020). While regime type is an important structural factor, in WACSOF's case, it has not posed serious constraint to WACSOF's national platforms either through legal restriction from registering as a civil society organisation, placing a ban on its activities, or denying civil society the access to both internal and external funding to promote regionalism and participation of civil society. For instance, Ghana was ranked 'Free' throughout the Freedom House's ten years' review of political freedom, as indicated in the above table, but according to the participants, WACSOF's national platform of Ghana was not set up or hosted prior to 2015 (Interviewee 32, interviewee 33). This delay was not attributed to any form of restriction by the prevailing regime in Ghana. One may think of lack of funding. Reinold also notes that 'even in contentious issue-areas such as good governance and election monitoring, the relationship between CSOs and ECOWAS has been one of healthy dissent' (2019:61). Another factor may also relate to the level of development. ECOWAS region is largely dominated by the least developed countries that also depend on loans and external grants to finance their developmental projects (UNCTAD 2016). So, civil society's access to funding internally to execute projects can sometimes prove difficult. Another point might be the impact of the neopatrimonial political culture which is sustained through personal connection with 'big men' in government offices in order to get access to public resources (Taylor and William 2008). Such culture tends to favour problem-solving civil society networks in regional governance over other organisations that are openly critical or counter-hegemonic to the political status quo in the region (Soderbaum 2007, 2016a). WACSOF shares a bit of a critical type in West Africa. Generally, the capacity of WACSOF both at the regional and national levels tends to relate more to the access to funding. While other structural constraints matter, the negative impact of the prevailing regimes of member states of ECOWAS seems to have a lesser negative impact on WACSOF's capacity.

Having considered the above, since 2003, in what ways has WACSOF been able to make an impact or contribute to the trajectory of regionalism/regional governance in West Africa? This will be the focus of the next section.

WACSOF's Societal Impact

This is the last analytical concept in the framework of this study, and the essence of which is to show the extent to which WACSOF's emergence has impacted on the trajectory of regionalism in West Africa. The assumption in the New Regionalism Approach is that transformation of regionalism often rests on the democratic forces of civil society (Mittelman 1999, Soderbaum 2002, 2004a, Fioramonti 2015, Iheduru 2015b, Godsater 2016). Since WACSOF represents one of such democratic forces in the West African regionalism, it is therefore logical to examine its impact based on this assumption.

In the 2008 Annual Report, Jubrin Ibrahim explained that 'WACSOF is committed to having a strong societal impact on all areas where peace, democracy and regional integration are a priority' (Ibrahim in WACSOF 2008:8). The conceptual understanding of societal impact has been clearly explained in Chapter 2. I will briefly highlight some key policy areas where WACSOF has made an impact despite its limited capacity as well as potential areas of weaknesses due to some structural factors.

Creating a voice for civil society in the ECOWAS Regionalism

Unlike the Forum of Associations Recognised by ECOWAS (FARE), the formation of WACSOF since 2003 has dramatically served as a source of inspirations and opportunities for civil society groups to channel their collective views on the activities of ECOWAS. Despite the challenges previously highlighted, WACSOF has contributed a civil society component for ECOWAS in which civil society actors across the region can deliberate on the issues of peace, security and development. Examples are WACSOF's People's Forums. Although the organisation of the Forum has not been regular, however, we cannot rule out the fact that the Forum has created a platform for the West African civil society organisations to engage with the top ECOWAS policymakers such as the Authority of ECOWAS Heads of States and Government, the ECOWAS Council of Ministers and other statutory bodies.

Operationalising ECOWAS Protocol on Democracy and Good Governance

As part of its conflict prevention contribution, the formation of WACSOF created an opportunity for civil society actors in the region by using the ECOWAS Protocol on Democracy and Good Governance as a tool for advocacy, monitoring and evaluating the level of compliance of the democratic processes in the ECOWAS member states. It is worth stressing that most of the avoidable conflicts in the region are sometimes traceable to electoral issues (Bappah 2018, Ihereduru 2015b, Adejumobi 2016). WACSOF, in collaboration with its local and international partners, has a record of participating in election observer missions with the view to deepening democratic processes in the region (WACSI 2009, Olonisakin 2009, Ismail 2011, Iheduru 2015b:145). In September 2015, with support from OSIWA, WACSOF also organised a successful training workshop to enhance the knowledge base of its members on advocacy against unconstitutional tenure elongation by political leaders in the ECOWAS member states (WACSOF 2015:25–26).

Collective Action against Child/Early Marriage

The United Nations' report has shown that West African states are among the highest in the world in the prevalence of girlchild/forced marriage/early marriage practices (UNICEF and UNFPA 2018:5). In response to this, WACSOF has been instrumental in creating awareness across the region through extensive advocacy programmes in ending early marriage of girls before the age of 18 (Interviewee 1, Interviewee 2, Interviewee 5, Madueke 2016). In 2014, WACSOF produced a documentary accessible on YouTube to sensitise the public and expose the prevalence of child marriage in the ECOWAS countries of Niger, Nigeria, Sierra Leone, Mali, Guinea and Burkina Faso – being the member states with prevalent records in forcing young girls into early marriages (WACSOF 2014). As at the time of writing this book, the YouTube version of the documentary had attracted over one million views with positive commentaries from the viewers.[8]

Other Notable Efforts of WACSOF

WACSOF has also helped to protect ECOWAS institutions, especially the ECOWAS Court of Justice. Despite its multiple challenges, the ECOWAS court has remained an important pillar for the promotion of regional human right regime in West Africa (Alabi 2016). When the former president of Ghana proposed to limit the jurisdictional power of the court, it was WACSOF's regional secretariat that mobilised against Yahya Jammeh's proposal to save the ECOWAS court (WACSOF 2009). Drawing from the WACSOF's report, justifying the reason for standing against the Yahya Jammeh's proposal:

> The request specifically sort that the court should require of community citizens to exhaust all domestic remedies before seizing the court for redress of grievances caused to them by any member state. WACSOF and its partners saw this as a deliberate attempt to kill one of the cradles of democracy in the region and quickly mobilised civil society in the region to lobby representatives from member states to oppose the move. At the end the motion failed and the court remains as strong as it had been in the past.
>
> (WACSOF 2009:15)

Considering the crucial role of the ECOWAS court, we can look at this WACSOF's intervention as a form of positive impact in the drive towards regional integration in West Africa. To substantiate this significant impact, the president of the ECOWAS Community Court of Justice, Honourable Judge Awa Nana Daboya acknowledged and appreciated the important role WACSOF's regional secretariat played in protecting the court in a letter dated 28 October 2009:

> Thanks to your actions of informing, communicating and lobbying, Legal Experts understood the danger of the said amendment, not just for the court, but over and above all to the citizens of our community space and therefore, they reject it with a landslide majority. Your citizen action demonstrates the critical role of civil society, in general, and your organisation in particular, in the consolidation of our achievements in regional integration.
>
> (President of the ECOWAS Court of Justice, in
> WACSOF 2009)

Moreover, WACSOF has also engaged in various relevant activities to its mandate in the region. For instance, in 2014, in collaboration with WACSI, and with the support of an external partner – the Commonwealth Foundation, WACSOF organised a post–MDGs training workshops in Ghana for civil society actors in West Africa (WACSI and WACSOF 2014). In addition, in 2013, WACSOF conducted fact-finding missions on the security challenges in Cote d'Ivoire, Mali, and Guinea Bissau (WACSOF 2013:7). Reflecting on the above, the evolution of WACSOF as a key actor has positively impacted on the processes of regional integration in West Africa. Unlike in the past, the presence of WACSOF has not only served as a check to ECOWAS, it has also helped to uphold key institutions of regionalism in West Africa. Broadly, WACSOF has made some positive impact as a regional civil society actor in a region largely populated by the least developed countries.

While acknowledging WACSOF's positive contributions so far, there are also notable areas of weakness that seemed to have structurally impeded the organisation to act effectively in making more meaningful impacts based on its founding principles. These notable areas are reflected in the highlighted observations below.

Weak National Presence

The presence is central to WACSOF's activities and whatever societal impact the organisation will make in the region. The available evidence within the timeframe of this study shows that WACSOF is still working to revamp its national platforms to be able to strengthen its national and local/subnational presence. Even though the national platforms are hosted by member organisations, the necessary governance structure needs to be put in place to ensure effective coordination of activities at the national levels. This includes election of the national Executive Committee. These regional spatial levels are really important for WACSOF in fulfilling its mandates. Addressing this weakness is likely to make WACSOF more inclusive and give opportunities to other civil society organisations to join WACSOF and contribute to regionalism in West Africa.

Contentious Identity, Ownership, Leadership and Governance

Part of the observations noted about WACSOF which I consider as weakness is the perception about its regional identity including the sense of its ownership. Since WACSOF was a joint creation of ECOWAS and civil society organisations, the issue of ownership of WACSOF has remained contentious to date. While one ECOWAS staff argued that 'WACSOF is not a statutory creation of ECOWAS', he claimed that ECOWAS only facilitated the creation of WACSOF'. According to this view, FERA was statutorily created by the ECOWAS Authority, whereas ECOWAS only had an MOU with WACSOF like other organisations (Interviewee 20). From another ECOWAS staff, 'WACSOF is a child of ECOWAS'. Although WACSOF has often seemed to assert its independence, however, a clear understanding of identity and ownership is likely to give the organisation a clear direction of its position and responsibilities for leadership. A critical reflection on WACSOF shows that its mandate is not so different from the work of the Economic, Social and Cultural Council (ECOSOCC) of the African Union. The ECOSOCC is recognised and part of the institutional structure of the African Union, whereas WACSOF is not, but only revolves around being jointly owned by ECOWAS and CSOs or created by ECOWAS, with a Herculean mandate of driving participatory regionalism in West Africa. Many analysts have not taken a critical look at this issue. There is a need to have a clear understanding of WACSOF's identity and ownership. This was probably part of what WACSOF's co-founder meant at the 2016 Biennial Forum when he said it was time to review WACSOF's mandate in the region. As WACSOF presently constituted, the impact in the area of effective engagement with regional policymakers is often dominated by the most powerful WACSOF member organisations without inclusive opportunities for those members at the grassroots.

Although WACSOF has recorded some reasonable and modest achievements, one may posit that WACSOF is still faced with many challenges in democratically fulfilling its mandate as an interface between civil society and ECOWAS in West Africa. The consensus at the 2016 Forum was to revitalise WACSOF which also complements one of the participants who said 'I see a new WACSOF [...] the same WACSOF revitalised, the same WACSOF standing up like a giant so that people can lean on' (Interviewee 8).

Conclusion

It is evident that the analytical framework employed in this study has provided us with clearer analytical understanding about the emergence of WACSOF as an actor in the West African regional integration. The framework uses WACSOF and ECOWAS to show a distinct interpretation of regional identity. Specifically, it elucidates how WACSOF's identity was formed as a group's identity for civil society in the region. The socially constructed identity of regional CSOs in most cases follows a bottom-up approach, with a clear idea of ownership, leadership and social interest as a form of response to the collective identity of the regional institutional structure (Bello 2011). As we can see, WACSOF's identity is contested. It did not also follow a bottom-up approach in its regional identity's formation. Although WACSOF has made some reasonable contributions to regionalism in West Africa, the top-down approach in forming its regional identity seems to have contributed to the difficulties in consolidating its regional presence at the meso and micro levels.

WACSOF's presence appears weak and we can hardly make sense of this weakness without a critical reflection on its identity which is imposed from top-down. It is not clear who owns WACSOF even though it tends to serve as a regional body of civil society in West Africa. There are various perspectives: 'WACSOF is a child of ECOWAS' (quoted by ECOWAS rep in WPForum 2016); 'WACSOF is a brainchild of ECOWAS' (Interviewee 13); 'ECOWAS

was involved in the formation of WACSOF' (Interviewee 27); 'ECOWAS facilitated the creation of WACSOF' (WPForum 2016); WACSOF was a joint creation of ECOWAS, development partners and civil society' (Interviewee 1, Interviewee 2, Interviewee 20). This confusion was further compounded by the fact that at some point there were cases of staff working in the WACSOF secretariat who thought ECOWAS was their employer instead of WACSOF (Interviewee 20). The perception of a regional civil society organisation of itself is as important as the perceptions of others of it. It is through this uncontroversial understanding of self and social interest in the region that we can be in a better position to make sense of civil society regionalism and the regional agency that gives life to it.

Furthermore, we cannot isolate the negative impact of the above factors on the capacity of WACSOF to act effectively in a region such as West Africa where the capacity of a regional civil society organisation is largely dependent on the support of external partners like development agencies and donors. These are mostly from the developed regions. It also emerged from the field that WACSOF enjoyed a good deal of support from external partners within the first five years of its establishment before the internal contradiction in its regional identity began to emerge, exhibiting unhealthy competition with its members, issue with its governance and leadership. In fact, Professor Oumar Ndongo, the former General Secretary of WACSOF, in the 2008 Annual Report, described 2007 as 'a year of deep crisis for WACSOF' and sought the need to rebuild confidence of the organisation and 'bring old partners and attract new ones' to support WACSOF activities (WACSOF 2008:9). It seemed something went wrong in the previous years when he re-emphasised that 'We hope that our partners will soon come back to help us materialise the ambitions we have for WACSOF' (WACSOF 2008:11). This may suggest that WACSOF has tended to rely on the reputation built through its various activities during those early days, which already had positive effects on the larger society. One participant referred to those early years as 'heydays of WACSOF' (Interviewee 20). Another participant in a 2016 interview also added that WACSOF just started to come back in the last few years to prove a point of relevance again in the region after years of inactivity (Interviewee 10).

WACSOF probably needs to seriously manage its regional identity. This chapter has shown that WACSOF is an evolving regional civil society actor in West Africa with most visible impact in operationalising the ECOWAS Protocol on Democracy and Good Governance. However, there is a need for more inclusive participation by revamping its national platforms. While the framework of the book is not prescriptive, it has helped to understand the extent to which WACSOF has evolved as an actor in democratising regionalism in the ECOWAS region through the analysis of its identity, presence, capacity and impact.

The next chapter provides a study of WANEP to see what differentiates it from WACSOF, and whether WANEP has been able to achieve what WACSOF is still struggling to achieve in the region.

Notes

1 The first consultation of interregional civil society networks, comprising WACSOF of West Africa, EACSOF of East Africa and SADC-CNGO of Southern Africa was convened in Abuja by the CCP-AU from 30 May 2012 to 1 June 2012. North Africa and Central Africa were not represented. See page 5 of the Minutes of the Meeting. Available online: http://ccpau.org/wp-content/uploads/2012/06/Communique-Reg -CSO-Networks-Mtg-1-June-2012-Abuja-Nigeria1.pdf [accessed 1/05/ 2017].

2 Additional information is provided in the following documents: WACSOF Charter 2003, WACSOF Annual Reports 2012, 2013, 2014, 2015.

3 Also available on YouTube: https://www.youtube.com/watch?v=_tsyvmofFMl [accessed 01/05/2017].

4 This view was based on my field research between 2016 and 2018. However, there might have been new developments between WACSOF and the ECOWAS parliament based on the signed MOU.

5 *Case SERAP v Federal Republic of Nigeria*: Judgement No ECW/CCJ/JUD/18/12, Accessible via http://www.courtecowas.org/site2012/pdf_files/decisions/judgements /2012/SERAP_V_FEDERAL_REPUBLIC_OF_NIGERIA.pdf [accessed 26/08/2017].

6 This is the extract from the IDEG call to establish/reactivate WACSOF Ghana in December 2014. Full details available at: https://www.facebook.com/wacsiorg/posts /685123624919483 [accessed 3/8/2017].

7 Ghana has ten regions as parts of the national governance structures. Each of the regions consists of administrative districts. In forming the national government, each regional produces a regional minister and deputy regional minister. According to the commentator, it is the same plan they want to set for WACSOF Ghana, which will comprise of the National Secretariat, Regional Coordinators and representatives in the various districts, but this has not been done. To familiarise with the regional political structure of Ghana, you may wish to see the official website of the country here: http:// ghana.gov.gh/index.php/governance/regional-ministers [accessed 3/8/2017]

8 See the YouTube video on the documentary on Ending the Child Marriage in West Africa: https://www.youtube.com/watch?v=xyum-QRM-VM [accessed 28/8/2017].

5 Civil Society and Regional Peacebuilding in West Africa

Assessing the Evolution of the West African Network for Peacebuilding (WANEP) as an Actor

Introduction

The previous chapter has helped us to make sense of West African Civil Society Forum (WACSOF) as an actor through the framework of this study. The chapter clearly shows that regional identities and their modes of social construction can play a significant role in the ability of civil society organisations to act in the region. This current chapter presents West African Network for Peacebuilding (WANEP) as another relevant regional civil society actor that is considered to have played a significant role in post-Cold War West Africa, but this has not been contextualised in the regionalism debates. This chapter interrogates the question: *to what extent and in what ways has WANEP evolved as a regional civil actor in West Africa?* In this case study, the interested area of regional activity is regional peacebuilding in West Africa. This is because WANEP is claimed to be a leading regional civil society organisation in peacebuilding in the region. Thus, the chapter analyses the extent to which WANEP has evolved as an actor and its contribution to regional integration in this given policy area.

In a strike difference to WACSOF, the chapter finds that WANEP has evolved as an effective regional civil society actor that has impacted on regionalism of peacebuilding in West Africa. WANEP started from below mainly for problem-solving in regional governance. The organisation was able to draw support internally and externally because of its focus on peace and security in the region. This has contributed greatly to its enhanced capacity in the region. The chapter begins with a brief historical background, the justifications of the case, and succinct discussions of WANEP's governance and organisational structure. Afterwards, the analysis of WANEP from the context of regionalism through the frame of this book is presented and inferences are drawn for the conclusion of the chapter.

Brief Historical Background of WANEP in a 'Troubled Region'

The origin of WANEP cannot be understood without drawing attention to the late 1980s and 1999s episode of conflicts and wars in West Africa (Interviewee 13, Interviewee 9, Interviewee 7). At the time, West African regional stability was persistently threatened by devastating violence and civil wars resulting in

DOI: 10.4324/9781003257288-6

monumental loss of hundreds of thousands of human lives, degradation of human values, violation of human rights and abuses of children in addition to irreparable destructions of properties that brought social, economic and political activities to a standstill in the affected states (Reuter 2008, 2011, UNDP 2006, Amnesty International 2008, Tom 2017, WANEP 2016c). Such were the experiences of wars in Liberia, Sierra Leone, Guinea Bissau, Côte d'Ivoire and the likes in this troubled era.

While these were parts of the post-Cold War baggage of rebellion and human tragedies, the normative elements of 1992 report: *An Agenda for Peace, Preventive Diplomacy, Peacemaking and Peacekeeping* of the first African Secretary General of the United Nations, Boutros Boutros-Ghali, cannot be isolated in understanding what the concept 'peacebuilding' meant in practice at the time (Boutros-Ghali 1992, Jenkins 2013, Tom 2017). According to Boutros-Ghali, peacebuilding refers to 'action to identify and support structures which will tend to strengthen and solidify peace in order to avoid a relapse into conflict' (1992:5). This definitive term was further expanded in the *1995 Supplement* to the Agenda for Peace (Boutros-Ghali 1995). While this definitive expansion, and contestations in academia about the term are noted, the main essence of drawing attention to the emergence of the term and Boutros-Ghali's (1992) definition here is to provide an idea of the historical and contextual embodiment of the term 'peacebuilding' as a regional identity for WANEP in West Africa.

The available accounts show that WANEP was a response to the post-Cold War civil strife in West Africa (Interviewee 9, Interviewee 10, Enchill 2011, Lederach 2016, WANEP 2016c). According to the organisation, the formation of WANEP took a form of conversation with the main aim to bring about social change in the conflict-ridden region of West Africa in the 1999s (Lederach 2016, WANEP 2003, WANEP 2016c). John Paul Lederach notes that:

> The WANEP pioneers began to travel across the region and engaged in hundreds of conversations that eventually led to the formation of what is now an organisation and regional network that exemplifies the very best of a visionary, grounded, and committed peacebuilding platform.
>
> (2016: xiv)

As explained by the participants, part of the key motivations of the pioneers was to create an opportunity for Africans to accept the responsibilities of partaking in the processes of dealing with and resolving their conflicts (WANEP 2003, Interviewee 7, Interviewee 13, Interviewee 9). In their 2003 report, the two founders of WANEP persuaded the analysts of African conflicts to rethink their assumptions about the regions and urged them to acknowledge some modest efforts on conflict preventions that had also emerged on the continent (Doe and Bomabande 2003). At the time, they asserted that 'If you think any good thing could not come from West Africa – the poorest subregion in the world, the most destabilised, and home to some of the oldest dictators in Africa – then think again' (Doe and Bombande 2003:6). This was a bold statement at the time. To what extent is this statement relevant today and how has WANEP evolved as an actor in the context of promoting peacebuilding in West Africa? WANEP may have exemplified a typical readiness of an African organisation, collaborating to address peace and security problems. However, it also behoves the analysts to acknowledge both internal and external sources of support for WANEP as an actor. The internal and external support cannot be isolated in terms of the capacity of WANEP to act in the region. In 2014, Maru describes WANEP in an independent report commissioned by SIDA as follows:

> With a network of more than 550 national organisations, spread across the region in the 15 ECOWAS member states, and linking state and non-state actors at local level with national and regional decision makers, WANEP has managed to achieve unique access and has gained an increased understanding over time, established expertise on local issues related to its work on conflict prevention, peace building and human security.
>
> (Maru 2014:5)

Founded in 1998, WANEP represents the West African civil society network, comprising 15 national chapters covering the ECOWAS member states (Enchill 2011, Maru 2014, Interviewee 7, Interviewee 13). The idea of WANEP originated from two citizens of West Africa, Mr Sam Gabaydee Doe, a Liberian, and Mr Emmanuel Bombande, a Ghanaian. The existing documented records and the findings from the field affirmed that the main purpose for establishing WANEP was in response to the seismic wave of violent conflicts ravaging the West African region at the time (Enchill 2011, Maru 2014, Interviewee 7, Interviewee 13, Interviewee 1, Interviewee 9, Interviewee 10). Among the violent conflicts or civil wars in the region included are those in Table 5.1.

Table 5.1 The Overview of the West African Conflicts

Conflicts/Wars	Period	Nature of Conflicts
Nigerian Biafra civil war	1967 to 1970	Political/secessionist
Casamance conflict in Senegal	Since 1982	Political/secessionist
Civil war in Liberia	Dec 1989 to 1996	Political
Tuareg rebellion in Mali	1990 to 1995	Political
Civil war in Sierra Leone	1991 to 2002	Political
Civil war in Guinea Bissau	1998 to 1999	Political
Second Liberian civil war	1999 to 2003	Political
Ivorian civil war	2002 to 2007	Political
Niger Delta insurgency in Nigeria	2004 to 2009	Resource control
Tuareg rebellion in Niger	2007 to 2009	Political
Boko Haram insurgency	Since 2009	Terrorism
Second Ivorian civil war	2010 to 2011	Political
Northern Mali uprising	2012 to 2013	Political/secessionist

Sources: Obasanjo (1981), Seyferth (2014), Benjaminsen (2008:819–836), Bøås (2005), Bah (2010), Obi (2009), Guichaoua (2013), Osumah (2013), Voor et al. (2017), Massey (2009), BBC (6/4/2012).

There are other silent inter-communal clashes and the emerging challenges of transhumance within the ECOWAS community such as clashes between herders and farmers in the West African Sahel that have resulted in incessant killing on both sides including civilians (FAO and ECOWAS 2016, UNOWAS 2018). According to United Nations Office for West Africa and the Sahel (UNOWAS), 'Conflicts between herders and farmers are of increasing concern to ECOWAS Member States. They have a devastating impact on human, national and regional security. They destroy the economic and social fabric of rural communities' (2018:16). Generally, post-Cold War West Africa produced some of the deadliest conflicts in the post-colonial African history, particularly with the Liberian civil wars (from 1989 to 2003) with the estimated death of about 250,000 people (Reuter 2011). Another closely related example is Sierra Leone where thousands of people died in the civil war (from 1991 to 2002) (Reuter 2008). According to the UNDP (2006), the figures relating to casualties during Sierra Leone civil war were not arrived at based on accurate statistics. However, 'conservative estimates suggest that 70,000 people were killed and roughly 2.6 million people …] were displaced from their homes' (UNDP 2006:6). In addition, other noted atrocities included amputation of limbs, ears and lips, mass raping, and forceful enlisting of children as fighters in the war (UNDP 2006). There are other cases as listed in the above table. Many scholars have devoted their attention to post-Cold War conflict analyses in West Africa (Adebajo and Rashid 2004, Jusu-Sheriff 2004, Kandeh 2004, Opoku 2007, Ismail 2011, Hoffman 2011, Kogbe 2012, Ezeokafor 2015, Mitton 2015, Marc et al. 2015:8, Ibrahim and Majeks-Walker 2015, Bombarde 2016, Eze 2016a, Tom 2017). According to a report from the United Nations' Economic Commission for Africa (UNECA):

> The West African sub-region remains one of the most unstable areas on the continent. Conflicts and rebellions have been recurring in the ECOWAS zone over the last 40 years, affecting more than half of the Member States: Liberia, Sierra Leone, Guinea, Guinea Bissau, Ivory Coast, Mali, Niger, Nigeria and Senegal. Several Member States have experienced military coups since 1977.
>
> (2013:69)

It was such a regional structure of fear and instability that informed the response of West African citizens which WANEP was meant to represent. Bombarde has consistently affirmed that, 'WANEP emerged within civil society in response to regional armed conflict' (2016:126). The data also suggest WANEP's idea was based on the research study on peace conducted in the region in 1997 by WANEP founders. It was the finding of that study that led to the formation of WANEP as a non-state peacebuilding organisation (Interviewee 7, Interviewee 10, Interviewee 24, Enchill 2011, Lederach 2016). According to one of the participants, the pioneers' main intention was to conduct research on peace and security to address the ravage of wars and conflicts in the region, but their finding revealed that a regional civil society organisation was needed to drive it. He explained that:

After conducting studies in seven countries and agreed on the structure of WANEP as an institution as we know it today, they started with seven countries where they did the research. And over the years they now expanded to cover the fifteen West African states. So, basically that is the background of WANEP. It was to respond to the civil wars that were ravaging in West Africa.

(Interviewee 7)

The above remark has been corroborated by other sources of data and interviews which suggest that WANEP is probably the first regional civil society initiative in the area of peacebuilding in West Africa (Doe 1998, Opoku 2007, Enchill 2011, Interviewee 11). Apart from the West African Action Network on Small Arms (WAANSA) established in 2002 (WPForum 2016), one similar organisation with a related mandate is the Kofi Anna International Peacekeeping Training Centre (KAIPTC). KAIPTC was established in 1998, though the Institute did not officially open until 2004. More so, KAIPTC was an initiative of the government of Ghana and its main objective was to provide training services mainly to the military and paramilitary personnel and other civilians from the ECOWAS member states and beyond.[1] Because of the perennial issues of conflicts in the region, the story of WANEP tends to be unique in the sense that it emerged out of necessity to contribute to conflict prevention when the stability of the region was being threatened (WANEP 2017, Interviewee 7, Interviewee 24, Adebajo and Rashid (2004), Adejumobi 2004, Ismail 2011, Ezeokafor 2015, Tom 2016). The contemporary history of peace and security of West Africa is mixed with misery, tragedy, triumph and emancipation. This history, according to Maru (2014), will remain incomplete without acknowledging the role of WANEP in it. One of the pointers to that role was its involvement in mobilising women as agents of peace and conflict prevention activities. Liberia is one example. Even though women were generally seen as victims of wars, in the case of WANEP, women formed part of WANEP's vital resources for peacebuilding (Amnesty International 2008, Wamai 2011, WANEP 2016c). This aspect will be expanded later in the chapter.

Justification of WANEP as a Case Study

WANEP has emerged to be one of the few prominent civil society actors on the continent of Africa today. The idea of the counter-hegemonic posture of civil society is widely accepted as the basis of transformative regionalism in the mainstream literature (Soderbaum and Shaw 2003, Grant and Soderbaum 2003, Fioramonti 2015, Soderbaum 2016a, Godsater 2016). Such a notion is relatively alien to the peacebuilding role that civil society plays today in regional governance in West Africa. The nature of its regional social identity in peacebuilding tends to support the stability of the political structure of the West African region based on the normative framework of ECOWAS. WANEP tends to have historical significance in the post-Cold War regional peace and security governance in West Africa. Also, the organisation has been actively engaging ECOWAS in the area of regional peace since 2002 in designing and implementing the West African Early Warning System as a part of the ECOWAS mechanism for peace and security. WANEP's organisational/operational objective is regional and this is aptly reflective in its institutional structure and operation. The organisation's attributes fit-in with the analytical criteria of a regional civil society actor. In addition, WANEP seems to offer an alternative perspective on the role of civil society when we compare it with WACSOF in terms of their identities and trajectories in the region.

WANEP's Governance and Organisational Structure

WANEP has a governance and organisational structure that reflects the scope and its operation in West Africa. The organisation is organised and governed at the regional, national and subnational levels. Its macro level comprises a regional board which acts as the board of trustees of the organisation. The membership of the board is often drawn from eminent citizens and scholars from the West African region (Interviewee 7, Interviewee 8, Interviewee 10, WANEP 2016a, WANEP 2017). At this level is the regional management that oversees the day-to-day affairs of the WANEP regional secretariat, currently located in Ghana. The management comprises an executive director, a programme director, an administrative manager and a finance manager (Interviewee 9, Interviewee 10, WANEP 2006, WANEP 2015a).

At the national level is another national board whose members are also appointed periodically. The national secretariat is headed by the WANEP national coordinator (WANEP 2006, WANEP 2015a, Interviewee 10). These are applicable to the ECOWAS member states. Each of the national secretariats have some degrees of autonomy but they are all under the oversight of the regional secretariat that reports annually on their operational performance in terms of prudence and adherence to the best practices, especially in financial management and reporting standards. The regional secretariat also evaluates and ranks their activities based on national early warnings and contribution to peace and security across the region in general.

At the local levels are also subnational coordinators of WANEP in respective member states. These are extensions of WANEP's presence at the local levels and form key membership organisations working collaboratively with the organisation on early warning at the local levels. A typical example is Nigeria where there are six zonal coordinators across the country's six geo-political zones and the coordinators of each of the 36 states of Nigeria including the Federal capital territory in Abuja (Interviewee 7, Interviewee 13, Interviewee 24). My understanding of WANEP's regional presence is viewed based on the activities that occur at each of the levels briefly explained above. Having clarified this, I use the next section to frame WANEP as a civil society actor in the context of regionalism/regionalisation with a focus on peacebuilding before presenting its analysis through the analytical framework.

Framing WANEP in the Context of Regionalism/ Regionalisation in Africa

Being a foremost regional civil society network, WANEP could be understood as part of the new waves of regionalism in post-Cold War West Africa. It cannot be overemphasised prior to the 1990s that ECOWAS reflected the interest and dominance of the West African states, a replica of what Jibrin Ibrahim once described as 'a club of dictators' (Madueke 2015). In this period, the activities of non-state actors did not attract the necessary attention that they deserved. The emergence of WANEP in 1998 represented the regional agency for the peace-loving West Africans and their organisations, earlier foreseen in the new regionalism literature and the Arusha Charter of 1990 (UNECA 1990:20, Fawcett and Hurrell 1994, Hettne, Initai and Sunkel 1999, Hettne and Soderbaum 2000). In one of the earliest works on new regionalism, Bjorn Hettne, a proponent of the New Regionalism Approach, observes that '[T]he new regionalism [also] presupposes the growth of a regional civil society, opting for regional solutions to some local, national and global problems' (Hettne 1999:10). The new regionalism perspective is not narrow unlike the old regionalism. It transcends the primary focus on state actors and embraces a pluralist understanding of regional agency and ideas (Soderbaum 2003:4, Fawsett 2005, Fioramonti 2014).

The pluralist view of new regionalism provides accommodation for the participation of non-state actors in the region (Shaw et al. 2003, Van Langenhove 2004, Acharya 2014a). So, WANEP came up based on the realisation of the limitation of the state actors in responding to the emerging threats in the region (Interviewee 7, Opoku 2003, Ismail 2011). Even though the issues of peace and security were often considered traditionally within the preserve of the states, post-Cold War West Africa saw active participation of civil society organisations and the women's movement in managing conflict and working together in the area of peacebuilding in the region (Adebajo and Rashid 2004, Olonisakin 2009, Iheduru 2015, Wamai 2011). In the context of the New Regionalism Approach, Hettne notes that:

> Whereas the old regionalism only concerned relations between formally sovereign states, the new regionalism forms part of the global structural transformation in which non-state actors are active, and manifest themselves at several levels of global system.

(1999:8)

While it is important to take note of the notable contributions of the post-Cold War reflectivist writers in the new approach to regionalism in this era, there was also a related African approach with a similar pluralist views of collective participation of citizens in political, economic and development of African states and their regions. So, one cannot ignore the influence of indigenous radical, or what could be called an alternative development approach for Africa between the mid-1980s and the 1990s. The framework was named the Arusha Charter. The Arusha Charter underscored the role of civil society groups/NGOs in the development of

Africa and transcended the state actors in its conception of key actors from local, national to the regional levels. With its people-centred approach to participation and governance of African affairs, part two, paragraph 13 of the Charter provides as follows:

> It is crucial that people and their popular organisations should develop links across borders to promote co-operation and inter-relationship on sub-regional, regional, south-south and south-north bases. This is necessary for sharing lessons of experience, developing peoples' solidarity and raising political consciousness for democratic participation.
>
> (UNECA 1990:20)

The Arusha Charter (1990) resonates with the New Regionalism Approach (NRA). It challenged the African government and policymakers and urged the African people and civil organisations to look beyond their respective national borders for cooperation in development matters (UNECA 1990). On the other hand, the New Regionalism Approach emphasises the need to transcend states as the main actors in the theorisation of regions and regionalisation by suggesting civil society and the market as co-regionalisers (Hettne, Inotai and Sunkel 1999, Hettne and Soderbaum 2000). The emergence of WANEP as a regional civil society network in 1998 was not a coincidence. Funmi Olonisakin, a notable expert on West African security, posits as follows:

> In the fluid immediate post-Cold War environment, addressing West Africa's multifarious security concerns required innovation, creativity and even gallantry, among a range of actors locally and regionally. Crucially, there was a critical mass of actors, which was instrumental in shaping the interaction between civil society and ECOWAS and helped create a credible formula for dealing with the exigency of the time.
>
> (2009:109)

Olonisakin (2009) does not conceptualise the above in the context of regionalism, but her point closely relates to the dominant characters of the post-Cold War phenomena of West Africa. However, in promoting regional human security, some scholars have also posited the need to involve civil society (Shaw et al. 2003, Van Langenhove 2004). While the emergence of WANEP was directly related to the context of the West African conflict, theoretically, it can also be explained through the emerging regionalisation of civil society and other non-state actors in the post-Cold War period (Iheduru 2003, Soderbaum 2004a, Shaw et al. 2003). If WANEP is considered as one of the civil society actors as postulated in the New Regionalism Approach, what makes WANEP an actor and to what extent has it evolved to shape regional peace and security governance in West Africa? In addressing this question, I analyse the actorship of WANEP in this policy area by focusing on its action-based identity, its regional presence based on the levels of its activities and the capacity and impact in West Africa.

Analysing WANEP as a Regional Civil Society Actor

This section provides an understanding of WANEP's actorship, starting with the cross-examination of the rationale behind its regional identity in West Africa. West Africa represented by ECOWAS has been a region with its peculiar challenges since the end of the Cold War. The development of regional norms based on democratic values, peace and security within the framework of ECOWAS was as a result of the perceived threats to peace and stability of the region (Stoddard 2017). David Aworawo vividly captures parts of the post-Cold War challenges in the ECOWAS region when he explained that:

> Political instability arising from lack of good governance has ensured that West Africa remains politically unstable. The original treaty of Lagos was silent on conflict management and prevention as well as good governance. It was however appreciated quite early in the life of the community that no meaningful cooperation could take place within the sub-region without peace and security.
>
> (2010:129)

Even with the earlier realisation of peace and security to meaningful cooperation and progress of the region, some of the earlier approaches of ECOWAS such as ECOWAS Monitoring Group (ECOMOG) and the likes were not without their flaws. This shortcoming has been acknowledged by some ECOWAS leaders (including former president Olusegun Obasanjo) who also shared the understanding that 'ECOMOG fell badly short of its ideals in many ways' (Aworawo 2010:130). These inherent flaws and the lessons learnt from state-centric approaches subsequently led to a new ECOWAS instrument tagged ECOWAS Mechanism for Conflict Prevention, Management, Resolution, Peacekeeping and Security, adopted in December 1999 among others later on (Adebajo and Rashid 2004, Aworawo 2010, Olonisakin 2009, Ismail 2011). It was through this gradual development of the West African peace and security architecture that WANEP emerged as an expression of a group of West African civil society, developing an action-based identity for peace in the region. A comprehensive understanding of WANEP's regional identity is detailed below.

WANEP's Regional Social Identity

As I have stressed, the idea of identity, especially in the study of regionalism or regionalisation, is impregnated with multiple nuances. To remind us, the idea of regional identity, as elucidated earlier, is often conceived as 'collective' (Scholte 2005, 2015, Godsater 2015, Iheduru 2015b, Godater and Soderbsum 2011, Bello 2011, Fioramonti 2015). The regional identity can also be 'social' (Bello 2011:44). Reflectively, does WANEP have an identity and how do we understand it in its regional context? Some scholars have focused predominantly on collective identity (Scholte 2005, 2015, Godsater 2015, Iheduru 2015, Godsater and Soderbaum 2011, Bello 2011, Fioramonti 2015). Godsater (2016:38) also looked at collective identity and argued that it is what the civil society networks form. However, another interpretation of civil society identity is what is referred to as social and action-based (Bello 2011). The understanding of WANEP's regional identity is advanced based on this understanding. According to Valeria Bello:

> Civil society associations and movements try to advocate particular interests which may be those of a specific category of people, such as fishermen or women. By coming together, groups of different nationalities can find common interest and can interact in such a way as to create the tools for constructing a social identity. Of course, this regional social identity is limited and holds a particular meaning for each individual and each group.
>
> (Bello 2011:44)

Coming together of diverse civil society organisations that formed the membership base of WANEP in West Africa underpins the interest in peace and security that these organisations share in the region. In E.A. Anyambod's words":

> WANEP was formally launched as a network organisation aimed at harnessing civil society and community-based peacebuilding efforts and initiatives in West Africa. The noble idea was borne out of the experience of a human disaster created by the mayhem of the wars in Liberia and Sierra Leone.
>
> (Anyanbod in WANEP 2007:4)

Anyanbod's statement tends to correspond with the above idea of social construction of a regional social identity for WANEP. As Checkel (2016) noted, there is no given or prescriptive explanation for identity. WANEP developed a regional network in the quest for peacebuilding in the region (Interviewee 9, Interviewee 10, Interviewee 21). This was not necessarily for counter-hegemonic reasons, or to alter the structural condition of the region (Interviewee 13). Rather, as the available data suggests, it was to lend support for regional structural stability on one hand, and for WANEP to coordinate civil society groups under one umbrella as a partner in instituting a complementary structure for peace and minimising the occurrence of violence or wars in the region (Interviewee 7, Interviewee 24, Interviewee 13).

WANEP's identity is not necessarily isolated nor is it completely independent. Some of the dominant social, political and economic problems that characterise the region are sources of constraints for the people and their organised groups. There is tendency for civil society actors like WANEP to strive within the structural conditions of the region when its main aspiration is based on problem-solving (Reinold 2019). In an interview with Accord, Emmanuel Bombande drew attention to the gaps in the practice of peacebuilding and how WANEP became a modernised platform to solving crises:

> In the 1990s [...] There was a need for peacebuilding and conflict prevention efforts but no organisation for coordinating these existed. When I was

growing up in Ghana, I would often see my grandfather convene early morn-
ing meetings where he sat with a group of elders in a circle. I later understood
that they were solving crises – today you would call it conflict prevention. We
advocate professionalising this sort of response capacity. It is indigenous and
integral to our way of living.

(Emmanuel Bombande in Accord 2011:22)

In an interview in Abuja in August 2016, one of the participants remarked that
'WANEP's identity is in peacebuilding and resembles the regional structure of
the ECOWAS as an institution' (Interviewee 7). In his view, WANEP's regional
identity is an identity for civil society in the sense that it is structured just like the
vision of ECOWAS. He even went further to compare how ECOWAS operates
from the regional to the national levels with how WANEP also operates from
its regional secretariat to the national offices within the region. He pointed at
ECOWAS Commission as a replica of WANEP regional secretariat while the
national offices of WANEP tend also to similarly represent the positions of
ECOWAS member states. (Interviewee 7). What is clear from the above is the
regional context that led to the formation of a civil society's action-based identity
for regional peacebuilding which now represents the image of WANEP today.
As I mentioned earlier, it is one thing for a perceived civil society actor to claim
a regional identity. It is another thing to have a regional presence filled with key
activities in the region. The next section looks at the extent to which WANEP has
evolved to act across the regional levels.

WANEP's Regional Presence

This section critically reflects on the regional presence of WANEP in West Africa.
The essence is to find out whether there is an empirical evidence of WANEP
at regional levels in West Africa. As explained in the analytical framework, the
regional levels refer to the macro-, meso- and micro-levels of regions. They can as
well refer to what Vleuten and Eerdwyk (2014) termed 'regional', 'national' and
'subnational' levels as units for governance of a particular region. These views
are not limited to the above. Andrew Grant (2017) is another illustrative example.
Grant takes *macro-regional* as a global level, *meso-regional* as a regional level,
State as a national level and *micro-regional* as a local level (Grant 2017:151–
154). Despite these varied views, the regional level/presence in this study is limited to the macro, meso and micro levels. This analytic concept helps to reveal key
activities of civil society in the region. The macro, meso and micro levels relating
to WANEP's activities are therefore discussed below.

WANEP's Macro-regional Presence

At the macro level, WANEP has maintained active regional presence in relations
to the ECOWAS Commission. WANEP relates operationally with ECOWAS

policymaking and implementation in the area of peace and security. WANEP's regional design was a bottom-up approach and has resulted in a sustained partnership with ECOWAS since the early 2000s (Odhiambo and Chitiga 2016, Bombande 2016, Eze 2016a). WANEP has a regional secretariat which is located in Accra in Ghana and a regional liaison officer in the Early Warning Department of ECOWAS Commission in Abuja who serves as the link between WANEP, civil society and the ECOWAS early warning directorate (Odhambo and Chitiga 2016). The memorandum of understanding that defines the partnership between WANEP and ECOWAS is based on operationalising the ECOWAS Early Warning and Response (Interviewee 7). The regional scope of WANEP can be explained through its activities as a civil society implementing partner in West Africa. Maru (2014) emphasised that the two organisations have mutually reinforced each other especially in developing regional early warning norm in West Africa. This understanding was also buttressed in one of the WANEP's reports that:

> The partnership between ECOWAS and WANEP is crucial for the success of an early warning and early response programme in West Africa since each partner serves to complement the effort of the other, thereby promoting much needed high-level collaboration.
>
> (2006:11)

Although the partnership is crucial, it is also important to note that WANEP's regional presence is not mainly determined by its relations with the ECOWAS. WANEP had already mapped out its regional presence from the macro-level to the micro-level, and this presence reflected its activities at those levels. An example is its West African Early Warning and Response (WARN) system which cuts across all the three regional levels in West Africa. WANEP's regional presence both institutionally and operationally can probably be illustrated by its WARN and ECOWARN programmes as a form of regional management/governance of peace and security within the ECOWAS community. According to a participant, providing an insight on the presence of WANEP at the macro level:

> WANEP manages the Early Warning System of ECOWAS, and this is because ECOWAS felt that it is going to be too burdensome for them to be going out there to collect data for monitoring conflicts. That it's better for them to work with WANEP, and I think that relationship was also greased by a very generous grant that USAID provided. So, USAID is the one paying. USAID pays, WANEP does the work and the ECOWAS uses the data generated.
>
> (Interviewee 13)

The participant explained that the system relied on two main sources of data which are collected on daily basis across ECOWAS member states. These are what the participant termed, 'open and close-source data' (Interviewee 13). He explained that the open-source data are collected by WANEP through its national networks while the close-source data are collected by the various Secret Service agencies of the ECOWAS member states (Interviewee 13). All these data are analysed and fed into the ECOWAS Early Warning and Response Data bank in preparedness for the management of conflicts before they degenerate into violence and civil wars. Since the national networks of WANEP play an important role in the gathering of open-source data for the early warning management in the region (Interviewee 13, Interviewee 7), it is important to take a close look at how WANEP's national networks determine the effectiveness of its presence at what we may call national levels or meso-regional levels in West Africa. Based on this, the next section looks at WANEP's presence at the meso-regional level.

WANEP's Meso-regional Presence

As explained in the analytical framework, the meso-regional levels are mainly to understand the activities of WANEP at the national levels in the region. WANEP seems to have presence nationally in the ECOWAS region as there are national chapters of WANEP that are covered by the operational structure of the organisation (WANEP 2017). According to an ECOWAS staff, 'WANEP has early warning system. They have what they called national early warning' (Interviewee 22). The national chapter is an extension of WANEP operational levels in the area of conflict prevention. Instead of waiting for conflict to happen or reacting to the occurrence of violence, the idea of early warning was first developed from the national levels and the aim was to take a proactive step in monitoring early warning signs in the region (interviewee 7). One of the participants explained that 'If you look at ECOWAS Early Warning System, it is actually a combination of WANEP's national early warning system plus ECOWAS regional early warning system that comes together to build ECOWARN' (Interviewee 9). Many of the ECOWAS staff interviewed in this study confirmed that WANEP has national offices in the ECOWAS member states for the purpose of operationalising the early warning system.

Looking at the role of WANEP at the national levels, it is mainly complementary to that of the states. From a new regionalism perspective, it resembles what Acharya (2018) calls participatory regionalism or what Godsater and Soderbaum (2011) describe as problem-solving role of civil society in regional governance. A WANEP staff clarifies that 'WANEP is not an activist-based organisation. We influence policy. We work day-to-day on the ground'. Iheduru also describes 'WANEP as the lead agency that mobilises other CSOs to collect and analyse data which is then fed into four zonal bureaus and the Observation and Monitoring Centre at the ECOWAS Secretariat in Abuja' (2015b:144). These activities are coordinated by the national network of WANEP in the ECOWAS member states. For instance, in Benin Republic, WANEP – Benin was established in June 2003 comprising member organisations that shared a common interest in the area of peace and human security in the country (WANEP 2016c). These organisations work together for peacebuilding under the coordination of the WANEP national network/secretariat. Benin's population is over 11 million (World Bank 2019a) and unlike Liberia, Sierra Leone, Guinea Bissau and Côte D'Ivoire, it has not experienced civil war. Parts of the activities of WANEP – Benin include building the capacity of its members on the dynamics of conflicts and analyses to enhance its national early warning system, peacebuilding and deployment of the African indigenous mechanism for resolving conflict (Interviewee 7).

In Burkina Faso, WANEP's national network was established in April 2003. Like in Benin, the network comprises civil society organisations with diverse thematic areas but share an expressed interest in working together with other stakeholders for the peace and stability of the country and West Africa in general (Peace Insight 2017). One of the recent crises in the country was the 2014 popular protest led by Citizens' Broom, a civil society movement that opposed the former President of Burkina Faso, Blaise Campaore, in his bid to extend his tenure through the attempted amendment of article 37 of the country's constitution (Dersso 2014, Saidou 2018). According to Saidou (2018), WANEP is present in Burkina Faso but its crucial role is mainly in the early warning. Through its national early warning, WANEP had earlier foreseen and warned against potential violence in Burkina Faso before the violence broke out (Jenner 2015, Bombande 2016). ECOWAS and UNOWAS subsequently swung into preventive diplomatic moves to avert the imminent civil war in the country (Jenner 2015, WANEP 2016c, Bombande 2016). Aside from the internal political tension, the geographical location of Burkina Faso in the Sahel region made it also vulnerable to the growing threats of violent extremism in the region (BBC 2019). Burkina Faso is part of a collective regional force – G5, joined in 2017 comprising Mali, Niger, Chad and Mauritania, to counter terrorist activities in the Sahel region (World Bank 2019b, BBC 2017b, 2018, 2019, CIA 2018). In Burkina Faso with an estimated population of over 19 million (World Bank 2019), WANEP's presence is felt as part of the civil society working in collaboration with the regional stakeholders to prevent violent conflict in the state (Jenner 2015, Interviewee 8).

In Côte d'Ivoire, WANEP's presence took its root in April 2003 and has been active since then. The tenth anniversary of WANEP's presence in Côte d'Ivoire was marked on 21 September 2013. The Central Intelligence Agency's (CIA) brief on Côte d'Ivoire provides an overview of the Ivorian conflict (CIA 2018) while USAID also acknowledged the involvement of WANEP in conflict management and conflict prevention in the country (USAID 2016, 2019). We should not forget that Côte d'Ivoire experienced its first military coup in December 1999. This was followed by a fraudulent election characterised by electoral malpractices (Onishi 2000). The leader of the junta, Robert Guei, consequentially declared himself the winner of the election (Economist 2000) but was subsequently forced to flee the country. WANEP-Côte d'Ivoire played a preventive diplomatic role through a bottom-up approach: 'WANEP-Côte d'Ivoire used its access and entry points among the various communities to engage in peacebuilding and conflict transformation' (Bombande 2016:133). The United States Institute for Peace (USIP) has also confirmed the presence of WANEP through its past activities in managing and preventing conflicts in Côte d'Ivoire (USIP 2007, USAID 2010). In addition, USIP 2007 report suggests an active presence of WANEP in Côte d'Ivoire. According to the report, the USIP and the West African Network for Peacebuilding – Côte d'voire (WANEP-CI) organised a workshop in Abidjan, Côte d'Ivoire, from 6 to 9 November 2007, on strategies to ensure a peaceful political transition and electoral process (USIP 2007). The workshop included nearly 50 civil society organisations (CSOs) from all parts of the country, representing the media, human rights and democracy advocates, economic development groups, and religious and traditional leaders (USIP 2007). Moving on from Côte d'Ivoire to Cape Verde, due to its location and relative stability, WANEP's presence in Cape Verde is fairly recent. According to the interview conducted in Abuja, the national secretariat of WANEP in Cape Verde was established in 2016 (Interviewee 7), although in another report, a WANEP national focal point has already been established in the country since 2008 (WANEP 2016c:44). The difference between Cape Verde and other member states of ECOWAS is that Cape Verde is more politically stable since its independence from Portugal in 1975 (Baker 2006, Asikiwe 2015). Based on the available data, Table 5.2 indicates the years that WANEP established its national offices in the EOWAS member states.

The next section provides an account of micro-regional conglomerations of the WANEP membership and discusses some of their activities at this level.

Table 5.2 Date of Establishment of the National Networks

Years	National Networks	No.
2000	Liberia	1
2001	Liberia & Sierra Leone	2
2002	Liberia, Sierra Leone, Ghana, Nigeria & Togo	5
2003	Liberia, Sierra Leone, Ghana, Nigeria, Togo, Benin, Burkina Faso, Côte d'Ivoire, the Gambia & Senegal	10
2004	Liberia, Sierra Leone, Ghana, Nigeria, Togo, Benin, Burkina Faso, Côte d'Ivoire, the Gambia & Senegal and Guinea Bissau (11)	11
2005	Liberia, Sierra Leone, Ghana, Nigeria, Togo, Benin, Burkina Faso, Côte d'Ivoire, the Gambia & Senegal, Guinea Bissau and Guinea	12
2006	Liberia, Sierra Leone, Ghana, Nigeria, Togo, Benin, Burkina Faso, Côte d'Ivoire, the Gambia & Senegal Guinea Bissau and Guinea	12
2007	Liberia, Sierra Leone, Ghana, Nigeria, Togo, Benin, Burkina Faso, Côte d'Ivoire, the Gambia & Senegal Guinea Bissau and Guinea	12
2008	Liberia, Sierra Leone, Ghana, Nigeria, Togo, Benin, Burkina Faso, Côte d'Ivoire, the Gambia & Senegal Guinea Bissau and Guinea (12) Focal Points established in Cape Verde, Mali & Niger	12
2009	Liberia, Sierra Leone, Ghana, Nigeria, Togo, Benin, Burkina Faso, Côte d'Ivoire, the Gambia & Senegal Guinea Bissau, Guinea, Cape Verde, Mali & Niger (15)	15

Source: WANEP (2016c:44).

WANEP's Micro-regional Presence

This section refers to the presence of WANEP at the micro-regional levels. This level is both compatible with the regional governance perspective (see Vleuten and Eerdwyk 2014:18), or as an acceptable level in the new regionalism analysis (see Soderbaum 2002, 2004a, Grant and Soderbaum 2003, Grant 2017). This can also be referred to as subnational or community presence in the 15 countries of West Africa. I will only discuss some of the examples of activities of WANEP at this level. According to the participants, WANEP's strength is drawn from its over five hundred member organisations that are working within the subnational regions and communities of each of the ECOWAS member states (Interviewee 7, Interviewee 13, Interviewee 24). Harsch complements this by noting that, 'WANEP is active through its own national affiliates' (Harsch 2012). An example of a strong micro-regional presence can be found in Nigeria. WANEP Nigeria has about three hundred (300) member organisations working across the subnational regions of the country with zonal coordinators who oversee the activities of zones or regions comprising South West, North West, North Central, South-South, South East and North East (Interviewee 7, Okechukwu and Dureke 2010, WANEP Nigeria 2019). Each of these zones or micro-national regions is identified with its peculiar security challenges which are regularly captured by the member organisation of WANEP in their community monitoring (Interviewee 7). The micro-regional presence of WANEP in Ghana covers seven out of ten micro-regions of the country. These are Upper West, Upper East, Northern, Brong Ahafo, Volta and Ashanti regions (Interviewees 10, Interviewee 11, WANEP 2013a, WANEP 2016c). For the Gambia, this micro-regional presence covers the Upper River region, Central River region, North Bank region, Western region and Lower River region (Interviewee 11, WANEP 2013b, WANEP 2016c). According to an ECOWAS staff:

> They [WANEP] are not only at the national levels in member states, even at the state levels. Like in Nigeria, they are virtually at every state level. If they are not, they have partnership with other CSOs who generate data for them and feed in their own structure also. I know they are very much involved in dialogue, community resilient peacebuilding effort in Jos. I know about that. In Guinea Bissau, I know they are on ground. Across all the region in all member states, not only at the national levels, they try to cascade down to the local levels.
>
> (Interviewee 21)

These few examples point to the WANEP's presence at local levels. The kind of role that CSOs play in the region requires that they are in constant contact with the people. As observed above, it is not the WANEP regional secretariat that always puts the boots on the ground, whether in gathering open-source data on security situations in the region (Interviewee 13, Interviewee 7) or promoting peace education in the schools or engaging in grassroots-based advocacy on peace-related matters (WANEP 2012, Interviewee 24). Some of these activities are carried out by the WANEP member organisations under the coordinated effort of the national secretariats. They contribute to the open-source data gathering on security situations across the country through the national early warning system (Interviewee 13, Interviewee 24), WIPNET programmes, peace education, electoral monitoring among others. An example is WANEP's peace education for secondary school teachers and higher institutions (WANEP 2010). WANEP has also responded to perennial religious crises in the Jos of the North Central, providing security situation reports on Boko Haram, dealing with violent conflict between herdsmen and farmers in the North Central, and working with national emergency management agency of Nigeria to respond to emergencies situations often anticipated in the national early warning reports (Interviewee 7).

For WANEP–Ghana, similar peacebuilding activities are taking place at the subnational regional and community levels (Ghana News Agency 2017), which include work to ameliorate clashes between farmers and herdsmen and training political actors to avoid the electoral violence that often leads to instability in Africa. WANEP tends to follow a problem-solving type of civil society actor in West Africa. As noted earlier, one of the key issues or problems in the region has to do with the election-related violence (Ebo 2004, Adejumobi 2004, 2016). The ECOWAS Protocol on Democracy and Good Governance is a framework with an operationalising link with the ECOWAS Mechanism for Conflict Prevention (ECOWAS 2001). The former made the role of civil society and the media explicit in collaboration with the national and regional stakeholders to ensure that elections in the region are devoid of fraud and violent conflicts (see especially, Article 8, Article 23(2), Article 28 (1-3) and article 30 of the protocol). What WANEP also does is 'a supporting function to complement the activities of ECOWAS' (Interviewee 24). Despite the democratic gains across the ECOWAS member states (Stoddard 2017), elections and electoral violence have partly been responsible for the instability in the region (Bappah 2018). Although this is not peculiar to the ECOWAS region alone, electoral violence/instability has characterised the post-Cold War democratisation project of the sub-Saharan Africa (WANEP 2016c, Shaw 2000). According to Timothy Shaw, a prominent academic voice on African politics:

> Africa has not benefited from any post-Cold War 'peace dividend'. Indeed, internal and regional conflicts have proliferated and escalated in the 1990s, with profound implications for regional and continental security and stability. Although almost all African conflicts are internal in 'origin', they invariably become regional in scale as they progress.

> (2000:405)

Perhaps complementary to Shaw's claim, the International Peace Institute, more than a decade later, called our attention to the situation in West Africa, when it posited that,

'Regrettably, the impact of electoral violence is also visible in West Africa. Democracy and stability have suffered from a culture of rigging, and elections remain challenged by a generation of leaders who refuse to see themselves out of office' (International Peace Institute 2011). The regional democratic norm of ECOWAS may have helped to deepen the democratic process in each of the member states, making it difficult for the military junta to seize political power and take over government unlike in the past (Stoddard 2017). However, conduct of election remains a sensitive exercise that needs to be managed with all seriousness (Adejumobi 2016). According to the participants, that is why ECOWAS and development partners such as USAID and the EU, including civil society bodies have taken the issues of election seriously to mitigate election-related violence in the region (Interviewee 7, Interviewee 9, Interviewee 21, Interviewee 22). An ECOWAS staff added that 'WANEP has early situation room, and their situation room always benefits ECOWAS. WANEP is always among ECOWAS election observation team. They monitor election together. They analyse situation which goes beyond only early warning' (Interviewee 21). WANEP mobilises its local member organisations and community stakeholders. It also provides capacity building for them to enhance their skills to be able to handle peace- and conflict-related issues in their communities (Interviewee 24, Interviewee 22, Interviewee 21, Interviewee 7).

Despite all these collaborative efforts, the ECOWAS region and its citizens still face multiple threats such as the rise of violent extremism, transhumance crises across the region, transnational organised networks of drugs smuggling, human trafficking/people smuggling, smuggling of small arms and light weapons, child trafficking, ritual killings, terrorism financing, cybercrime, endemic poverty, environmental pollution, among others (Tom 2016, Osumah 2013). Some of these problems may appear transnational in scope. They all have implications at the national, local or community levels. While WANEP tends to be active, it has its limitations as a civil society actor. I will refer to these limitations in the next section. WANEP is relevant here because it is affirmed that its acclaimed regional presence can be empirically substantiated. Dealing with all these challenges especially those relating to human security across regional levels is beyond the complimentary role of a problem-solving civil society actor like WANEP. Based on the available data, this section has empirically substantiated WANEP's presence across the regional spatial levels in West Africa. The next section examines what constitutes WANEP's regional capacity and the extent to which it has enabled it to act in West Africa.

WANEP's Regional Capacity in West Africa

The term 'capacity' is frequently used in the civil society and development literature (Bratton 1994, Lewis 2002, Mercer 2002, Kilonzo et al. 2015, Soderbaum 2016a, Armstrong et al. 2011, Fioramonti 2015, Godsater 2015, 2016, IMF 2018, Lindvall 2017, Olowu 2003). For Lindvall (2017:1–4), it is used to determine the effective implementation of public policy reforms by political actors while Olowu

(2003) considers the term in relation to the ability of African states and non-state actors in the 'developmental public policies and good governance' (Olowu 2003:1–6). The UK Department for International Development (DFID) has also defined capacity as 'the ability of the people, organisations and society to manage their affairs successfully' (DFID n.d.:2). The effectiveness of any civil society organisation depends on its capacity to act in regional governance (Armstrong and Gilson 2011:3). The capacity of CSOs like WANEP is often tied to a cause or a policy area of activity.

Assessing WANEP's Regional Capacity

One interviewee asserts that, 'WANEP has the required capacity to carry out its activities in the region' (Interviewee 13). His claim is based on the three key factors that have enabled WANEP to effectively act on the regional levels. These are characterised by its awareness of the cultural practices and complexity of West African conflicts; its recognition and application of 'soft power' of the West African Women; and its strategic internal collaboration and external support. Most interviewees among the civil society and ECOWAS institutions agree that WANEP has constantly demonstrated technical and strategic awareness of the complexities of conflicts and peacebuilding processes in the region (Interviewee 24, Interviewee 20, Interviewee 13, Interviewee 7, Interviewee 1, Interviewee 10). Consequently, this awareness has impacted effectively on peace-related activities WANEP has been undertaking in the region. Building peace does not only depend on the material capability of the actors (Jenkins 2013, Tom 2017). The ideational awareness of the cultural practices and sensitivity to conflicts in their respective context is of great essence for any peacebuilding actor (Tom 2017, Jenkins 2013, Brusset et al. 2016, UNICEF 2016). According to UNICEF (2016), such awareness of the complexity and context of conflicts can form part of the capacity of the actors in analysing conflict, resolving conflict and building peace. Brusset, de Coning and Hughes explain that complexity thinking capability provides a deeper insight into conflict by paying attention to the context. They note that, 'understanding the conflict from that perspective is the most significant paradigm shift that peacebuilding needs to adopt for it to be in a position to affect meaningful change' (Brusset, et al. 2016:276). Technically, WANEP seems to have been able to build support among the states and non-state organisations in the region, as well as considerable support from external donor agencies. According to Maru, 'WANEP programmes on human security, conflict prevention and peace-building are strongly supported by ECOWAS, national governments, CSOs and local institutions' (2014:43). Perhaps its ability to draw this capacity support cannot be isolated from the fact that its main interest as represented by its identity is neither agitational nor counter-hegemonic against the prevailing structural order of the region. Rather, it works collaboratively as a partner to the states and ECOWAS for the purpose of regional stability via conflicts minimisation or preventions. Empirical evidence for this can be related to the Ivorian Ambassador, Youssuofou Bamba's comment about WANEP in September 2014:

let me take this opportunity to mention the outstanding work done by the Ivorian chapter of the West African Network for Peacebuilding (WANEP-CI), which has set up an independent national early warning system, including dissemination of monthly reports of the collection of data relating to human security, and aims of course, at supporting actions to prevent conflict and promote peace in Cote d'Ivoire. The NGO (WANEP-CI) should be better supported with substantial resources to increase its effectiveness.

(2014:2)

Unlike many other regional CSOs, WANEP seems to enjoy a cordial relationship with a vast majority of states and regional stakeholders in West Africa. When reflecting on the capacity of WANEP in the region, this wider support is of great significance for the organisation as an actor (Interviewee 21, Interviewee 22, Interviewee 24). According to an ECOWAS staff, 'having regional presence in ECOWAS member states is a form of capacity for WANEP' (Interviewee 24). Another point is that WANEP's identity did not seem to pose any threat to the states in the region. This non-counter-hegemonic value of WANEP was attested to by at least four participants in this study (Interviewee 13, Interviewee 10, Interviewee 9, Interviewee 7). From this understanding, WANEP is rather seen as a friendly problem-solving partner in entrenching peace and stability in the region. This in turn allows it especially in its regional activities to support both national and regional government to provide what it describes as 'robust information to enhance human security in the region by monitoring and reporting on sociopolitical situations that could degenerate into violent conflicts' (WANEP 2015:14). Institutionally, WANEP national networks form essential parts of its regional capacity as it can hardly act as a regional actor if those national networks are not functionally responsive (Interviewee 7, Interviewee 24). Apart from building those national networks from below, WANEP also provides an oversight and coordination of their activities in the region. According to an interviewee:

> WANEP developed its own networks. For example, in Nigeria, WANEP brought several civil society organisations together in manner that is of mutual benefits. If you are a civil society organisation operating in Nigeria, if you belong to WANEP Nigeria, as a civil society organisation, WANEP will organise free training for you. WANEP will involve you in the implementation of projects. So, it is of mutual benefits. So, the civil society organisations that have relationship with WANEP, they get some direct benefit.

(Interviewee 13)

WANEP may have national offices. However, without the network of member organisations, it is most likely that WANEP would not be able to function effectively in the region. Even though some of these network members of over 500 organisations may have divergent interests, they are indirectly sources of capacity in their own rights for the activities of WANEP. According to another participant, it is nearly impossible without involving the people and organisations at the grassroots (Interviewee 9). They are stakeholders and empowering them as peacebuilders across the community adds to the capability of WANEP to build and sustain peacebuilding practices in the region (Interviewee 9, Interviewee 7, Interviewee 24, Interviewee 22). As the respondent pointed out, 'You can't sustain peace without the people working in those countries, in those communities being parts of the solution' (Interviewee 9). Through this collaboration, WANEP tends to exhibit a considerable capability for wider participations of its member organisations within the programmatic areas. These are the National and Regional Early Warning and Response Programme; the West African Peacebuilding Institute (WAPI) that focuses on the training and retraining of peacebuilders within the civil society organisations, the personnel of the national governments, and the staff of regional organisations such as ECOWAS and African Union (Interviewee 24, Interviewee 20, Interviewee 7, Interviewee 13).

Another point about WANEP's regional capacity is the recognition of the 'soft power' of the West African Women as an instrument for peace (WANEP 2003, Wamai 2011, WANEP 2016c, Interviewee 7). This is represented institutionally in the Women in Peacebuilding Network (WIPNET), which is WANEP's programme that trains and empowers women in the region to become active peacebuilders/agents of peace instead of being the objects or victims of violent conflicts in the region (Opoku 2007, Maru 2014, Bombande 2016). The realisation of the vulnerability of women in the time of conflicts also led to facilitating a platform to bring out the agency of women in preventing, mediating and resolving conflicts in West Africa (Interviewee 7, Interviewee 24). As at 2006, civil society groups belonging to WIPNET accounted for more than half of the total members in WANEP (Dixon and Reyes 2007:11). Dixon and Reyes (2007) explained that there was a rift between WIPNET and WANEP in the year 2006 due to the women's demand for decision-making positions within WANEP and expansion of WIPNET membership beyond West Africa. Dixon and Reyes capture it as follows:

> WIPNET's members chose to seek full legal autonomy from WANEP, its parent organisation, which disputed WIPNET's right to break away, ultimately resulting in a court ruling that the name 'WIPNET' belongs to WANEP. In response, the bulk of WIPNET's members have decided to leave WANEP and regroup as the Women's Peace and Security Network-Africa (WPSN).
>
> (2007:11)

Several visits to the website of WPSN show that the organisation has not been updating its activities for some years. Traore (2017) also confirms lack of activity of WPSN in recent years. However, WIPNET has proven to be a source of capacity for WANEP with a considerable positive impact in Liberia, Sierra Leone, Côte d'Ivoire, The Gambia and Nigeria (Interviewee 24, Interviewee 7, WANEP and GPPAC 2007:22). Another area where WANEP has showed a considerable capability is in its project on the Civil Society Coordination and Democratic Governance that focuses on preventing electoral-related violent conflicts that could lead to political instability in the concerned member states (WANEP 2015:16). WANEP operated Election Situation Rooms and monitored the general elections of countries such as Ghana (Eze 2016b), Nigeria, Côte d'Ivoire, Guinea, Burkina Faso, Liberia, Togo, Benin and Sierra Leone (WANEP 2015:17). As a civil society organisation, it lacked the capacity to conduct this monitoring alone. WANEP over the years has mutually enhanced its capability by collaborating with CSOs, national governments, and organisations within and outside the region (WANEP 2017b, USAID and WANEP 2018). These include ECOWAS, AU, UNOWA, USAID West African Office, the EU and UNDP (WANEP 2017b).

The study shows that WANEP has enjoyed a good reputation from the development partners and this has been sustained from the initial recognition of its activities during the civil wars in the region to the present time with new forms of security threats from electoral violence and terrorism. Table 5.3 shows the ealier grants received by WANEP from 2002 to 2005.

We should also note that this period marked the peak of the post-Cold War violent conflicts in the region. It should therefore not be a surprise if WANEP as a key regional civil society organisation was able to garner financial support to aid its peace activities at the time. In February 2015, USAID announced the award of the sum of US$2.5 million to WANEP to support its early warning and early response system (US Embassy in Ghana 2015). The grant was aimed at strengthening WANEP's national presence across the 15 ECOWAS member states to prevent election violence in the region for a period of five years (US Embassy in Ghana 2015). WANEP also reported that it had signed a three-year (2018–2021) contract with the European Union to implement a project on election monitoring in seven countries – Burkina Faso, Côte d'Ivoire, the Gambia, Guinea Bissau, Senegal and Togo (2019:8). Through this form of support over the years, it cannot be overemphasised that WANEP has showed some considerable capabilities through its regional activities in West Africa (Maru 2014, Eze 2016, WANEP 2012). All these are parts of institutional signifiers of WANEP's capacity in moving beyond constructing its regional identity in West Africa. It has worked towards the transformation of the so-called identity as a peacebuilder into a peacebuilding action. While considering the nature of WANEP's role in the region, it may be antithetical for it to act as a counter-hegemonic actor. Without being a counter-hegemonic from a regional sense, there are shared views both from documented evidence and interviews that WANEP has partly helped to contribute to civil

Table 5.3 The Earlier Grants Received by WANEP

Years	Grants Received (US$)
2002	780,988
2003	1,497,459
2004	1,400,154
2005	1,190,315

Source: WANEP.

society regionalism in West Africa in the area of peace and security, at least, in terms of its consistent and collaborative activities on early warnings (Interviewee 24, Interviewee 20, Interviewee 7, Interviewee 21, Interviewee 10, Maru 2014). WANEP's involvement in regional peacebuilding tends to mirror what Acharya (2018) describes as 'participatory regionalism'. This does not mean there are no divergent interests within its network. However, regional peacebuilding seems to have become a participatory avenue for local organisations to take part in region-alism despite multiple impediments they are likely to face, most especially resist-ance from the existing states' structure in the region.

The Impact of the Political Regime in the ECOWAS Member States on WANEP

As explained in Chapters 2 and 5, the types of regime of member states of a regional organisation may determine the trajectory of a regionalist project, includ-ing the access for civil society participation (Hulte el at. 2018, Reinold 2019, Soderbaum 2007, 2016). However, the emerging empirical evidence has indi-cated that civil society organisations like WANEP that engage in problem-solving activities tend to have access to participate in regional governance (see Collins 2015, Godsater 2016). Apart from the fact that ECOWAS is open to civil soci-ety participation (Olonisakin 2009, Ismail 2011), WANEP's activities in regional early warning are based on collaboration with states and other critical stakehold-ers in promoting peace and security of the region (Iheduru 2015b, Jenner 2015, Maru 2014, Interviewee 7, Interviewee 13). Since it is not necessarily counter-hegemonic in its approach, WANEP's complementary role is basically monitor-ing early warning signs of conflicts before they result in violence or war. The data generated through the early warning analysis are used by ECOWAS and member states. This kind of role makes WANEP less likely as a target of any undemocratic regime to the extent of constraining its capacity as a partner in the region.

The next section focuses on how WANEP's regional activities have impacted on regionalism in the area of peacebuilding in West Africa.

WANEP's Societal Impact

What do we mean when we refer to impact in peacebuilding? A shared under-standing of what constitutes impact when we assess a peacebuilding organisation may be needed. Of course, there are different interpretations from peace practi-tioners dealing with the effects of positive or negative peace and whether absence of war or violence is enough as presence of peace among others (Jenkins 2013, Tom 2017). My understanding of impact here is what Boutros-Ghali (1992, 1995) refers to as the outcome of peacebuilding in terms of the institutional structure put in place to guard against falling back into violent conflicts. My aim is to relate WANEP's involvement to both direct and indirect impact that manifests WANEP's activities through the institutions put in place for peacebuilding in West Africa. I have relied on the participants' views to make sense of the impact of WANEP's activities in the last two decades. One of such views expressed by a staff of ECOWAS is quoted below:

> Comparing West Africa with other African regions, if there is any network doing well in Africa, present in 15 member states, you would not see two organisatons. The one that you will see is WANEP. And if you compare the peace we are enjoying today (in West Africa) despite some new challenges, WANEP's contribution to peace is invaluable. WANEP can claim ownership of being part of the process through its presence with ECOWAS, which is also doing really well compared to other regions.
>
> (Interviewee 24)

What the above comment tends to suggest is that the impact of WANEP is based on the peacebuilding network of the civil society groups the organisation has created in the ECOWAS member states. However, what also matters is the implication of the network for the stability of the region in which member states are still confronted with multiple security challenges. No matter how weak or strong WANEP has been, it still has a limited role to play as a civil society actor in the region. The complexity of the security challenges in West Africa underscores the presence of multiple stakeholders. An understanding of WANEP's impact can only make sense within the limited role civil society actors are permitted to play in regional governance. According to an ECOWAS staff, 'the member states are the actual implementors of all ECOWAS policies and the civil society now provides supporting function because you will discover that at the Commission, we cannot do everything. Where there is gap in going deep into the grassroots that is where civil society comes in' (Interviewee 20). From this limited civil society's role, the views about WANEP's impact are explained in five key areas as an outcome or a form of structure to sustain civil society peacebuilding activities in West Africa.

The first example is institutionalised national and regional conflict early warning system. The reason for this is that early warning arrangement never existed before WANEP was established in 1998 (Interviewee 7, Interviewee 8, Interviewee 24). This is a flagship activity of WANEP. Early warning system has become a centre-point of the post-Cold War transformation of the regional conflicts in West Africa. It is also based on this activity that a commissioned report of the SIDA described WANEP as 'the godfather of peacebuilding in West Africa' (Mari 2014:5). Participants in this study also mentioned that, President Barack Obama of the United States of America publicly acknowledged and commended ECOWAS Early Warning System (ECOWARN) (Interviewee 7, Interviewee 9, Interviewee 10). In the SIDA report, it has been posited that 'whatever impact ECOWAS had registered in the early warning and early response programme, it is shared with WANEP' (Maru 2014:5). Another ECOWAS staff added 'For me, WANEP is a very credible civil society organisation. If not I am not sure they would not be able to maintain a long relationship with ECOWAS for about 15 to 20 years' (Interviewee 21). A WANEP staff also clarified that it was after President Obama's remarks about ECOWARN that USAID called WANEP and gave a direct grant to WANEP to look after election-related conflicts in West Africa for a five-year term (Interviewee 9). From the above perspective, institutionalising national and regional early warning system that promotes collaborations between civil society and ECOWAS Commission tends to top the list of impact of WANEP's activities in West Africa. Even though WANEP may lay a claim to its achievement in this area, I don't think the organisation would have been able to make much progress in this area without the financial support of external donors (see Appendix 2).

The second area of impact through WANEP's involvement in regionalism in the area of peacebuilding in West Africa is the enhanced women's participation in peacebuilding across all levels. WANEP's WIPNET is the best example of this. As noted earlier, the Liberian civil war was one of the deadliest wars in recent West African history from 1989 to 2003 (Kramer 1995). Leyman Gbowee who was a leading figure in mobilisation of women of Liberia happened to be the coordinator of WANEP's WIPNET at the time. Existing studies have acknowledged the instrumental role of these women before the peace agreement was signed between the Charles Taylor's government and the rebel's group at the Accra peace talks in Ghana in 2003 (Amnesty International 2008, Wamai 2011, WANEP 2003, 2016c, Interviewee 7). Since 2003, WANEP has buttressed that 'The Women in Peacebuilding Network of WANEP-Liberia led women to provide the moral force needed to reawaken the degenerated country. That force followed the warlords to Ghana and ensured that they signed a peace deal' (2003:5). Also, during my fieldwork, at least two interviewees stressed that Leymah Gbowee was a WANEP's staff during her peace activities and mobilisation of women of Liberia (Interviewee 7, Interviewee 9). This claim was also reiterated in a special report of WANEP (see WANEP 2016c). A participant in this study specifically mentioned that:

> Leymah Gbowee of Liberia is a Nobel Peace Prize winner. She was a WANEP's staff. All that work she did to get that (prize) it was a WANEP's work. You need to see the movie called 'PRAY THE DEVIL BACK TO HELL'. You will see the WANEP's t-shirts. You will see everything. So, at that level, we organised women and directed her to hand a letter to Charles Taylor and directed her to go to Accra for the peace talks. She agreed and she went, and the peace talks held and we succeeded, and that is one of the legacies of WANEP in mobilising grassroots women, Christians and Muslims.
>
> (Interviewee 7)

The role of WIPNET (women's wing of WANEP) has remained a milestone for the organisation even though there was a rift between some members of WIPNET and the WANEP management which resulted in the formation of a new group, the Women Peace and Security Network Africa (WIPSEN) on 8 May 2006 by some former members of WIPNET. WIPNET's proactive role in restoration of peace in Liberia remains significant for WANEP. The victims of the Liberian war were not only Liberians in Liberia, many of them were ECOWAS citizens which underscores the regional dimension of the conflict (Aworawo 2010, Ezeokafor 2015, Adedeji 2007). A unique civil society's role like this appears as a significant contribution to the contemporary history of peace and security in West Africa (Interviewee 7, Interviewee 9). In addition, in 2016, during the opening of the WANEP's new regional office in Ghana, the United Nations Secretary General's Special Representative for UNOWA, Dr Mohamed Ibn Chambers, also acknowledged the positive role of WANEP during the Sierra Leonean civil war (Africanews 2017). Many of the participants believed that WANEP's successful collaboration in peacebuilding activities reflects its impact empirically in countries such as Côte d'Ivoire, Benin, Guinea, Guinea Bissau, The Gambia, Burkina Faso, Ghana, Niger, Nigeria, Mali, Senegal and Togo, especially through the national and regional Early Warning and Response System (WANEP 2016c, Maru 2014, Interviewee 7, Interviewee 13, Interviewee 24, Interviewee 22). Other areas include peace education for youth and creating opportunities for them to act as peace agents, introduction of Election Violence Monitoring, Analysis and Mitigation (EMAM) programme to reduce the election-related violence in the region (Interviewee 22, Interviewee 21, Interviewee 24, Interviewee 35). West Africa is not totally free of conflicts. In fact, Iwilade and Agbo are of the view that 'ECOWAS will always have to, now and then, resolve large-scale violent conflicts that it has neither the capacity nor the need to engage with' (2012:372). However, unlike more than two decades ago, one can say that the evolving culture of conflict prevention/peacebuilding through the participation of civil society actors like WANEP has contributed significantly to monitoring early signs of potential conflicts in the ECOWAS member states before they result into a full-blown violence or instability. Being a leading civil society actor in this area of activity, WANEP has enjoyed a good reputation among local and international actors. According to one of the ECOWAS officials, WANEP is described as 'a reliable and key regional NGO involving in efforts at resolving conflicts in the region' (Interviewee 22). The 2014 SIDA report about WANEP also noted a similar observation that:

> national, regional and international institutions that have been approached during this evaluation have found WANEP to be reliable and credible partner. WANEP exudes confidence both with non-state actors and state members of the ECOWAS, particularly as its extremely relevant and high demand projects have significant impact on the ground.
>
> (Maru 2014:6)

The conflict in Casamance province in Senegal is an example. The province has experienced a protracted low-intensity conflict between the Government of Senegal and the Movement of Democratic Forces of Casamance (MFDC) spanning close to four decades since 1982 (Lewis 2012). WANEP is reportedly trying to bring all parties together to resolve the conflict. According to the report of the News Ghana of 25 August 2015, WANEP organised a two-day consultative meeting of relevant stakeholders on Casamance conflict held in Accra, Ghana, from

21 to 22 August 2015 (News Ghana 2015). The rationale for this was to 'develop new strategies and operational techniques' (WANEP 2015b:1) in finding a solution to the Casamance conflict (News Ghana 2015, WANEP 2015b, Interviewee 9). WANEP has also intervened in the Jos crises of North Central Nigeria to stem the incessant violence and maiming (WANEP and IPCR 2010) that once claimed lives of 'more than 1000 people [...] in just six days' (Human Right Watch 2001). In Ghana where the regional secretariat is located, WANEP is recognised as a contributor to conflict prevention activities in the country especially in northern Ghana with protracted issues of interethnic or intra-ethnic conflicts (Mahama and Felix 2013:123, Interviewee 22, Interviewee 7). Another notable reference made by the participants has to do with WANEP's contribution to the establishment of Ghana's National Peace Council as an institutional structure that now works with other stakeholders to promote peaceful co-existence in the country (Interviewee 24, Interviewee 10, Interviewee 22).

The possible inference from the above empirical evidence draws attention to the participatory nature of regionalism of peacebuilding in West Africa. Whether this can be said to be an indirect democratic regionalism or what Acharya (2018) calls 'participatory regionalism', what is evident so far is that WANEP's network has made it possible for small groups and individuals within civil society to participate in regionalism that focuses on peacebuilding in West Africa.

Conclusion

This chapter has examined the extent to which WANEP has evolved as an actor in the area of peacebuilding or conflict prevention in West Africa. The chapter analysed the origins of WANEP's social identity based on the views of its pioneers and interactions across the region. We can understand that these conversational and interactional practices were employed by the initiators to socialise discrete groups in their respective countries into a regional platform for promoting peace and security in West Africa. This is regarded as a local promotion/bottom-up orientation of WANEP's idea. In a sense, this greatly helped in its evolution at the early stage in the region. One key lesson from such methodical approach is that it reinforces the significance of a bottom-up process of identity construction for civil society. Since this has not been captured in previous studies, it is important to pay a close attention to this new insight in understanding the evolution of civil society as an actor in regional integration in West Africa. Also, the framework buttresses the inclusive application of policy or interest-based identity as a driving force of action for civil society activities in regional integration. In that sense, the framework clearly shows that the regional social identity of WANEP came about as a response to the threats to the West African people and political stability in the ECOWAS region.

The analytical significance of WANEP's case is that researchers can make a much clearer sense and understanding of regional civil society actors by showing awareness of the action-based identity to explain the regional agency of civil society in regionalisms or regional integration. Second, what constitutes 'regional' is often underplayed as to interrogate the spatial levels of regional actors. This framework underscores regional presence as another analytic concept that complements our understanding of regional civil society actors in this case. The regional presence shows the extent to which WANEP has evolved across the regional levels such as the micro (local), the meso (national) to the macro (ECOWAS) levels. Even though WANEP is regional, the strength of the organisation lies locally with various civil society groups in the network. WANEP's capacity was also examined through the framework which pointed to its institutional and operational capacity especially in collaborations with internal and external actors. Through this capacity, the factors that enable it to implement its key regional activities are clearly elucidated. It is through these activities that people form their views about its actorship. For instance, in the eyes of the ECOWAS officials, WANEP is seen as a 'credible' partner in peace and security in West Africa (Interviewee 22). One participant even described it as 'a leading regional CSO that sees itself as a supportive and facilitating actor in peace and security' (Interviewee 24). Reflecting on WANEP as a relevant civil society actor seems to indicate how much importance the ECOWAS policymakers and states attach to peace and stability of the region. The emerging civil society regionalism literature has acknowledged that civil society has more opportunities to participate in regional governance in West Africa than their counterparts in Southern and East Africa (see Reinold 2019, Glas and Balogun 2020). This does not mean that all ECOWAS member states are more democratic, hybrid or authoritarian in terms of their prevailing regime locally. The driving force for civil society in regional democratic and security governance is in line with the regional instruments of ECOWAS such as Protocol on Democracy and Good Governance as well as the Framework on Conflict Prevention. As Glas and Balogun (2020) persuasively explain, it is the regional norm or quest for 'people-centred governance' that reinforces the openness of ECOWAS to encourage active participation of civil society in the regional policymaking especially in the area of peace and security. In turn, civil society actors like WANEP may also serve as a cover for the ECOWAS bureaucrats when the regional demands tend to conflict with the national interests. According to an anonymous ECOWAS staff:

> not exactly that we are using WANEP [as a cover]. It is not ECOWAS in this case, Of course staff of ECOWAS have certain limitations. We are on oath. Being an NGO, they (their staff) have no allegiance to member states except ordinary man. They say things we can't be able to say or do.

WANEP may have evolved and maintained a healthy relationship within the political dynamics of the region. Despite its acclaimed stake, one finds that the test of leadership of WANEP has successively been managed by its co-founders. Since 1998, WANEP had only three executive directors. The first director was Sam Gbaydee Doe who led the organisation from 1998 to 2004. Emmanuel Bombade took over as executive director in 2004 and headed it until 2015 and left after becoming a deputy foreign minister of Ghana. The current executive director,

Chukwuemeka Eze, has been leading WANEP since 2015 (WANEP 2016c:93–96). WANEP's leadership has always been in the hands of those who understood its vision and aspirations. This can be a contributing factor to WANEP's credibility. Even the current executive director was the regional programme director from 2010 to 2015, having previously served at WANEP Nigeria as programme officer (2003–2005) and national coordinator (2005–2010).

More so, WANEP may have institutionalised participation of women (WIPNET) as a source of influence for peace but so far it has not produced a female executive director in its historical evolution. This may work against the organisation in the future if gender sensitivity is not given a priority in its succession planning. Another key area of observation relates largely to the organisation's reliance on external donors to support peace processes in the region. Without considering alternative sources of financing its regional projects, the sustainability of the organisation in the region may be threatened, especially now with the new dynamics of perennial experiences of terrorism in the West African Sahel. Despite this, WANEP still envisions itself among the stakeholders working for a 'West Africa region characterised by just and peaceful communities' (WANEP 2015:5). For instance in 2015, its present executive director said, 'West Africa by many objective indicators is more stable, peaceful and prosperous compared to 20 years ago, when consultations over the formation of WANEP was ongoing across the region' (WANEP 2015:5) 'We have more stable democracies, predictable electioneering cycles and increased voices of citizens in governance' (WANEP 2015:5). The above tends to reinforce the idea of liberal peace often championed by norm entrepreneur and largely funded by external donors (see four strands of liberal peace in Richman 2006). While WANEP may have evolved as a credible civil society actor in West Africa, as some participants have described it, the organisation is likely to continuously remain relevant in the current regional order, playing a complementary role of a problem-solving civil society actor in peace and security in West Africa.

Note

1 See the mandate of KAIPTC. Available online: www.kaiptc.org/about-us/history [accessed 31/12/2017].

6   Conclusion

Introduction

This study has dealt with civil society regionalism in West Africa. It has become clear that what constitutes regional actorship of civil society is beyond the four-dimensional typology of legitimation, partnership, resistance or counter-hegemonic and manipulation that recently emerged from the new regionalism literature (see Godsater and Soderbaum 2011, Fioramonti et al. 2015, Soderbaum 2016a). In the beginning, I argued that we can transcend such a typology by offering a framework to analyse what is regional in the regional civil society actors in Africa. I attempted this by offering four analytical concepts (identity, presence, capacity and impact) to understand the actorship of WACSOF and WANEP. This is a clear innovation in the regionalism literature, which I would argue has proved to be very useful in understanding the extent to which the two cases have evolved as civil society actors in regional integration and governance in West Africa. In addition, West Africa as a region, previously at the margin of the debates, is now situated at the centre of regionalism analysis. By this token, a significant empirical contribution is added to the literature, offering much clearer perspectives on rethinking civil society regionalism.

On that note, the aim of this chapter is to discuss the findings and draw attention to the original contributions of this research. The chapter draws attention to the main aims of the project, the contributions to knowledge and acknowledgement of the limitations of the study. In addition, it highlights some salient areas that could be explored for future research.

Fulfilling the Book's Aims and Contributions to the Literature

This project has built on the new regionalism literature that combines reflectivism with constructivism to make sense of the agency of regionalism in the non-Western regions such as Africa in the context of civil society regionalisation. Within the last three decades, while scholars have all acknowledged civil society as an actor in the new regionalism literature, there seemed to be less emphasis on what constitutes *the regional* about regional civil society actors in such debates. Based on the West African analysis, this book attempts to move the scholarship forward

DOI: 10.4324/9781003257288-7

in this regard. First, it addressed the lacuna in the existing works on civil society regionalism that placed little emphasis on the regional attributes of these civil society actors. It testifies to the new understanding of what regional civil society is and addressed what is analytically 'regional' in the so-called civil society and its actorship in regionalism.

Regionalism has always been mired by multiple ambiguities and concepts. These have led to a disjuncture between civil society regionalism scholarship and implications for practice in the African regions. This study has transcended this by clarifying some of these complicated concepts of regionalism and making them accessible for further academic applications and regional policymaking. This book made the study of civil society in regionalisms/regional integration clearer and understandably accessible to experts and laymen/women in a way they can relate with in their respective regions.

Second, West Africa is a region which has remained at the margin of regionalism debates on civil society as most reflectivist writers such as Fredrik Soderbaum (2002, 2004a, 2007, 2016a, 2016b), Andreas Godsater (2013a, 2015, 2016), and Zajontz and Leysens (2015) with significant voices, have mainly focused on Southern Africa and partly East Africa. Focusing on the West African experience of civil society and on specific cases of these actors has contributed to fill the existing empirical gaps in the region. The book also enriches the research agenda of Global International Relations (GIR) by offering new analytical perspectives and a reinterpretation of existing concepts to make sense of regional civil society actors in Africa. Particularly, this third point is a response to Amitav Acharya and Barry Buzan's call for a Global International Relations which is founded on multiple narratives of IR (Acharya 2018, Acharya and Buzan 2019). Global IR challenges emerging scholars from the Global South to engage in theory building by drawing from their local and regional practices to offer alternative or adaptive understanding on how we make sense of international relations in its regional and global contexts.

Theoretical Contributions of This Study

This study contributes to the extant literature on the regional dimension of civil society actorship in line with the new phase of rethinking regionalism. The framework of this book starts by interrogating the regional identity of civil society actors to find out against whom it has been constructed. The regional identity is recast in a way that shows how regional civil society actors emerge in response to the social issues emanating from the region. The analysis offers two distinct understandings of identity at the regional levels; the regional social identity that is action-based (agency) and the regional collective identity that is structure based (see also Bello 2011). This study shows that the identity of a regional civil society actor is action-based and socially constructed and represents the interests and certain values shared by citizens who organised themselves into voluntary associations in pursuance of those values. There seems to be no given values or preferences for civil society. These need to be discovered by researchers in problematising what a given regional civil society actor stands for and what interest it seeks to pursue or is pursuing at the regional level. This has to do with the civil society organisations' perception of 'self' and how others perceive them. A reflective researcher is expected to unequivocally show awareness of this. In this study, this conceptual idea of regional identity becomes clearly understood by showing how it manifests in WACSOF and WANEP within the dynamics of the ECOWAS region (see Chapters 4 and 5).

Second, the framework also uses regional presence to understand the extent to which the two cases have evolved spatially, comprising the macro-, the meso- and the micro-regional levels. Apart from allowing a vivid appreciation of what a regional bottom is, spatially, the framework also shows the linking level between the micro-bottom and the macro-level (upper) to unpack the regional levels for civil society. Even though this study shows how these spatial levels help us to make sense of what constitutes the regional presence for WACSOF and WANEP in West Africa, it can also be used to provide a clearer typology of regional civil society actors by levels. It should be noted that it could be used to potentially suggest that there are broadly three types of regional civil society actors, namely macro-, meso- and micro-regional civil society actors.

The framework also presents regional capacity as the third analytic concept. In this context, the framework interrogates the capacity of civil society to act to transform its social identity into a regional action or activity(ies) at its prevailing regional levels in order to bring about a desirable impact or change in the given regional policy area. In many instances, the normative tendencies of most civil societies at the regional levels aim to influence or transform regionalism. The framework makes it possible to interrogate the impact or contributions in the given regional policy area of civil society activity. Analytically, identity, presence, capacity, and impact are used as the bases of evaluating the actorship of WACSOF and WANEP in democratic participation and regional peacebuilding, respectively.

Empirical Contributions of This Study

Civil society actors' intention is usually framed in a way that shows that they want to influence the activities of regional organisations such as ECOWAS. Specifically, the cases of WACSOF and WANEP show that the interests of these organisations are to democratise regional security activities of ECOWAS in the context of conflict prevention. While WACSOF fits in well with the criteria of the framework, it appears weak as an actor in the region. WANEP also fits in well with the criteria of the framework but the finding shows that it tends to be more proactive in regional integration in West Africa. The striking difference in the evolution of the two organisations can be understood through the formation of their respective regional identities. Although WANEP was established five years before WACSOF was conceived, what is more significant is not the difference in the years of establishment, but the mode and the rationale behind their creations. These are the main factors that have influenced the trajectories of the two organisations. The finding shows that the formation of WANEP was based on a necessity or an institutional gap in regional peacebuilding in West Africa at the time. Thus, the formation of its regional identity as an organisation, started from below by socialising various groups of actors working independently into a regional network for peace. WANEP has since transformed the initial country-centric practice of peacebuilding into an institutionalised regional mode. The name 'West African Network for Peacebuilding' was not an accident. It rather provides the justification for the rationale behind WANEP's formation in 1998. In other words, WANEP was a response to the crisis of conflicts in the region. Although the 2003 WACSOF Charter covered wide areas of governance in the region, the majority of participants in this research study confirmed that WACSOF was established to provide a democratic input through civil society participation in regional integration in West Africa. Although WACSOF was supposed to serve as an umbrella body of all civil society organisations in West Africa, it has consistently been faced with an identity crisis. Part of the explanations for this was because WACSOF's formation was based on a top-down approach comprising the ECOWAS Secretariat (now Commission) and two civil society organisations. The ECOWAS Secretariat was reported to have facilitated the formation of WACSOF in 2003 with other organisations such as the Centre for Democracy and Development represented by Dr Kayode Fayemi, a Nigerian, and Nana K.A.Busia, a Ghanaian who was the director for West African programmes of International Alerts at the time. What WACSOF has become cannot be completely isolated from its regional identity and the mode of its social construction. The study reveals that WACSOF's identity was not only imposed from the top but the ownership and leadership of the organisation also became unclear in its perception of self and how others in the region perceived it. The study shows that this contradiction did not manifest itself early, but it subsequently contributed to the difficulties WACSOF would face in building a strong regional presence to be able to popularise regionalist activities in West Africa. By the virtue of its mandate, WACSOF was meant to serve as a coordinator for civil society participation in regional integration. Instead, it also engaged in competitions for projects ordinarily meant for its member organisations. As a result, it tends to lack respect and recognition among the regional networks of civil society in the region, which see it as a competitor rather than a civil society leader. Also, unlike WANEP that has institutionalised its regional presence within the ECOWAS community in the area of peacebuilding, WACSOF still requires an active regional presence and has continually remained in quest to revamp itself as a more relevant organisation in the region. This study has demonstrated that there is a significant link between the contradiction in WACSOF's regional identity and its weak regional presence in West Africa.

Resulting from this weak regional presence is the weakness of WACSOF's capacity to act as expected in the region, including the coordination of the activities of civil society participation in the ECOWAS programmes. In recognition of these weaknesses, revamping the ideal of WACSOF was the aspiration of the 6th WACSOF's Biennial People Assembly held in Abuja in August 2016.

I made a follow-up trip to find out what had changed two years later and found that the organisation is still in the process of revamping itself. During this period, WACSOF's activities remained in the lull (although there are some new activities lately, mostly virtual). As a result, this has been attributed to the organisation's weak institutional and operational capacity to act in pursuance of its normative goals.[1] Of course, capacity is a key factor, but attention also needs to be paid to the evolution of WACSOF as a regional civil society actor to understand the challenges the organisation is presently facing. This evolution takes us back to the analytic concepts such as the construction of its regional identity which looks like an imposition from the top that made support from the local/community levels so difficult for WACSOF, hence contributing to its weak presence. Another key factor is that WACSOF appears to be too ambitious. Perhaps, this was the reason why its co-founder, Dr Kayode Fayemi called for a review of its mandate at the 2016 Biennial People's Forum. All these concerns are justifiable reasons that persistently hinder WACSOF to make the visible impact in opening up ECOWAS to wider participations of civil society groups and West African people. Although the organisation has recorded some reasonable impact especially in election monitoring, what WACSOF is today is clearly antithetical to the view that Jibrin Ibrahim, its former president, made in the 2013 Annual Report that:

> Since 2003, WACSOF has striven to develop a credible system and institutional framework to best organize civil society in West Africa. That journey has taken the organisation through several twists and turns, through which the organisation has progressively evolved into a better stronger and more results-oriented organisation.
>
> (WACSOF 2013:2)

This is not to negate the fact that WACSOF is a regional civil society actor in West Africa. Arguably, it has not yet evolved into 'a better, stronger and more results-oriented organisation' (WACSOF 2013:2) with the requisite capacity to democratically influence the regionalist activities in the region. In 2016, the WACSOF's 6th Biennial People's Assembly concluded with the hope of revamping WACSOF to take its rightful place in the West African regionalism. Paragraph 5 of the Communique of the 6th Biennial People's Forum captures WACSOF's situation as follows:

> Since its inception in 2003, WACSOF has worked to deliver on this mandate, and efforts are on-going to strengthen the organisation's capacities toward this. However, a host of obstacles have been in the way of a truly successful delivery on its mandate.
>
> (WACSOF 2016)

There is currently an ongoing effort by the regional secretariat to reposition WACSOF. However, the WACSOF that exists in West Africa[2] is not yet a revamped WACSOF that its members and stakeholders had craved for because of concerns about its capacity in delivering on its mandate in the region.

Contrary to the findings in the WACSOF's case, the study of WANEP offers different empirical insights on how regional civil society actors evolve and the role they play in the region of West Africa. Although WANEP was not conceived to democratise ECOWAS per se, however, one can observe that the organisation has contributed to democratic regionalism or what Acharya (2018) calls 'participatory regionalism' in the area of peacebuilding in West Africa. The reason for this cannot completely be isolated from what its regional identity stands for and how it was initially formed. As the idea and values of WANEP began to spread within the region, it started by socialising other civil society practitioners with similar values of collaborative work. It was those early social interactions that resulted in the formation of a civil society regional identity for peace and security in West Africa (Interviewee 22, Interviewee 24). Unlike WACSOF whose identity was imposed from the top, WANEP's identity emerged from below and was able to build a *regional presence* gradually and gained popularity across the 15 ECOWAS member states (Interviewee 20, Interviewee 13, Interviewee 24). The finding confirmed that it was ECOWAS that invited WANEP to work as a civil society component in addressing violent conflicts and preventable wars in the region (Interviewee 22, Interviewee 21, Interviewee 13, Interviewee 11, Interviewee 7). It must be understood that WANEP did not begin by claiming to be a regional civil society actor. Unlike WACSOF, what its pioneers did first was to come to terms with the post-Cold War issues of conflicts at the local level in West Africa. This became a discursive tool for them as they engaged in conversations from the micro-levels while rallying round the key actors and stakeholders within the states and non-state organisations to create a culture of peacebuilding. Apart from strengthening its presence from local to regional levels, the findings also show that WANEP enjoys reputation with regional capacity due to its ability to draw support from local and external actors. WANEP's capacity enables it to institutionalise its regional presence and put in place key regional activities related to conflict preventions.

These key activities include the West African early warning system, peace education, mediation and conflict resolution, civil society coordination, democracy and good governance, WIPNET programmes and the training activities of its West African Peacebuilding Institute. All these activities have translated into its positive contribution to the regional peace and security architecture of West Africa.

WANEP has evolved within the last two decades, constructing regional identity around peace and security, building regional presence from the local to the national and the regional levels, enhancing its regional capacity through partnership and collaboration with local and external actors, and opening up regionalism of peacebuilding to civil society participation in West Africa. In a sense, WANEP has contributed to popularising the culture of peace within the region. One can infer that there is a clear difference in terms of peace and stability between the West African region of today and the West African region of more than 20 years ago. And when telling the contemporary history of relative peace and stability of West Africa, WANEP is most likely to be one of the referent civil society actors. This is an empirical statement that is verifiable. At this juncture, it is evident that WANEP has contributed to democratising regionalism in the area of peace and security. Inspite of the new emerging threats, one can note that part of the impact WANEP has made can be linked to the restoration of relative peace and stability in West Africa. There is a documented record of its contribution to the efforts that ended the brutal civil war in Liberia. This was the war that had kept the country under the siege for 14 years (Interviewee 30, Dargis 2008, WANEP 2016c, Interviewee 24, Interviewee7).

General Lessons from Regional Civil Society Activities in West Africa

To understand the extent to which regional civil society has evolved in West Africa and unravel its influence or impact on the region, the most significant examples are the two cases that this study has examined, analysed and presented in response to the research question. Simply put, regional civil society has evolved as an actor socially constructing regional identities around wider democratic participation in the ECOWAS activities and promoting human security/conflict prevention in the region. The better understanding of such regional social identities can be framed in the context of democratising regional security governance or (Popuar Regional Security) in West Africa. This is a way of popularising regionalism in a manner that accommodates the intentional democratic inputs of citizens and civil society organisations in framing popular narratives around regional governance. This includes the security architecture of the region which places a premium on the security of the people in its broadest sense. The security of the people in this context does not necessarily negate the security of the state but the emphasis is placed on the people as the most significant referent objects of security policy formulations across regional levels. A proper framing of this participatory understanding may be part of a future research. The ECOWAS Conflict Prevention Framework that underwrites a wider participation of ECOWAS citizens and civil society groups (ECOWAS Commission 2008:16) can also serve as a supporting instrument that aligns with this ideational understanding. The ECOWAS Conflict Prevention Framework has 14 components that aim to strengthen human security in the region. What regional CSOs now do is developing interest and identities within the components. Examples include the early warning, democracy and good governance, human rights and rule of law, natural resource governance/environment, women, peace and security, youth empowerment, humanitarian assistance, and peace education (ECOWAS Commission 2008:21).

The above has further substantiated the first analytic concept of the framework. As it is now, a systematic study in the future can explore this idea with a proper framing that captures civil society regionalism underlying the intersection between what appears as aspirations of civil society movements in West Africa and the reality on the ground. Perhaps the idea may offer new insights into a new social construction of civil society and West Africa as a region, just as *Africapitalism* seeks a new way of looking at the practice of entrepreneurship, African development and relation between the states and markets in the African continent.

Relating to the Existing Study of Civil Society Regionalisation

The study has dealt with civil society as serious subjects in regionalism. The study of civil society as part of regions and regionalism is not restricted to the West African region that I have reflected upon in this project. Rather, it is a global phenomenon that has become a practice since the end of the Cold War (see Chapter 1). Beyond a single region, civil society organisations have been continuously responding at regional levels to influence various regionalist policies (Fioramonti 2015, Soderbaum 2016a, Acharya 2018). Within Africa alone, there are varied manifestations of these regional civil society actorships. An example is EACSOF, a regional civil society network, seeking to influence the activities of the East African Community (Khadiagala 2016, Reinold 2019). Another example is SADC-CNGO working to check the policy excesses of SADC in Southern Africa (Soderbaum 2007, Godsater 2016). Interregional networks of civil society also exist at the African Union level, acknowledging the increasing role of civil society actors in African regionalism. Beyond Africa is the civil society participation in the European Union's policymaking in diverse areas (Bello 2011, Armstrong et al. 2011, Kohler-Koch 2009, Garcia 2015). An example is the European Peacebuilding Liaison Office (EPLO), a regional civil society network working to influence EU's policy on peacebuilding practices in Europe and beyond. Another example is the European Citizens' Platform, a civil society network popularising the European citizenship and rights from the national to the regional levels (Garcia 2015). In South East Asia, an example of such a civil society network is AADMER Partnership Group, working with ASEAN Committee on Disaster Management (Collins 2015:103). These emerging regional civil society networks are not empirically limited to a single region. There has been an evolving interregional manifestation of these civil society movements. The best example is the African Union-EU Civil Society Forum, seeking to influence policy programmes in interregional relations between the two regional organisations. Therefore, civil society regionalism has rather become a global phenomenon in a wide range of regions around the world. Focusing on two of its kinds in West Africa is not to reduce the scope of study to a single region. Rather, it has helped to generate both analytical and empirical insights about the West African regional civil society that could serve as inspirations for a similar research in other regions such as South East Asia, the East African Community, Southern Africa and the European Union.

The concepts such as regional identity (as action-based), regional presence, regional capacity, and societal impact could probably serve as analytical tools for making sense of regional civil society actors for the students and scholars of regions and comparative regionalism. The study relates analytically well with the current trends of regionalism which is comparatively oriented. I must state that the concepts are not a prescriptive category. They were employed because they serve the purpose of this study.

In response to important questions about the problems of comparative regionalism made by De Lombarde, Soderbaum, Langenhove and Baert (2009), such as, what to compare and how to compare, this study has made a contribution to that effect. As students and researchers of comparative regionalism, one of '*the whats*' to probably compare is civil society regionalism focusing on its regional attributes. Depending on the context and the aim of such research, one of the concepts used in this book could be used or combined with other alternative concepts to undertake a comparative study of regional civil society organisations. These are concepts that are already accessible in the regionalism literature.

Another area where this study lies is in a grounded understanding of African regionalism in the context of Africa and societies by providing narratives of African civil society actors on the regional levels from the perspectives of the people. A significant amount of knowledge of regionalism in Africa has largely originated from the Global North. This does not imply the knowledges produced are meaningless even though they often seek to confirm or refute certain theories or hypotheses that originated from the Global North. This book moves one step ahead by providing the African stories of civil society regionalism as they are while also paying a close attention and feeding their analytic narratives complementarily to the emerging global study of regions and regionalism. On the one hand, it resonates with the idea of Global International Relations introduced in Amitav Acharya's speech in 2014 as president of the International Studies Association (Acharya 2014a, Acharya 2018, Acharya and Buzan 2019). On the other hand, it is an affirmation of an ideational agency of the African narrative in the global understanding and knowledge production. While the essence of Global IR is to transcend the dominated approaches of IR (and regionalism), it does not aim to create a division between what is Western and what is non-Western. Rather, Global IR aims to make the study of regions and international relations more global by encouraging the discovery of new concepts and reinterpretations of the existing concepts both from the Global North and the Global South (Acharya 2014a). The Global IR assumes that for international relations to be truly global, a mutual learning between the Global North and Global South is a core necessity. Therefore, both the established scholars and emerging scholars from the Global South have been challenged to pay attention to their societal contexts to enrich our global understanding of the discipline (Acharya 2014a). The contributions of this study could serve as a source of critical reflections and understanding for students of African politics, comparative regionalism, peace studies and global politics by learning from the West African context of civil society regionalism.

Limitations

As there is no given research that is completely free of limitations, for this reason, I highlight below what I consider as this study's limitation. Methodologically, the case study of this research is limited to two main organisations. This can be considered as a limitation of this study because West Africa as a study area comprises several potential regional civil society organisations which have not been studied in this project. Although the two cases examined in the study provided some new empirical insights about civil society activities in the region, there are other organisations not covered that can be expanded in the future work. These organisations such as West African Women Association (WAWA), West African Civil Society Institute (WACSI), Open Society for West Africa (OSIWA), West African Action Network on Small Arms (WAANSA), West African Bar Association (WABA), Media Foundation for West Africa (MFWA), Mano River Women's Peace Network (MARWOPNET) and others. They will further enrich empirical insights in other policy areas not covered in this book and build on the existing findings in the region.

Apart from the above, West African regional civil society actors could have been compared with the Southern African regional civil society actors or the East African regional civil society actors. Since no single research can cover all conceivable areas of study, such a comparative study in the future may look at the issues of regional human rights and civil society in Africa. For instance, Khadiagala (2016) has acknowledged the increasing role of the East African Civil Society Forum in promoting human rights in solidarity with the East African Court of Justice. Such an area can be compared with West Africa in the context of civil society activism and the ECOWAS Community Court of Justice in the area of human rights. While it is important to note the above limitations, they did not in any way undermine the credibility of this study other than the obligation that the researcher must acknowledge them as an ethical practice. Thus, some of these limitations could form potential areas for future areas.

Potential Areas for Future Research

This research project can be developed further in many ways. It should be re-affirmed that the study of regional civil society actors in African regionalism is still at a very infant stage with many promising opportunities for future research. With the framework newly introduced in this study, future research may focus on the potential cases that are not covered in this research. There is a wide range of opportunities using the framework introduced in this study to deepen our understanding of key actors in African regionalism. Because the framework encompasses the key actors identified in the New Regionalism Approach, such as states, civil society, market and external actors, it can really help to transcend the predominantly state-centric preoccupations of regional integration research in Africa to rediscover the agency of other key actors driving or resisting regionalist projects in the continent.

This framework can also be used to study regional civil society organisations from the level of the African Union to the Regional Economic Communities like ECOWAS, EAC and SADC and the national levels of their member states. The idea of a continental regional civil society of Africa is already in vogue and this study has offered a timely framework to make sense of it. Apart from this, the relational study between regional civil society and regional parliaments in Africa is another potential area for future research. This includes a study of the relationship between the regional civil society organisations in West Africa and the ECOWAS parliament, or regional civil society organisations in East Africa and the East African Legislative Assembly or SADC Parliamentary Forum. Another potential area is the role of external actors in enhancing regional agency of citizens in West Africa. A key reference is the increasing role of the European Union as an external actor in peace and security in the region. In addition to this, there has been an increasing role of non-Western actors such as China in Africa. A comparative study of the influence of the Western and Non-Western external actors in African regionalism may be a potential area for future research. Also, micro-regional integration from below is a key arena that may be a focus of future research. An example is the study of the Regional Integration of the Development Agenda for the Western Nigeria's (DAWN Commission) principle of integration of 'unsovereign states.' It would be observed that the European Union has mapped out micro-regions across its 28-member states (pre-Brexit), but ECOWAS has not. The role of micro-regions in regional integration in West Africa may be another possible area to be taken up in the future. The highlighted themes above are viable research areas for the future research engagement.

This study therefore posits that despite the ECOWAS-Civil Society's conflict prevention efforts and relative stability of West Africa within the last two decades, the region is no doubt currently faced with the emerging threats of internal rife relating to transhumance/farmers/herders' clashes, extremism, transnational terrorism, drug trafficking, human trafficking, irregular migration, statelessness, internal displacement, massive youth unemployment, political corruption, food insecurity and environmental degradations, among other human-security challenges. It can as well be stated that the configurations of the highlighted issues are hardly isolated from the political economy of the region, considering that out of the 15 member states of ECOWAS, 11 members are classified as the least developed countries as highlighted in the 2018 report of the United Nations. The attendant regional dynamics of human insecurity in the region bedevilled by relative weaknesses of most of the ECOWAS member states as pivotal pillars of a development-driven regional integration in West Africa is one of the justifiable reasons to pave a new way of collaboration for the future of the region and its people. The relative weaknesses must be critical concerns for all stakeholders including civil society networks in order to pave a way for a new ECOWAS.

The role of regional networks of citizens and societies is ever important than before to attend to the pressing security of the West African people across the border. As some scholars have noted, regionalism of the non-West is development driven (Grant and Soderbaum 2003, Asante 2016, Shaw 2016, Adebajo 2016). Of course, ECOWAS regionalism is not an exception in that respect as some of the development instruments and various institutions of governance in the region have shown. Of relevance are the components of the ECOWAS Conflict Prevention Framework that cover all the essentials of human security. Another evidence to substantiate this is the ECOWAS 2020 which was adopted by the ECOWAS Authority in 2007 towards a transition from 'the ECOWAS of States' to the ECOWAS of the People'. The ECOWAS Vision 2020 comprises five main pillars expected to be transformed and implemented by states, citizens and other regionalist stakeholders in West Africa. The first pillar focuses on exploitation of abundant regional resources (such as vast arable land, millions of hectares of pastoral land, river basins, deposits of gold and diamond, oil and gas, iron, baux-ite and manganese) for the benefit of the region and its people. The second pillar focuses on peace and security which is underpinned by the ECOWAS Conflict Prevention Framework aimed at ascertaining a stable and peaceful region at all levels. The third pillar focuses on good and democratic governance from the national to regional levels. The fourth pillar is economic and monetary integration and the fifth pillar is the West African region with striving private sectors. As it is now, the ECOWAS of the People that the ECOWAS Vision 2020 aims to achieve by the year 2020 – involving citizens, civil society and other key stakeholders – no doubt remains a popular aspiration.

Post-Vision 2020 Insights into ECOWAS Regionalism

At present, we are looking forward to the roll-out of a new vision, the ECOWAS Vision 2050, which seeks to build 'a community of peoples fully integrated in a peaceful, prosperous region, with strong institutions that respect fundamental freedoms and work for inclusive and sustainable development'.[3] According to an informant in the ECOWAS Commission, the ECOWAS Vision 2050 is not a completely new vision. It is rather an extension of the ECOWAS Vision 2020. It has the same number of pillars like the Vision 2020 and the aim is to bring about an inclusive integration of the region where citizens play more active role dealing with challenges of regional integration in West Africa. The five pillars of the new vision are: (i) a secure, stable and peaceful region; (ii) a region endowed with strong institutions with the rule of law and fundamental freedoms; (iii) a fully integrated and prosperous region; (iv) a region mobilised for transforma-tion, inclusive and sustainable development; (v) a community of peoples fully inclusive of women, the youth and children. However, in the face of emerging challenges in post-pandemic West Africa, ECOWAS stakeholders such as states, citizens, business organisations, civil society, educational and research institu-tions, and development partners must therefore come to realise the need to reflect on the lessons on what was achieved in the ECOWAS Vision 2020 and what was not. They must be bold in the will and deeds in the next successive actions. As the plan to implement the ECOWAS Vision 2050 commences soon, it is impor-tant to take into consideration the continued challenges of terrorism in the Sahel with consequential threat to democratic governance as we witnessed in Mali from 2020 and the newer cases of Guinea and Burkina Faso. The ECOWAS regional democratic order is currently being threatened by the new waves of coup d'Etat in the region. As regards COVID-19, one would have expected ECOWAS institu-tions, especially the West African Health Organisation to have learnt lessons from the outbreak of Ebola in being not just reactional in response to the new health challenge such as COVID-19 pandemic (and variants such as Delta and Omicron) but also in being an active part of scientific efforts in the global search for the solution to the disease. According to the president of the African Development Bank, Dr Akinwumi Adesina, 'Africa should not be begging for vaccines. Africa should be producing vaccines'. There is an urge to rediscover the agency of Africa in seeking solutions to the challenges that are facing Africa. Out of adversity, there could be opportunities. Tolling the line of thought of Dr Akinwumi Adesina about vaccines production in Africa is a call for investment on the African soil that will generate jobs for the teeming population that will add value to collaborative research between Africa and the world; it is a call to confront the challenges of the 21st century with active agency for solution within or through international collaboration that places Africa at the centre of the table. In the post-Vision 2020, we should not just look at the challenging side of the problems such as COVID-19 pandemic, but we should endeavour in a reasonable manner to also explore the opportunities that are characterised by such health security challenges. The use of modern technology in providing quality health delivery, the use of telemedicine, exploration of local medicinal plants by the West African scientists, higher institutions and allied agencies should be awakened to proffering solutions to local, national, regional and global health crises. The partnership of ECOWAS and development donor agencies should be tailored towards technology transfer and hybridisation of innovative solutions to addressing myriad of problems in the collective quest for socio-economic development of the region.

Climate change is also a big factor in the ECOWAS/Sahel region, posing a serious threat to food security and fuelling violent conflicts between the herders and farmers in countries such as Nigeria, Niger, Mali and Burkina Faso.[4] Another concern is the increasing rate of irregular migration, human trafficking, trafficking of drugs, small arms and light weapons which need to be tackled, alongside with the issues of corruption, citizens data protection, cyber insecurity, energy security, poverty, discrimination against women, forced/child marriage, declining agency of higher education in development, excessive reliance on external actors in funding regionalist projects and reawakening the consciousness of the sleeping regional giant, Nigeria, in West Africa. In the above, there is a sense of a region of fear and wants. As the new vision 2050 portends, the ECOWAS has begun again to transform itself into a *Region of Freedom and Wealth*. Regionlism is not all about integration of states alone. It is a project to collectively confront a common problem for the collective good of the region and its people.

Final Comment

This study has thoroughly examined how regional civil society organisations have evolved in West Africa within the last three decades, the impact they made and the challenges they encountered, and sign-posted emerging issues that are likely to shape their engagement in the post-2020 era of ECOWAS regionalism with the ECOWAS Vision 2050. The attempts to promote democratic participation of civil society actors in regional integration as well as regional peacebuilding in West Africa are presented through the analysis of WACSOF and WANEP. The evidence shows that the emergence of WACSOF would have laid a foundation for a transformative regionalism with active civil society's participation in regional integration in West Africa. WACSOF has had notable contributions as a platform for civil society engagement in ECOWAS activities including in conflict preventions. However, the organisation has become relatively weak due to a lack of required regional capacity especially in providing leadership and coordination for a wider participation of civil society in the ECOWAS programmes. The second is in the area of peace and security, otherwise termed regional peacebuilding in the case of WANEP, which suggests a positive pointer to the sustained role of civil society in contributing to peace and security through the early warning system in the region. This is not to pretend as if the region is free from many emerging challenges as stated in the earlier analysis. However, this form of collective participation points to what citizens of the region can achieve together by using their regional agency to drive development-focused regionalism in West Africa. The critical role of civil society in regional governance as checks to intergovernmental organisations is as important as also engaging in problem-solving in West Africa. WACSOF is not necessarily weak because the organisation is constrained by the prevailing regime. WACSOF is weak because it requires necessary support to enhance its capacity to be able to play a more popular role in West Africa. Through the emerging digitalisation of civic space and increasing support of stakeholder organisations like African Development Banks with willingness to partner with civil society in development coupled with the new idea of Africapiatlism, spreading of faith-based organisations and Nollywood or 'ECOwood' – all these could serve as enablers for popularising participatory regionalisms in West Africa and opening space for opportunities for the individual ECOWAS citizens, corporate bodies, governments and international stakeholders.

Notes

1 As at February 2019.
2 Let me clarify that I am referring to the timeframe from 2016 to 2019.
3 See Press Release of the ECOWAs Parliament, available online via: https://parl.ecowas .int/ecowas-moves-from-vision-2020-to-vision-2050/ [accessed 27/3/2022].
4 See World Economic Forum (2019) 'The Sahel is engulfed by violence: Climate change, food insecurity and extremists are largely to blame'. Available online via: https://www.weforum.org/agenda/2019/01/all-the-warning-signs-are-showing-in-the -sahel-we-must-act-now/ [accessed 20/3/2022].

Bibliography

Acharya, A. (1997) 'Ideas, Identity, and Institution Building: From the "ASEAN Way" to the "Asia Pacific Way"?', *The Pacific Review*, Vol. 10, No. 3, pp. 319–346.

Acharya, A. (2003) 'Democratisation and the Prospects for Participatory Regionalism in Southeast Asia', *Third World Quarterly*, Vol. 24, No. 2, pp. 375–390.

Acharya, A. (2012) 'Comparative Regionalism: A Field Whose Time has Come?', *The International Spectator*, Vol. 47, No. 1, pp. 3–15.

Acharya, A. (2014a) 'Global International Relations: A New Agenda for International Studies', *International Studies Quarterly*, Vol. 58, No. 4, pp. 647–659.

Acharya, A. (2014b) *The End of American World Order*, Cambridge, Polity Press.

Acharya, A. (2016a) 'Regionalism Beyond EU Centrism', in Borzel, T. and Risse, T. (eds.), *The Oxford Handbook of Comparative Regionalism*, Oxford, Oxford University Press, pp. 88–109.

Acharya, A. (ed.) (2016b) *Why Govern? Rethinking Demand and Progress in Global Governance*, Cambridge, Cambridge University Press.

Acharya, A. (2017) 'After Liberal Hegemony: The Advent of a Multiplex World Order', *Ethics and International Affairs*, Vol. 31, No. 3, pp. 271–285.

Acharya, A. (2018) *Constructing Global Order: Agency and Change in World Politics*, Cambridge, Cambridge University Press.

Acharya, A. and Buzan, B. (2019) *The Making of Global International Relations: Origin and Evolution of IR at its Century*, Cambridge, Cambridge University Press.

Acharya, A., Singhdeo, S. K. and Rajaretnam, M. (eds.) (2011) *Human Security: From Concept to Practice: Case Studies from North East India and Orissa*, Singapore, World Scientific Publishing Co. Pte Ltd.

Adebajo, A. (2002) *Building Peace in West Africa: Liberia, Sierra Leone, and Guinea-Bissau*, London, Lynne Rienner Publishers Inc.

Adebajo, A. and Rashid, I. (eds.) (2004) *West Africa's Security Challenges: Building Peace in a Troubled Region*, Boulder, Lynne Rienner Publishers.

Adebajo, A. (2005) 'The Curse of Berlin: African Security Dilemma', in IPG/2005. Available online: http://library.fes.de/pdf-files/id/ipg/03044.pdf [Accessed 10/05/2018].

Adebajo, A. (2016) 'A Tale of Three Cassandras: Jean Monnet, Raúl Prebisch, and Adebayo Adedeji', in Levine, D. H. and Nagar, D. (eds.), *Region-Building in Africa*, New York, Palgrave Macmillan, pp. 53–67.

Adebajo, A. and Rashid, I. (eds.) (2004) *West African Security Challenges: Building Peace in a Troubled Region*, London, Lynne Rienner Publishers Inc.

Adebanwi, W. (2014) *Yoruba Elites and Ethnic Politics in Nigeria: Obafemi Awolowo and Corporate Agency*, New York, Cambridge University Press.

Adebanwi, W. (2015) 'Rethinking Knowledge Production in Africa', *Africa*, Vol. 86, No. 2, pp. 350–353.

Adedeji, A. (1970) 'Prospects of Regional Economic Co-Operation in West Africa', *The Journal of Modern African Studies*, Vol. 8, No. 2, pp. 213–231.

Adedeji, A. (2004) 'ECOWAS: A Retrospective Journey', in Adebajo, A. and Rashid, I. (eds.), *West African Security Challenges: Building Peace in a Troubled Region*, London, Lynne Rienner Publishers Inc., pp. 21–49.

Adedeji, E. (2007) 'Non-State Actors, Peacebuilding and Security Governance in West Africa: Beyond Commercialisation', *Journal of Peacebuilding & Development*, Vol. 3, No. 2, pp. 53–69.

Adejumobi, S. (2004) 'Conflict and Peace Building in West Africa: The Role of Civil Society and the African Union', *Conflict, Security & Development*, Vol. 4, No. 1, pp. 59–77.

Adejumobi, S. (ed.) (2010) *Governance and Politics in the Post Military Nigeria: Changes and Challenges*, New York, Palgrave Macmillan.

Adejumobi, S. (2016) 'Region-Building in West Africa', in Levine, D. H. and Nagar, D. (eds.), *Region-Building in Africa*, New York, Palgrave Macmillan, pp. 213–230.

Adi, H. and Sherwood, M. (2003) *Pan-African History: Political Figures from Africa and the Diaspora Since 1787*, London, Routledge.

Adler, E. and Barnett, M. (2000) 'Taking Identity and Our Critics Seriously', *Cooperation and Conflict*, Vol. 35, No. 3, pp. 321–329.

Afadzinu, N. (2015) 'The Role of Civil Society in Regional Integration: The West African Experience', in Akoutou, A., Sohn, R., Vogl, M. and Yeboah, D. (eds.), *Migration and Civil Society as Development Drivers: Regional Perspectives*, WAI ZEI Paper, No. 23, pp. 9–40. Available Online: https://www.zei.uni-bonn.de/dateien/wai-zei-paper/wai -zei_paper_no_23_en [Accessed 20/03/2017].

Africanews. (2017) 'Ibn Chambas: NGOs should Support Transition Process in the Gambia', Available online: http://africanelections.org/new_news.php?nid=1968 [Accessed 05/04/2018].

African Development Bank. (2012) 'Cape Verde: A Success Story', Available online: https://www.afdb.org/sites/default/files/documents/projects-and-operations/cape_ verde_-_a_success_story.pdf [Accessed 30/05/2020].

African Union. (2016) 'Ghana and Uganda Launches ECOSOCC National Chapters', Press Release No: 314/2016. Available online: https://au.int/web/sites/default/files /pressreleases/31388-pr-20160916_pr_national_chapters_ghana_uganda-1.pdf [Accessed 07/07/2017].

Agbiboa, E. D. (2018) 'Eyes on the Street: Civilian Joint Task Force and the Surveillance of Boko Haram in Northeastern Nigeria', *Intelligence and National Security*, pp. 1023–1093.

Aidara, I. (2015) 'Civil Society in Senegal: Institutional Arguments and Challenges for Participatory Governance', in WACSI (ed.), *Civil Society and Development in West Africa: Regional Perspective*, Accra, WACSI, pp. 158–167.

Ake, C. (1976) 'Explanatory Notes on the Political Economy of Africa', *The Journal of Modern African Studies*, Vol. 14, No. 1, pp. 1–23.

Akínrìnádé, S. (2004) 'On the Evolution of Civil Society in Nigeria', in Glasius, M., Lewis, D. and Seckinelgin, H. (eds.), *Exploring Civil Society : Political and Cultural Contexts*, New York, Routledge, pp. 125–131.

Akintoye, S. A. (2010) *A History of Yoruba People*, Dakar, Amalion Publishing.

Akinyeye, Y. (ed.) (2010) *Nation-States and the Challenges of Regional Integration in West Africa: The case of Nigeria*, Paris, Karthala.

Akwei, I. (2017) 'ECOWAS has Issued an Order for Military Intervention in the Gambia to Oust President Yahya Jammeh at the Stroke of Midnight Thursday when his Mandate Ends', *AfricanNews*. Available online: http://www.africanews.com/2017/01/18/ecowas-okays-military-intervention-in-gambia-joint-troop-stationed-at-border// [Accessed 27/07/2017].

Alabi, M. O. A. (2016) *ECOWAS Court and Regional Integration in West Africa*, Saarbruchen, Scholar's Press.

Alao, A. and Olonisakin, F. (1998) 'Post-Cold War Africa: Ethnicity, Ethnic Conflict and Security', in Oyabade, A. and Alao, A. (eds.), *African After Cold War: The Changing Perspectives on Security*, Asmara, African World Press Inc, pp. 117–142.

Al Jazeera. (2012a) 'ECOWAS Troops for Guinea Bissau and Mali', Available online: http://www.aljazeera.com/news/africa/2012/04/201242704130728252.html [Accessed 27/07/2017].

Al Jazeera. (2012b) 'ECOWAS Agrees to Mali Intervention Force', Available Online: http://www.aljazeera.com/news/africa/2012/11/20121111192710305682.html [Accessed 03/01/2018].

Al Jazeera. (2017a) 'ECOWAS Holds Off on Troop Deployment to the Gambia', Available online: http://www.aljazeera.com/news/2017/01/ecowas-holds-troop-deployment-gambia-170107211600920.html [Accessed 27/07/2017].

Al Jazeera. (2017b) 'Gambia: The People Who Stood Against Yahya Jammeh', Available online: https://www.aljazeera.com/programmes/talktojazeera/inthefield/2017/09/gambia-people-stood-yahya-jammeh-170914093543378.html [Accessed 06/04/2018].

Al Jazeera. (2019) 'Nigerian Police Battle a Growing Kidnapping Crisis', Available online: https://www.youtube.com/watch?v=xWCodT9hRFo [Accessed 24/09/2019].

Alou, M. T. (2015) 'Civil Society in the Face of Socio-Political Changes in Niger: Role and Opportunities', in WACSI (ed.), *Civil Society and Development in West Africa: Regional Perspective*, Accra, WACSI, pp. 138–145.

AllAfrica. (2015) 'Mano River Peace Network Launched', Available Online: http://allafrica.com/stories/201506241149.html [Accessed 31/01/2017].

Alusa, D. (2013) 'Multipolar Politics and Regional Integration in East Africa: Opportunities and Challenges for Non-state Actors', in Omeje, K. and Hepner, T. R. (eds.), *Conflict and Peacebuilding in African Great Lakes Region*, Bloomington, Indiana University Press, pp. 65–84.

Amaeshi, K. and Idemudia, U. (2015) 'Africapitalism: A Management Idea for Business in Africa?', *Africa Journal of Management*, Vol. 1, No. 2, pp. 210–223.

Amaeshi, K. (2018) 'AFRICAPITALISM: Rethinking the Riole of Business in Africa', Online, https://www.tonyelumelufoundation.org/research-publications/africapitalism-rethinking-the-role-of-business-in-africa-by-prof-kenneth-amaeshi [Accessed 03/08/2022].

Amnesty International. (2008) 'Women of Liberia: Fighting for Peace', Available online: https://www.youtube.com/watch?v=sOoR1Ta_4Nc [Accessed 21/04/2020].

Ang, S. and Dyne, L. V. (2008) 'Conceptualisation of Cultural Intelligence: Definition, Distinctiveness, and Nomological Network', in Ang, S. and Dyne, L. V. (eds.), *Handbook of Cultural Intelligence: Theory, Measurement, and Application*, New York, Routledge, pp. 3–15.

Aning, E. K. (2004) 'Investing in Peace and Security in Africa: The Case of ECOWAS', *Conflict, Security & Development*, Vol. 4, No. 3, pp. 533–542.

Anyambod, E. A. (2007) 'A Decade of Peacebuilding: 1998–2008', in *2007 WANEP Annual Report*, p. 4, Available online: http://wanep.org/wanep/index.php?option=com

_content&view=article&id=45:chairpersons-message-2007&catid=1:board&Itemid =12 [Accessed 23/01/2018].

Anyanwu, C. D. (2015) 'Can Caribbean Civil Society Effectively Influence Regional Policy: Overcoming National and Regional Challenges in CARICOM', in Fioramonti, L. (ed.), *Civil Society and World Regions: How Citizens Are Shaping Regional Governance in Times of Crisis*, Lindon, Lexington Books, pp. 63–76.

Armstrong, D. Bello, V. Gilson, J. and Spini, D. (eds.) (2011) *Civil Society and International Governance: The Role of Non-State Actors in the Regional Regulative Frameworks*, New York, Routledge.

Asante, M. F. (2019) *The History of Africa: The Quest for Eternal Harmony*, 3rd Edition, New York, Routledge.

Asante, S. K. B. (1997) *Regionalism and Africa's Development: Expectations, Reality and Challenges*, London, Macmillan Press Limited.

Asante, S. K. B. (2016) 'The Political Economy of Africa's Region-Building and Regional Integration' in Levine, D. H. and Nagar, D. (eds.), *Region-Building and Regional Integration*, New York, Palgrave Macmillan, pp. 127–140.

ASEAN People. (n.d.) 'Background About ASEAN People', Available online: http:// aseanpeople.org/about/background/ [Accessed 17/04/2017].

Asiwaju, A. I. (2010) 'Cross-Border Initiatives and Regional Integration in West Africa: The Nigerian Experience', in Akinyeye, Y. (ed.), *Nation-States and the Challenges of Regional Integration in West Africa: The case of Nigeria*, Paris, Karthala, pp. 137–148.

Asobie, H. A. (2010) 'Conceptual and Theoretical Issues in Regional Integration in West Africa: The Nigerian Perspective', in Akinyeye, Y. (ed.), *Nation-States and the Challenges of Regional Integration in West Africa: The case of Nigeria*, Paris, Karthala, pp. 21–40.

Assah, G. (2015) 'Civil Society in Benin: Issues, Challenges and Prospects', in WACSI (ed.), *Civil Society and Development in West Africa: Regional Perspective*, Accra, WACSI, pp. 22–29.

Atlantic Report. (2013) 'Two Years After Civil War's End, Cote D'Ivoire is Still Unstable', Available Online: https://www.theatlantic.com/international/archive/2013 /07/two-years-after-civil-wars-end-c-te-divoire-is-still-unstable/278210/   [Accessed 03/01/2018].

Atuguba, R. A. (2015) 'Civil Society: The Key to Ghana's Democratic Transformation and Consolidation', in WACSI (ed.), *Civil Society and Development in West Africa: Regional Perspective*, Accra, WACSI, pp. 82–91.

Aworawo, D. (2010) 'Challenges of Regional Integration: National Interest and Nigeria's Contribution', in Akinyeye, Y. (ed.), *Nations States and the Challenges of Regional Integration in West Africa: The Case of Nigeria*, Paris, Karthala, pp. 121–135.

Ayoob, M. (2002) 'Inequality and Theorizing in International Relations: The Case for Subaltern Realism', *International Studies Review*, Vol. 4, No. 3, pp. 27–48.

Azikiwe, I. (2015) *AFRICA: Conflict Resolution and International Diplomacy*, Central Milton Keynes, AuthorHouse.

Bach, D. (2003) 'New Regionalism as an Alias: Regionalisation through Trans-State Networks', in Grant, A. and Soderbaum, F. (eds.), *The New Regionalism in Africa*, Aldershot, Ashgate, pp. 21–30.

Bach, D. C. (2004) 'The Dilemmas of Regionalization', in Adebajo, A. and Rashid, R. (eds.), *West Africa's Security Challenges: Building Peace in a Troubled Region*, Boulder, Lynne Rienner.

Bach, D. (2015) *Regionalism in Africa: Genealogies, Institutions and Trans-State Networks*, London, Routledge.

Bach, D. C. (2016) *Regionalism in Africa: Genealogies, Institutions and Trans-State Networks*, London, Routledge.

Baert, S. and Soderbaum, F. (eds.) (2014) *Intersecting Interregionalism: Regions, Global Governance and the EU*, United Nations University Series on Regionalism, Vol. 7, New York, Springer.

Bah, A. B. (2010) 'Democracy and Civil War: Citizenship and Peacemaking in Côte d'Ivoire', *African Affairs*, Vol. 109, No. 437, pp. 597–615.

Baker, B. (2011) 'Justice and Security Architecture in Africa: The Plans, the Bricks, the Purse and the Builder', *The Journal of Legal Pluralism and Unofficial Law*, Vol. 43, No. 63, pp. 25–47.

Baker, B. (2006) 'Cape Verde: The Most Democratic Nation in Africa?', *The Journal of Modern African Studies*, Vol. 44, No. 4, pp. 493–511.

Baker, B. (2017a) 'African Police: Failing Agents of Human Security', in Mclintosh, M. and Hunter, A. (eds.), *New Perspectives on Human Security*, New York, Routledge, pp. 220–234.

Baker, B. (2017b) 'A Conversation with Professor Bruce Baker', on 17th May 2017 at Coventry University.

Baldet, O. (2015) 'Contribution of Civil Society to National Development in Guinea-Socio-Economic and Democratic Challenges, the Need for Repositioning', in WACSI (ed.), *Civil Society and Development in West Africa: Regional Perspective*, Accra, WACSI, pp. 92–103.

Ball, N. and Fayemi, K. (eds.) (2004) *Security Sector Governance in Africa: A Handbook*, Centre for Democracy and Development. Available online: http://www.gsdrc.org/docs/open/GFN-SSR-SecuritySectorGovernanceInAfrica-AHandbook.pdf [Accessed 19/01/2015].

Balogun, M. J. (2011) *Hegemony and Sovereign Equality: The Interest Contiguity Theory in International Relations*, New York, Springer.

Bamidele, O. (2016) 'Civilian Joint Task Force' (CJTF) – A Community Security Option: A Comprehensive and Proactive Approach to Counter-Terrorism', *Journal of Deradicalisation*, No. 7, pp. 124–144.

Banfield, J. (2015) 'TELL IT LIKE IT IS: The Role of civil society in responding to serious and organised crime in West Africa', Available online: https://www.international-alert.org/sites/default/files/CVI_CivilSocietyWestAfrica_EN_2015.pdf [Accessed 25/05/2020].

Bappah, Y. A. (2018) 'ECOWAS Protagonists for Peace: An Internal Perspective on Policy and Community Actors in Peacemaking Interventions', *South African Journal of International Affairs*, Vol. 25, No. 1, pp. 83–98.

Bar, A. S. (2013) 'ECOWAS and Legitimacy Question: A Normative and Institutional Approach', in Zaum, D. (ed.), *Legitimating International Organisations*, Oxford, Oxford University Press, pp. 88–110.

Barros, M. D. (2015) 'Grassroots Support and the Rule of Law in Guinea-Bissau: Highlights on Civil Society Achievement', in WACSI (ed.), *Civil Society and Development in West Africa: Regional Perspective*, Accra, WACSI, pp. 104–113.

BBC Report. (2012) 'Mali Taureg's Rebel Declare Independence in the North', Available online: http://www.bbc.co.uk/news/world-africa-17635437 [Accessed 03/01/2018].

BBC. (2017a) 'Gambia's President Jammeh Refuses to Leave Office as Deadline Passes', Available online: http://www.bbc.co.uk/news/world-africa-38672840 [Accessed 27/07/2017].

BBC. (2017b) 'Burkina Faso Gun Attack Kills 18 People at Café', Available online: http://www.bbc.co.uk/news/world-africa-40920338 [Accessed 20/02/2018].

BBC. (2018) 'Burkina Faso Profile - Timeline', Available online: http://www.bbc.co.uk/news/world-africa-13072857 [Accessed 20/05/2018].

BBC. (2019) 'Burkina Faso Fight Against Islamic Militant', Available online: http://www.bbc.co.uk/news/world-africa-39279050 [Accessed 18/06/2019].

Bedjauoi, M. (2012) 'Brief Historical Overview of Steps to African Unity', in Yusuf, A. A. and Ouguergouz, F. (eds.), *The African Union: Legal and Institutional Framework: A Manual of Pan African Organisation*, Leiden, Koninklijke Brill, pp. 9–23.

Bello, V. (2011) 'Collective and Social Identity: A Theoretical Analysis of the Role of Civil Society in the Construction of Supra-national Societies', in Armstrong, D., Bello, V. Gilson, J. and Spini, D. (eds.), *Civil Society and International Governance: The Role of Non-State Actors in the Regional Regulative Frameworks*, New York, Routledge, pp. 16–31.

Benjaminsen, T. (2008) 'Does Supply-Induced Scarcity Drive Violent Conflicts in the African Sahel? The Case of the Tuareg Rebellion in Northern Mali', *Journal of Peace Research*, Vol. 45, No. 6, pp. 819–836.

Bervis, M. (2010) *Democratic Governance*, Princeton, Princeton University Press.

Blaike, N. (2007) *Approaches to Social Enquiry: Advancing Knowledge*, 2nd Edition, Cambridge, Polity Press.

Bierschenk, T. (2009) 'Democratization without Development: Benin 1989–2009', *International Journal of Politics, Culture, and Society*, Vol. 22, No. 3, pp. 337–357.

Bøås, M. (2005) 'The Liberian Civil War: New War/Old War?', *Global Society*, Vol. 19, No. 1, pp. 73–88.

Bøås, M. Marchand, M. H. and Shaw, T. M. (2003) 'The Weave-World: The Regional Interweaving of Economies, Ideas and Identities', in Soderbaum, F. and Shaw, T. M. (eds.), *Theories of New Regionalism*, New York, Palgrave Macmillan, pp. 197–2010.

Boejie, H. (2014) *Analysis in Qualitative Research*, London, Sage Publications Limited.

Bombande, E. (2011) 'Regional Civil Society Peacebuilding in West Africa', *Interview in Accord*, Vol. 23, No. 4. Available online: http://www.c-r.org/downloads/CON1222_Accord_23_4.pdf [Accessed 27/01/2018].

Bombande, E. (2016) 'The Role of WANEP in Crafting Peace and Security Architecture in West Africa', in Cortright, D., Greenbert, M. and Stone, L. (eds.), *Civil Society, Peace and Power*, London, Rowman and Littlefield, pp. 119–142.

Booth, K. (1991) 'Security and Emancipation', *Review of International Studies*, Vol. 17, pp. 313–326.

Börzel, T. and Risse, T. (eds.) (2016) *The Oxford Handbook of Comparative Regionalism*, Oxford, Oxford University Press.

Börzel, A. T. and Risse, T. (2020) 'Identity Politics, Core State Powers and Regional Integration: Europe and Beyond', *Journal of Common Market Studies*, Vol. 58, No. 1, pp. 21–40.

Boutros-Ghali, B. (1992) *An Agenda for Peace, Preventive Diplomacy, Peacemaking and Peacekeeping*. Available online: https://www.un.org/ruleoflaw/files/A_47_277.pdf [Accessed 03/05/2020].

Boutros-Ghali, B. (1995) 'Supplement to an Agenda for Peace: Position Paper of the Secretary-General on the Occasion of the Fiftieth Anniversary of the United Nations'. https://digitallibrary.un.org/record/168325?ln=en#record-files-collapse-header [Accessed 03/05/2020].

Bratton, M. (1989) 'Beyond the State: Civil Society and Associational Life in Africa', *World Politics*, Vol. 41, No. 3, pp. 407–430.

Bratton, M. (1994) 'Civil Society and Political Transition in Africa', *Institute for Development Research Report*, Vol. 11, No. 6, pp. 1–21.

Brown, S. A. W. (2018) *Power, Perception and Foreign Policymaking: US and EU Responses to the Rise of China*, New York, Routledge.

Bryman, A. (2008) *Social Science Research Method*, 3rd Edition, New York, Oxford University Press.

Bryman, A. (2016) *Social Research Methods*, 5th Edition, Oxford, Oxford University Press.

Brysk, A. (2013) *Speaking Rights to Power: Constructing Political Will*, New York, Oxford University Press.

Buckley, K. M. (2013) *Global Civil Society and Transversal Hegemony: The Globalisation Nexus*, New York, Routledge.

Brusset, E., de Coning, C. and Hughes, B. (2016) 'Conclusion', in Brusset, E., Coning, C. and Hughes, B. (eds.), *Complexity Thinking for Peacebuilding Practice and Evaluation*, London, Palgrave Macmillan, pp. 273–284.

Bruszt, L. and Palestini, S. (2016) 'Regional Development Governance', in Borzel, T. and Risse, T. (eds.), *The Oxford Handbook of Comparative Regionalism*, Oxford, Oxford University Press, pp. 374–404.

BTI. (2020) 'West and Central Africa: BTI Transformation Index', Available online: https://www.bti-project.org/en/reports/regional-dashboard-WCA.html?&cb=00000 [Accessed 05/09/2020].

Burns, B. R. (2000) *Introduction to Research Methods*, 4th Edition, London, Sage Publications Limited.

Buzdugan, R. S. (2013) 'Regionalism from Without: External Involvement of the EU in Regionalism in Southern Africa', *Review of International Political Economy*, Vol. 20, No. 4, pp. 917–946.

Buzan, B. (2003) 'Regional Security Complex Theory in the Post-Cold War World', in Soderbaum, F. and Shaw, T. (eds.), *Theories of New Regionalism*, New York, Palgrave Macmillan Limited, pp. 140–159.

Buzan, B. (2004) 'A Reductionist, Idealistic Notion that Adds Little Analytical Value', *Security Dialogue*, Vol. 35, No. 3, pp. 369–370.

Buzan, B. and Waever, O. (2003) *Regions and Power: The Structure of International Security*, Cambridge, Cambridge University Press.

Buzan, B., Waever, O. and Wilde, J. (1998) *Security: A New Framework for Analysis*, London, Lynne Rienner Publishers Inc.

Carter, C. and Pasquier, R. (2010) 'Introduction: Studying Regions as "Spaces for Politics": Re-Thinking Territory and Strategic Action', *Regional & Federal Studies*, Vol. 20, No. 3, pp. 281–294.

Ceccorulli, M. and Lucarelli, S. (2013) 'Conceptualising Multilateral Security Governance', in Lucarell, S., Van Langenhove, L. and Wouters, J. (eds.), *The EU and Multilateral Security Governance*, New York, Routledge, pp. 11–25.

Ceesay-Ebo, A. (2010) 'The Gender Dimensions of Peace and Security Architecture: A Regional Perspective on UNSCR 1325', in Olonisakin, F., Barnes, K. and Ikpe, E. (eds.), *Women, Peace and Security: Translating Policy into Practice*, New York, Routledge, pp. 184–198.

Central Intelligence Agency. (2018) 'World Factbook: Africa Burkina Faso', Available online: https://www.cia.gov/library/publications/the-world-factbook/geos/uv.html [Accessed 20/02/2018].

Centre for Systemic Peace. (2014) 'Polity IV Individual Country Regime Trends, 1946–2014', Available online: https://www.systemicpeace.org/polity/polity4x.htm [Accessed 05/09/2020].

Checkel, T. J. (2016) 'Regional Identities and Communities', in Börzel, A. T. and Risse, T. (eds.), *The Oxford Handbook on Comparative Regionalism*, Oxford, Oxford University Press, pp. 559–578.

Cheru, F. (2012) 'Democracy and People Power in Africa: Still Searching for the "Political Kingdom"', *Third World Quarterly*, Vol. 33, No. 2, pp. 265–291.

CIVICUS (2006) *A Diagnostic Study of Togolese Civil Society: CIVICUS: Civil Society Index Report for Togo*. Available online: https://www.civicus.org/media/CSI_Togo _Country_Report.pdf [Accessed 20/10/2021].

Civicus. (2011) *Guinean Civil Society: Between Activity and Impact*. Available online: https://www.civicus.org/images/stories/csi/csi_phase2/guinea%20acr.pdf   [Accessed 01/06/2020].

Collins, A. (2015) 'Building a People-Centred Community in Southeast Asia: Lessons from ASEAN's Engagement with Civil Society', in Fioramonti, L. (ed.), *Civil Society and World Regions: How Citizens Are Shaping Regional Governance in Times of Crisis*, Lindon, Lexington Books, pp. 91–106.

Commonwealth Foundation. (n.d.) 'Strengthening West African Civil Society Engagement', Available   online: http://commonwealthfoundation.com/project/strengthening-west -african-civil-society-engagement-with-ecowas-and-national-governments/ [Accessed 22/08/2017].

Corlazzoli, V. and White, J. (2013) 'Measuring the Un-Measurable: Solutions to Measurement', Department for International Development. Available online: https://www.sfcg.org/wp-content/uploads/2014/04/0812_DFID-Measuring-the -Unmeasurable_FINAL-2013_16-July.pdf [Accessed 20/04/2020].

Corre, G. (2003) 'Non-state Actors in Guinea Bridges Between a National Dialogue Process and a Thematic Platform', in *ECPDM Brief No. 3A*, Available online: https:// ecdpm.org//wp-content/uploads/2013/10/IB-3A-Non-State-Actors-Guinea-2003.pdf [Accessed 28/05/2020].

Coulibaly, S. (2015) 'From Availability to Accessibility of Resources: The Role of Civil Society in the Promotion of Sustainable Development in Burkina Faso', in WACSI (ed.), *Civil Society and Development in West Africa: Regional Perspective*, Accra, WACSI, pp. 30–39.

Cox, R. (1981) 'Social Forces, States and World Orders: Beyond International Relations Theory', *Millennium - Journal of International Studies*, Vol. 1, No. 10, pp. 126–155.

Daddieh, K. C. (1996) 'Universities and Political Protest in Africa: The Case of Côte d'Ivoire', *A Journal of Opinion*, Vol. 24, No. 1, pp. 57–60.

Daniel, B., Kumar, V. and Omar, N. (2018) 'Postgraduate Conception of Research Methodology: Implications for Learning and Teaching', *International Journal of Research & Method in Education*, Vol. 41, No. 2, pp. 220–236.

Dargis, M. (2008) 'Unsung Heroines of Liberia, Making Guns Yield to Words: Pray the Devil Back to Hell', *The New York Times*. Available online: https://www.nytimes.com /2008/11/07/movies/07pray.html [Accessed 26/03/2019].

De Lombaerde, P. (2011) 'The Good, the Bad and the Ugly of Comparative Regionalism: A Comment on Sbragia', *The Journal of Common Market Studies*, Vol. 49, No. 3, pp. 675–681.

De Lombaerde, P., Soderbaum, F., Langenhove, V. L. and Baert, F. (2009) 'The Problems of Comparison in Comparative Regionalism', *Jean Monnet/ Robert Schuman Paper Series*, Vol. 9, No. 7, April, Miami-Florida European Union Center.

Department for International Development. (n.d.) 'How to Note Capacity Building', Available online: https://www.gov.uk/government/uploads/system/uploads/attachment _data/file/224810/How-to-note-capacity-development.pdf [Accessed 22/08/2017].

Department of State. (2010) *Country Reports on Human Rights Practices for 2008*, Vol. 1, Washington, United States Government.

Derrick, J. (1977) 'West African Worst Years of Famine', *African Affairs*, Vol. 76, No. 305, pp. 537–586.

Derrick, J. (1984) 'West African Worst Years of Famine', *African Affairs*, Vol. 83, No. 332, pp. 281–299.

Dersso, S. A. (2014) 'Protests have Ended Blaise Compaoré's Reign; but What Does this Mean for the AU's Approach to Unconstitutional Changes of Government?', Available online: https://issafrica.org/iss-today/the-au-on-burkina-fasos-arab-spring [Accessed 17/02/2018].

Doe, S. (1998) 'WANEP: West African Network for Peacebuilding', HPN Humanitarian Practice Network. Available online: http://odihpn.org/magazine/wanep-the-west -african-network-for-peace-building/ [Accessed 03/10/2017].

Doe, S. and Bombande, H. E. (2003) 'Management Report', in *2003 WANEP Annual Report*. Available online: http://www.wanep.org/wanep/attachments/article/115/ ar2003.pdf [Accessed 01/11/2017].

Dokubo, C. (2010) 'Regional Integration and National Security: A Nigerian Perspective', in Akinyeye, Y. (ed.), *Nation-States and the Challenges of Regional Integration in West Africa: The Case of Nigeria*, Paris, Karthala, pp. 103–120.

Dickovick, T. J. (2012) *The World Today Series: Africa*, 47th Edition, Lanham, Stryker-Post Publications.

Dixon, L. and Reyes, D. (2007) *Do No Harm in Senegal: Missed Opportunities and Future Possibilities*. Available online: https://www.cdacollaborative.org/wp-content/uploads /2016/02/Do-No-Harm-in-Senegal-Missed-Opportunities-and-Future-Possibilities.pdf [Accessed 25/07/2020].

Draper, P. (2012) 'Breaking Free from Europe: Why Africa Needs Another Model of Regional Integration', *The International Spectator: Italian Journal of International Affairs*, Vol. 47, No. 1, pp. 67–82.

East African Community. (1999) *The Treaty for the Establishment of the East African Community*. Available online: file:///C:/Users/okogbe/Downloads/EAC%20TREATY .pdf [Accessed 02/06/2018].

East African Community. (2017) 'EAC to Start Issue EA e-Passport January 2018', Available online: https://www.eac.int/press-releases/148-immigration-and-labour/754 -eac-to-start-issuing-ea-e-passport-january-2018%20= [Accessed 29/09/2018].

Ebo, A. (2004) 'Security Sector Reform as an Instrument of Sub-Regional Transformation in West Africa', in *Reform and Reconstruction of the Security Sector*, pp. 65–92.

Ebrimah, A. and Weisband, E. (eds.) (2007) *Global Accountabilities: Participation, Pluralism and Public Ethics*, New York, Cambridge University Press.

ECOWAS. (1975) *The Treaty of the Economic Community of West African States*, Abuja, ECOWAS Secretariat.

ECOWAS. (1993) *Revised Treaty*. Available Online: https://www.ecowas.int/wp-content/ uploads/2015/01/Revised-treaty.pdf [Accessed 02/06/2018].

ECOWAS. (1996) 'Regulation C/REG.5/11/96 Establishing a Forum of Associations Recognised by ECOWAS (FARE)', *The Official Journal of ECOWAS*, Vol. 32, p. 17.

ECOWAS. (1999a) *Protocol Relating to the Mechanism for Conflict Prevention, Management, Resolution, Peace-Keeping and Security*, Abuja, The ECOWAS Secretariat.

ECOWAS. (1999b) *Twenty-Second Session of the Authority of Heads of State and Government Lome, 9–10 December 1999: Final Communique*. Available Online: https://www.ecowas.int/wp-content/uploads/2015/02/22nd-ECOWAS-Summit-Lome-9-10-Dec-1999.pdf [Accessed 01/06/2020].

ECOWAS. (2001) *Protocol A/SP1/12/01 on Democracy and Good Governance Supplementary to the Protocol relating to the Mechanism for Conflict Prevention, Management, Resolution, Peacekeeping and Security*. Available online: http://www.internationaldemocracywatch.org/attachments/350_ECOWAS%20Protocol%20on%20Democracy%20and%20Good%20Governance.pdf [Accessed 03/03/2018].

ECOWAS. (2005) 'Twenty-Eighth Summit of the ECOWAS Heads of States and Government: Final Communique', (Held in Accra, Ghana on 19th January, 2005). Available online: http://hubrural.org/IMG/pdf/cedeao_final_communique_accra_summit_2005.pdf [Accessed 23/01/2017].

ECOWAS. (2016a) 'ECOWAS, African Union and UN Statement on the Gambian December 1 Presidential Election', Available online: http://www.ecowas.int/ecowas-african-union-and-un-statement-on-the-gambian-december-1-presidential-election/ [Accessed 27/07/2017].

ECOWAS. (2016b) 'ECOWAS Ministers adopt Action Plan to Address Illicit Drug Trafficking, Organized Crimes and Drug Abuse in West Africa', Available online: http://www.ecowas.int/ecowas-ministers-adopt-action-plan-to-address-illicit-drug-trafficking-organized-crimes-and-drug-abuse-in-west-africa/[Accessed 23/05/2017].

ECOWAS Commission. (2008) *ECOWAS Conflict Prevention Framework*, Abuja, The ECOWAS Commission.

ECOWAS Commission. (2010) *Economic Community of West African States (ECOWAS): Revised Treaty*, Abuja, The ECOWAS Commission.

ECOWAS Commission. (2011) *ECOWAS Vision 2020: Towards A Democratic and Prosperous Community*, Abuja. Available online: http://www.spu.ecowas.int/wp-content/uploads/2010/03/ECOWAS-VISION-2020-THEMATICTIC-PAMPHLETS-in-English.pdf [Accessed 20/12/2014].

ECOWAS Commission. (2013) 'Ecowas Urges Strong Media Support Against Human Trafficking, Child Abuse', Press Release 305/2013. Available online: http://news.ecowas.int/presseshow.php?nb=305&lang=en&annee=2013 [Accessed 24/02/2015].

ECOWAS CTS Tracker. (2016) 'Report', Available online: http://healingnationsconsult.org/counter/about-us/ [Accessed 06/03/2017].

Enchill, K. (2011) 'WANEP: Our Story', Available online: https://www.youtube.com/watch?v=8jHriq2ToOY [Accessed 30/02/2017].

Euro News. (2017) 'Tension Rises in the Gambia as Adama Barrow is Set to be Sworn-in as New President', Available online: http://www.euronews.com/2017/01/19/tension-rises-in-gambia-as-adama-barrow-is-set-to-be-sworn-in-as-new-president [Accessed 27/07/2017].

Evora, I. and Costa, S. (2015) 'Civil Society and Development in Cape Verde', in WACSI (ed.), *Civil Society and Development in West Africa: Regional Perspective*, Accra, WACSI, pp. 40–51.

Eze, B. C. (2016a) 'The Role of CSOs in Promoting Human Rights Protection, Mass Atrocities Prevention, and Civilian Protection in Armed Conflicts', *Global Responsibility to Protect*, Vol. 8, No. Special Issue, pp. 249–269.

Eze, B. C. (2016b) 'Press Release: WANEP Hopeful for Peaceful Election in Ghana', Available online: http://www.wanep.org/wanep/files/2016/nov/pr_nov_2016_gh_elections_hope_for_peace.pdf [Accessed 02/04/2018].

Eze, M. O. and Wal, K. V. D. (2020) 'Beyond Sovereign Reason: Issues and Contestations in Contemporary African Identity' *Journal of Common Market Studies*, Vol. 58, No. 1, pp. 189–204.

Ezeokafor, E. (2015) 'Securitization Processes and West African Security: Regime-led Neo-Patrimonial Threats?', Unpublished PhD Thesis, submitted to the School of Humanities, University of Dundee.

Falola, T. and Essien, K. (eds.) (2015) *Pan-Africanism, and the Politics of African Citizenship and Identity*, London, Routledge.

Fanon, F. (1983) *The Wretched of the Earth*, Harmondsworth, Penguin.

FAO and ECOWAS (2016) 'The Cross Border Transhumance: A Proposal for Action,' Available online: https://ecpf.ecowas.int/wp-content/uploads/2016/01/CrossBorder -Transhumance-WA-Final-Report-1.pdf [Accessed 03/01/2018].

Fawcett, L. and Hurrell, A. (1994) 'Conclusion: Regionalism and Global Order', in *Regionalism in the World Politics: Regional Organization and International Order*, Oxford, Oxford University, pp. 309–328.

Fawcett, L. (2005) 'Regionalism from an Historical Perspective', in Langehove, L. V., Hettne, B. and Farrel, M. (eds.), *Global Politics of Regionalism: Theory and Practice*, London, Pluto Press, pp. 21–37.

Fawcett, L. (2016) 'Region-Building Debates in a Global Context', in Levine, D. H. and Nagar, D. (eds.), *Region-Building in Africa*, New York, Palgrave Macmillan, pp. 21–36.

Featherstone, K. (1994) 'Jean Monnet and the Democratic Deficit in European Union', *Journal of Common Market Studies*, Vol. 32, No. 2, pp. 147–170.

Ferguson, Y. H. and Jones, R. B. (2002) *Political Space: Frontiers of Change and Governance in a Globalizing World*, Albany State, University of New York Press.

Fini, T. W. (2015) 'Reflection on Civil Society in the Ivory Coast: Issues, Institutional Challenges and Post-Crisis Sensitivities', in WACSI (ed.), *Civil Society and Development in West Africa: Regional Perspective*, Accra, WACSI, pp. 52–67.

Filmer, D. and Fox, L. (2014) 'Overview: Youth Employment in Sub-Saharan Africa', Report, Washington, World Bank.

Fioramonti, L. (2014) 'The Evolution of Supranational Regionalism: From Top-Down Regulatory Governance to Sustainability Region', UNU-CRIS Working Paper, W-2014/2. Available online: http://www.cris.unu.edu/fileadmin/workingpapers/W -20142__revised_.pdf [Accessed 08/01/2015].

Fioramonti, L. (ed.) (2015) *Civil Society and World Regions: How Citizens Are Reshaping Regional Governance in Times of Crisis*, London, Lexington Books.

Fioramonti, L. and Matheis, F. (2016) 'Is Africa Really Following Europe? An Integrated Framework for Comparative Regionalism', *Journal of Common Market*, Vol. 54, No. 3, pp. 674–690.

Firchow, P. and Ginty, R. M. (2017) 'Measuring Peace: Comparability, Commensurability, and Complementarity Using Bottom-Up Indicators', *International Studies Review*, Vol. 19, No. 1, pp. 6–27.

Fortune, F., Ismail, O. and Stephen, M. (2015) *Rethinking Youth, Livelihood, and Fragility in West Africa: One Size Doesn't Fit All*, Washington, World Bank.

Fox, L., Senbetb, L. W. and Simbanegavib, W. (2016) 'Youth Employment in Sub-Saharan Africa: Challenges, Constraints and Opportunities', *Journal of African Economies*, Vol. 25, AERC Supplement 1, pp. i3–i15.

Frank, M. T. (1992) 'The Emerging Right of Democratic Governance', *The American Journal of International Law*, Vol. 86, No. 1, pp. 46–91.

Freedom House. (2015) *Freedom in the World*. Available online: https://freedomhouse .org/sites/default/files/2020-02/Freedom_in_the_World_2015_complete_book.pdf, [Accessed 05/10/2020].

Freedom Newspaper. (2016) 'Gambia: Pressure Mount on Gambia Over Prolonged Political Crisis', Available online: http://www.freedomnewspaper.com/gambia -pressure-mounts-on-gambia-over-prolonged-political-crisis/ [Accessed 03/08/2017].

Furlong, P. and Marsh, D. (2010) 'A Skin Not a Sweater: Ontology and Epistemology in Political Science', in Marsh, D. and Stoker, G. (eds.), *Theory and Method in Political Science*, New York, Palgrave Macmillan, pp. 17–41.

Garcia, L. B. (2015) *Participatory Democracy and Civil Society in the EU: Agenda-Setting and Institutionalisation*, London, Palgrave Macmillan.

Genna, G. M. and Hiroi, T. (2015) *Regional Integration and Democratic Conditionality: How Democracy Clauses help Democratic Consolidation and Deepening*, New York, Routledge.

Gerring, J., Thacker, S. C. and Moreno, C. (2005) 'Centripetal Democratic Governance: A Theory and Global Inquiry', *American Political Science Review*, Vol. 99, No. 4, pp. 567–581.

Glas, A. and Balogun, E. (2020) 'Norms in Practice: People-Centric Governance in ASEAN and ECOWAS', *International Affairs*, Vol. 96, No. 4, pp. 1015–1032.

Glenn, J. (2008) 'Global Governance and Democratic Deficit: Stifling the Voice of the South', *Third World Quarterly*, Vol. 29, No. 2, pp. 217–238.

Global Legal Monitor. (2010) 'Nigeria: Regional Court Says Government has Legal Obligation to Provide Free and Compulsory Education to Children', Available online: http://www.loc.gov/law/foreign-news/article/nigeria-regional-court-says-government -has-legal-obligation-to-provide-free-and-compulsory-education-to-children/ [Accessed 26/08/2017].

Gobo, G. (2011) 'Ethnography', in Silverman, D. (ed.), *Qualitative Research: Issues of Theory, Method and Practice*, 3rd Edition, London, Sage Publications Limited, pp. 16–34.

Godsater, A. and Soderbaum, F. (2011) 'Civil Society in Regional Governance in Eastern and Southern Africa', in Armstrong, D., Bello, V., Gilson, J. and Spini, D. (eds.), *Civil Society and International Governance: The Role of Non State Actors in the Regional Regulative Framework*, New York, Routledge, pp. 148–165.

Godsater, A. (2013) 'Regional Environmental Governance in the Lake Victoria Region: The Role of Civil Society', *African Studies*, Vol. 72, No. 1, pp. 64–85.

Godsater, A. (2015) 'Regionalisation "From Below" in Southern Africa: The Role of Civil Society in Regional Trade and HIV/AIDS Policy Making', in Fioramonti, L. (ed.), *Civil Society and World Regions: How Citizens Are Reshaping Regional Governance in Times of Crisis*, London, Lexington Books, pp. 123–136.

Godsater, A. (2016) *Civil Society Regionalisation in Southern Africa: The Case of Trade and HIV/AIDS*, New York, Routledge.

Godsater, A. and Soderbaum, F. (2011) 'Civil Society in Regional Governance in Eastern and Southern Africa', in Armstrong, D., Bello, V., Gilson, J. and Spini, D. (eds.), *Civil Society and International Governance: The Role of Non-State Actors in Global and Regional Regulatory Frameworks*, New York, Routledge, pp. 148–165.

Grant, A. and Soderbaum, F. (eds.) (2003) *The New Regionalism in Africa*, Aldershot, Ashgate.

Grant, A. J. (2017) 'The Kimberley Process on Conflict Diamonds, New Regionalisms and the Dynamics of (De/Re)territorialisation', in Engel, U., Zinecker, H., Mattheis, F., Dietze, A. and Plottze, T. (eds.), *The New Politics of Regionalism: Perspectives from Africa, Latin America and ASIA-PACFIC*, New York, Routledge, pp. 146–158.

Gray, J. (2017) 'Liberia: From 14 year of Brutal War to the 14 Years of Uninterrupted Peace: A Recollection of the Nation's Dark Past', in *Global News Network – Liberia*. Available online: http://gnnliberia.com/2017/08/20/liberia-14-years-brutal-war-14 -years-uninterrupted-peace-recollection-nations-dark-past/ [Accessed 04/04/2018].

Grebrewold, B. (2009) *Anatomy of Violence: Understanding the System of Conflict and Violence in Africa*, London, Ashgate Publishing Limited.

Gregorescu, A. (2013) 'International Organisations and their Bureaucratic Oversight Mechanism: The Democratic Deficit, Accountability and Transparency', in Reinalda, B. (ed.), *Routledge Handbook on International Organisations*, New York, Routledge, pp. 176–188.

Guichaoua, Y. (2012) 'Circumstantial Alliances and Loose Loyalties in Rebellion Making: The Case of Tuareg Insurgency in Northern Niger (2007–2009)', in Guichaoua, Y. (ed.), *Understanding Collective Political Violence*, New York, Palgrave Macmillan, pp. 246–266.

Haastrup, A. A. A. (2010) *Security as Change? An Institutional View of Contemporary EU-Africa Relations*. PhD Thesis, University of Edinburgh. Available online: https://era .ed.ac.uk/bitstream/handle/1842/14228/Haastrup2011.pdf?sequence=1&isAllowed=y [Accessed 30/03/2020].

Haastrup, T. (2013a) *Charting Transformation through Security Contemporary EU-Africa Relations*, London, Palgrave Macmillan.

Haastrup, T. (2013b) 'EU as Mentor? Promoting Regionalism as External Relations Practice in EU-Africa Relations', *Journal of European Integration*, Vol. 35, No. 7, pp. 785–800.

Haastrup, T. and Lopez, E. (2014) *Nigeria and Regional Security*, EUIRSCAS, 2014/49, Global Governance Programme-103, European, Transnational and Global Governance, Available online: https://cadmus.eui.eu/bitstream/handle/1814/31311/RSCAS %202014_49%5b1%5d.pdf?sequence=1&isAllowed=y [Accessed 09/05/2020].

Harding, G. (2014) 'Mind the Gap: How to Close the EU's Democratic Deficit', *Foreign Affairs*, June 4, 2014. Available Online: http://www.foreignaffairs.com/articles/141529 /gareth-harding/mind-the-ga [Accessed 17/03/2015].

Harsch, E. (2012) 'Building Peace from the Ground Up: Key Roles for Civil Society in Keeping Violence at Bay', Available online: http://www.un.org/africarenewal/ magazine/august-2012/building-peace-ground [Accessed 27/02/2018].

Heilbrunn, J. R. (1993) 'Social Origins of National Conferences in Benin and Togo', *The Journal of Modern African Studies*, Vol. 31, No. 2, pp. 277–299.

Hettne, B. (2003) 'The New Regionalism Revisited', in Söderbaum, F. and Shaw, T. M. (eds.), *Theories of New Regionalism*, London, Palgrave Macmillan, pp. 22–42.

Hettne, B. (2006) 'Beyond the 'New' Regionalism', in Payne, A. (ed.), *Key Debates in New Political Economy*, New York, Routledge, pp. 136–168.

Hettne, B. and Inotai, A. (1994) *The New Regionalism: Implications for Global Development and International Security*, Helsinki, UNU/WIDER.

Heywood, A. (2011) *Global Politics*, 2nd Edition, New York, Palgrave Macmillan.

Horn, D. M. (2013) *Democratic Governance and Social Entrepreneurship: Civic Participations and the Future of Democracy*, New York, Routledge.

Hearn, J. (2001) 'The Uses and Abuses of Civil Society in Africa', *Review of African Political Economy*, Vol. 28, No. 87, pp. 43–53.

Hettne, B. (1999) 'Globalization and the New Regionalism: The Second Great Transformation', in Hettne, B. Inotai, A. and Sunkel, O. (eds.), *Globalism and the New Regionalism*, London, Macmillan Press Limited, pp. 1–24.

Hettne, B. (2005) 'Beyond the "New" Regionalism', *New Political Economy*, Vol. 10, No. 4, pp. 543–571.

Hettne, B., Inotai, A. and Sunkel, O. (eds.) (1999) *Globalism and the New Regionalism*, London, Palgrave Macmillan.

Hettne, B. and Söderbaum, F. (2000) 'Theorising the Rise of Regionness', *New Political Economy*, Vol. 5, No. 3, pp. 457–472.

Hoffman, D. (2011) *The War Machines: Young Men and Violence in Sierra Leone and Liberia*, Durham, Duke University Press.

Hübschle, A. (2014) 'Of Bogus Hunters, Queenpins and Mule: The Varied Role of Women in Transnational Organised Crime in Southern Africa', *Trends Organised Crime: Women and Transnational Organised Crime*, Vol. 17, No. 1–2, pp. 31–51.

Hulse, M. et al. (2018) *Civil Society Engagement in Regional Governance: A Network Analysis* in Southern Africa: Discussion Paper No. 30/2018. Available online: https://www.die-gdi.de/uploads/media/DP_30.2018.pdf [Accessed 30/07/2020].

Hultin, N. (2014) 'Civil Society and Conflict in West Africa', in Obadare, E. (ed.), *The Handbook of Civil Society in Africa*, New York, Springer, pp. 199–212.

Human Rights Watch. (2001) 'Jos: A City Torn Apart', Available online: https://www.hrw.org/report/2001/12/18/jos/city-torn-apart [Accessed 06/04/2018].

Human Rights Watch. (2017) 'Gambia: Truth Commission to Uncover Jammeh Abuses', Available online: https://www.hrw.org/news/2017/12/12/gambia-truth-commission-uncover-jammeh-abuses [Accessed 02/03/2019].

Hurrell, A. (1995) 'Regionalism in Theoretical Perspective', in Fawsett, L. and Hurrell, A. (eds.), *Regionalism in World Politics: Regional Organisations and International Order*, New York, Oxford University Press, pp. 37–73.

Hurrell, A. (2005) 'Hegemony and Regional Governance in the Americas', in Fawcett, L. and Serrano, M. (eds.), *Regionalism and Governance in the Americas*, London, Palgrave Macmillan.

Ibekwe, N. (2012) '"ECOWAS should rein in Obasanjo"- West African Civil Society Forum', December 15, 2012, Available online: https://www.premiumtimesng.com/news/111310-ecowas-should-rein-in-obasanjo-west-african-civil-society-forum.html [Accessed 30/06/2020].

Ibrahim, F. A. and Majeks-Walker, N. (2015) 'Civil Society and the Democratic Transformation of Sierra Leone', in WACSI (ed.), *Civil Society and Development in West Africa: Regional Perspective*, Accra, WACSI, pp. 168–177.

Ibrahim, M. A. (2012) *The Role of Civil Society in Africa's Quest for Democratization*, New York, Springer.

Idemudia, U. and Amaeshi, K. (eds.) (2019) *Africapitalism: Sustainable Business and Development in Africa*, New York, Routledge.

Iheduru, O. C. (2003) 'New Regionalism: States and Non-State Actors in West Africa', in Grant, A. and Soderbaum, F. (eds.), *The New Regionalism in Africa*, Aldershot, Ashgate, pp. 47–66.

Iheduru, O. C. (2012) 'Regional Integration and the Private Authority of Banks in West Africa', *International Studies Review*, Vol. 14, No. 2, pp. 273–302.

Iheduru, O. C. (2013) 'The New ECOWAS: Implications for the Study of Regional Integration', in Cornelissen, S. Grant, J. A. and Shaw, T. M. (eds.), *The Ashgate Research Companion to Regionalism*, Burlington, Ashgate Publishing Limited, pp. 213–240.

Iheduru, O. C. (2015a) 'Organized Private Sector and Regional Integration in Africa', *Review of International Political Economy*, Vol. 22, No. 5, pp. 910–940.

Iheduru, O. C. (2015b) 'Civil Society and Regional Integration in West Africa: Partners, Legitimizers and Counter-Hegemonic Actors', in Fioramonti, L. (ed.), *Civil Society and World Regions: How Citizens Are Reshaping Regional Governance in Times of Crisis*, London, Lexington Books, pp. 137–160.

Iheduru, O. C. (2018) 'The African Corporation, 'Africapitalism' and Regional Integration in Africa', in Nölke, A. and May, C. (eds.), *Handbook of the International Political Economy of the Corporation (Handbooks of Research on International Political Economy Series)*, Camberley, Edward Elgar Publishers, pp. 329–345.

Iheduru, O. C. (2019) 'Africapitalism, Business and Social Construction of Regional Identity', in Idemudia, U. and Amaeshi, K. (eds.), *Africapitalism: Sustainable Business and Development in Africa*, New York, Routledge, pp. 37–59.

International Monetary Fund. (2018) *FY 2018 Mid-Year Report*, East African Regional Technical Assistance Centre. Available online: http://www.eastafritac.org/servlet/servlet.FileDownload?file=00P4100000H9KtGEAV [Accessed 07/03/2018].

International Peace Institute. (2011) 'Elections and Stabilities in West Africa', Available online: https://www.ipinst.org/wpcontent/uploads/publications/ipi_e_pub_praia__2_.pdf [Accessed 03/03/2018].

Ismail, O. (2011) 'ECOWAS and Human Security', in Jaye, T. Garuba, D. and Amadi, S. (eds.), *ECOWAS and the Dynamics of Conflict and Peace-building*, Dakar, CODESRIA, pp. 165–182.

Imodu, P. B. and Igbatayo, S. (2010) 'Fostering Regional integration in Africa: Case of Economic Community of West African States', *International Journal of Applied Economics and Econometrics*, Vol. 18, No. 1, pp. 75–94.

Iwilade, A. and Agbo, U. J. (2012) 'ECOWAS and the Regulation of Regional Peace and Security in West Africa', *Democracy and Security*, Vol. 8, No. 4, pp. 358–373.

Jarwolo, E. and Cummeh, J. (2015) 'Strengthening Effective Stakeholders Engagement to Promote Durable Development in Liberia', in WACSI (ed.), *Civil Society and Development in West Africa: Regional Perspective*, Accra, WACSI, pp. 114–127.

Jenkins, R. (2013) *Peacebuilding: From Concept to Commission*, New York, Routledge.

Jenner, A. (2015) 'WANEP/WAPI, 1998: Keeping Tensions from Escalating Into Chaos', Available online: https://emu.edu/now/peacebuilder/2015/07/wanepwapi-1998-keeping-tensions-from-escalating-into-chaos/ [Accessed 30/07/2020].

Jensen, M. N. (2006) 'Concepts and Conceptions of Civil Society', *Journal of Civil Society*, Vol. 2, No. 1, pp. 39–56.

Jessop, B. (2003) 'The Political Economy of Scale and the Construction of Cross-Border Micro-Regions', in Söderbaum, F. and Shaw, T. M. (eds.), *Theories of New Regionalism*, London, Palgrave Macmillan, pp. 197–196.

Jobarteh, M. (2015) 'Strengthening the Citizens' Voices: Strategic Engagement Towards National Development in The Gambia', in WACSI (ed.), *Civil Society and Development in West Africa: Regional Perspective*, Accra, WACSI, pp. 68–81.

Jusu-Sheriff, Y. (2004) 'Civil Society', in Adekeye, A. and Ismail, R. (eds.), *West Africa's Security Challenges: Building Peace in Troubled Region*, Boulder, Lynne Rienner Publishers, Inc., pp. 265–290.

Kacowicz, A. and Press-Barnathan. (2016) 'Regional Security Governance', in Borzel, T. A. and Risse, T. (eds.), *The Oxford Handbook on Comparative Regionalism*, Oxford, Oxford University Press, pp. 297–322.

Kandeh, J. D. (2004) *Coups from Below: Armed Subalterns and State Power in West Africa*, New York, Palgrave Macmillan.

Kane, I. and Mbelle, N. (2007) *Towards a People-Driven African Union: Current Obstacles and New Opportunities*, Cape Town, African Minds.

Karbo, T. (2018) 'Introduction: Towards a New Pax Africana', in Karbo, T. and Virk, K. (eds.), *The Palgrave Handbook of Peacebuilding in Africa*, Cham, Plagrave Macmillan, pp. 3–28.

Karbo, T. and Virk, K. (eds.) (2018) *The Palgrave Handbook of Peacebuilding in Africa*, Cham, Plagrave Macmillan.

Kasfir, N. (1998) 'Civil Society, the State and Democracy in Africa', *Commonwealth & Comparative Politics*, Vol. 36, No. 2, pp. 123–149.

Kasfir, N. (ed.) (2009) *Civil Society and Democracy in Africa: Critical Perspectives*, London, Routledge.

Kaunert, C. and Leonard, S. (2013) 'Introduction: European Security Governance after the Lisbon Treaty: Neighbours and New Actors in a Changing Security Environment', in Kaunert, C. and Leonard, S. (eds.), *European Security Governance and European Neighbourhood After the Lisbon Treaty*, New York, Routledge, pp. 1–10.

Kaunert, C. and Zwolski, K. (2010) 'The European Parliament and the Democratic Deficit: The Right Solution to the Wrong Problem', in Hug, A. (ed.), *Reconnecting European Parliament and its People*, London, Foreign Policy Centre, pp. 52–59.

Kirschner, V. and Stapel, S. (2011) 'Does Regime Type Matter? Regional Integration from the Nation States' Perspectives in ECOWAS', in Borzel, T. A., Goltermann, L., Lohaus, M. and Striebinger, K. (eds.), *Roads to Regionalism: Genesis, Designs and Effects of Regional Organisations*, London, Routledge, pp. 141–158.

Khadiagala, G. M. (2016) 'Region-Building in Eastern Africa', in Levine, D. H. and Nagar, D. (eds.), *Region-Building in Africa*, New York, Palgrave Macmillan, pp. 175–190.

Kilonzo, H., Bukanya, D. and Mwangi, J. (2015) 'Measuring Organizational Capacity: Developing Tools to Measure Civil Society Organisations Capacity to Receive Grants for HIV/AIDS Response in Kenya', *International Review of Management and Business Research*, Vol. 4, No. 1, pp. 152–162.

Kin, S. and Fiori, A. (2015) 'The Potential of Civil Society in Regional Governance in East Asia', in Fioramonti, L. (ed.), *Civil Society and World Regions: How Citizens Are Shaping Regional Governance in Times of Crisis*, Lanham, Lexington Books, pp. 77–90.

Kizito, E. U. and Patrick, U. N. (2012) 'The Role of Parliament on Economic Integration in Africa: Evidence from ECOWAS Parliament', *Journal of Humanities and Social Science*, Vol. 4, pp, 1–10.

Klandermans, B., Roefs, M. and Olivier, J. (eds.) (2001) *The State of the People: Citizens, Civil Society and Governance in South Africa*, Pretoria, HSRC Press.

Knack, S. (ed.) (2003) *Democracy, Governance and Growth*, Ann Arbor, University of Michigan Press.

Köchler, H. (2012) 'Regionalisation, Transnational Democracy and United Nations Reform: A Viewpoint', in De Lombaerde, P., Baert, F. and Felicio, T. (eds.), *The United Nations and the Regions: Third World Report on Regional Integration*, UNU Series 3 on Regionalism, New York, Springer.

Koehane, R. O. (1988) 'International Institutions: Two Approaches', *International Studies Quarterly*, Vol. 32, No. 4, pp. 379–396.

Koehane, R. O. and Nye, J. S. (2012) *Power and Interdependence*, 4th Edition, Boston, Longman.

Kohler-Koch, B. (2009) 'The Three Worlds of European Civil Society—What Role for Civil Society for What Kind of Europe?', *Policy and Society*, Vol. 28, No. 1, pp. 47–57.

Kohler-Koch, B. and Quittkat, C. (2009) 'What is Civil Society and Who Represents Civil Society in the EU? — Results of an Online Survey among Civil Society Experts', *Policy and Society*, Vol. 28, pp. 11–22.

Kofi Annan Foundation. (2013) 'Kofi Annan Launches West African Commission on Drugs', Available online: http://kofiannanfoundation.org/newsroom/press/2013/01/kofi-annan-launches-west-africa-commission-drugs [Accessed 13/02/2015].

Kogbe, O. (2012) *Why has Regional Integration been Slow in West Africa?: The Case of ECOWAS*, MA Dissertation, Coventry University, Coventry.

Kogbe, O. (2017) 'Participatory Democracy and Civil Society in the EU: Agenda-Setting and Institutionalisation', *European Politics and Society*, Vol. 18, No. 4, pp. 564–566.

Kogbe, O. (2018) 'Book Review: Rethinking Regionalism by Fredrik Soderbaum', *GlobalPolicy Journal*. Available online: htps://www.globalpolicyjournal.com/blog/10/09/2018/book-review-rethinking-regionalism [Accessed 10/09/2018].

Kramer, R. (1995) 'Liberia: A Casualty of the Cold War's End', *AllAfrica*, 1 July. Available online: http://allafrica.com/stories/200101090216.html [Accessed 04/04/2018].

Kuorsoh, P. K. (2017) 'WANEP Builds Capacity of Frontline Peace Actors', *Ghana News Agency*. Available online: http://www.ghananewsagency.org/social/wanep-builds-capacity-of-front-line-peace-actors-119737 [Accessed 03/03/2018].

Lamont, C. (2015) *Research Methods in International Relations*, London, Sage Publication Limited.

Landsberg, C. (2006) 'People to People Solidarity: Civil Society and Deep Integration in Southern Africa', *Transformation: Critical Perspectives on Southern Africa*, Vol. 61, No. 1, pp. 40–62.

Lansford, T. (2014) *Political Handbook of the World 2014*, London, Sage Publications Inc.

Lederach, J. P. (2016) 'Forward', in *The Strive and Strain in Civil Society Organisation in West Africa: The WANEP Story*. Available online: https://www.wanep.org/wanep/files/2019/Dec/OUR_STORY_Wanep_English.pdf [Accessed 23/04/2020].

Lederer, M. and Muller, P. (eds.) (2005) *Criticising Global Governance*, New York, Palgrave Macmillan.

Lelieveldt, H. and Princen, S. (2011) *The Politics of The European Union*, Cambridge, Cambridge University Press.

Lewis, D. (2002) 'Civil Society in African Context: Reflections on the Usefulness of a Concept', *Development and Change*, Vol. 33, No. 4, pp. 569–586.

Lewis, D. (2012) 'Casamance Conflict is Unhealed Sore for Senegal', *Reuters*, 25 February. Available online: https://www.reuters.com/article/us-senegal-casamance-idUSTRE81O09C20120225 [Accessed 05/05/2020].

LindVall, J. (2017) *Reform Capacity*, Oxford, Oxford University Press.

Lo, M. (2006) 'Re-Conceptualizing Civil Society: The Debate Continues With Specific Reference to Contemporary Senegal', *African and Asian Studies*, Vol. 5, No. 1, pp. 91–118.

Lo, M. (2010) *Civil Society-Based Governance in Africa: Theories and Practices: A Case of Study of Senegal*, Khartoum, Society Studies Center.

Lucarelli, S., Langenhove, L. V. and Wouters, J. (eds.) (2013) *The EU and Multilateral Security Governance*, New York, Routledge.

Madueke, U. (2015) 'The First Presentation at WACSOF Regional Partners', Meeting with the Support of OXFAM, held at the Nicon Luxury Hotel, Abuja, from 17th to 18th March 2015. Available online: https://www.youtube.com/watch?v=iPG9qQySRas [Accessed 24/05/2017].

Madueke, U. (2016) 'A Documentary on Child/Early Marriage Produced by the West African Civil Society Forum', Available on YouTube: https://www.youtube.com/watch?v=xyum-QRM-VM [Accessed 28/08/2017].

Mahama, S. E. and Longi, T. F. (2013) 'Conflicts in Northern Ghana: Search for Solutions, Stakeholders and Way Forward', *Ghana Journal of Development Studies*, Vol. 10, No. 1 & 2, pp. 112–129.

Mamdani, M. (2001) 'Beyond Settler and Native as Political Identities: Overcoming the Political Legacy of Colonialism', *Comparative Studies in Society and History*, Vol. 43, No. 4, pp. 651–664.

Maru, I. M. T. (2014) *Mid-Term Review of the West African Network for Peacebuilding (WANEP): Decentralised Evaluation for the Swedish International Development Cooperation Agency (SIDA)*. Available online: https://www.sida.se/contentassets/b90 03394b16e4d48b7246b0617b6f54f/15519.pdf [Accessed 01/02/2018].

Marsh, D. and Furlong, P. (2002) 'A Skin, not a Sweater: Ontology and Epistemology in Political Science', in Marsh, D. and Stoker, G. (eds.), *Theory and Methods in Political Science*, 2nd Edition, Hampshire, Palgrave Macmillan, pp. 17–41.

Massey, S. (2009) 'Multi-Party Mediation in the Guinea-Bissau Civil War', in Furley, O. and May, R. (eds.), *Ending Africa's Wars*, Hampshire, Ashgate Publishing Limited, pp. 83–97.

Macfarlane, S. N. and Khong, Y. (eds.) (2006) *Human Security and the UN: A Critical History*, Bloomington, Indiana University Press.

Maclean, R. (2017) 'Troops Enter the Gambia after Adama Barrow is Inaugurated in Senegal', *The Guardian*, 19 January. Available online: https://www.theguardian.com/world/2017/jan/19/new-gambian-leader-adama-barrow-sworn-in-at-ceremony-in-senegal [Accessed 27/07/2017].

Macnabb, D. E. (2015) *Research Method for Political Science: Quantitative and Qualitative Approaches*, 2nd Edition, New York, Routledge.

Mamattah, T. (2013) 'Building Civil Society in West Africa: Notes from the Field', in Obadare, E. (ed.), *The Handbook of Civil Society in Africa*, New York, Springer, pp. 143–156.

Marc, A., Verjee, N. and Mogaka, S. (2015) *The Challenge of Stability and Security in West Africa*, Washington, International Bank for Reconstruction and Development/The World Bank.

Mattheis, F. (2017) 'Repositioning Europe in the Study of Regions: Comparative Regionalism, Interregionalism and Decentred Regionalism', *Journal of European Integration*, Vol. 39, No. 4, pp. 477–482.

Matthews, B. and Ross, L. (2010) *Research Methods: A Practical Guide for Social Sciences*, Essex, Pearson Education Limited.

Mazrui, A. (1995) 'Pan-Africanism: From Poetry to Power', *Journal of Opinion*, Vol. 23, No. 1, African Studies, pp. 35–38.

Mbrou, L. A. (2015) 'The Contribution of Civil Society to the Upsurge of Democracy in Togo: Challenges for Internal Mobilisation and National Development', in WACSI (ed.), *Civil Society and Development in West Africa: Regional Perspective*, Accra, WACSI, pp. 178–187.

Mercer, C. (2002) 'NGOs, Civil Society and Democratisation: A Critical Review of the Literature', *Progress in Development Studies*, Vol. 2, No. 1, pp. 5–22.

Media Foundation for West Africa. (2014) 'ECOWAS Court Ruling on Deyda Hydara – Commendable', Available online: http://www.mfwa.org/ecowas-court-ruling-on-deyda-hydara-commendable/ [Accessed 13/05/2017].

Media Foundation for West Africa. (2016) *West African Free Expression Monitor.* Available online: http://www.mfwa.org/wp-content/uploads/2016/09/MFWA-FoE -Monitor-January-June-2016-1.pdf [Accessed 02/07/2017].

Mittleman, H. J. (1999) 'Rethinking the "New Regionalism" in the Context of Globalisation', in Hettne, B., Inotai, A. and Sunkel, O. (eds.), *Globalism and the New Regionalism*, London, Macmillan Press Limited, pp. 25–53.

Mitton, K. (2015) *Rebels in a Rotten State: Understanding Atrocity in the Sierra Leone Civil War*, New York, Oxford University Press.

Mitrany, D. (1948) 'The Functional Approach to World Organization', *International Affairs*, Vol. 24, No. 3, pp. 350–363.

Momoh, A. (2013) 'The Election in Lagos State as Political Monologue', in Ayoade, J. A. and Akinsaya, A. (eds.), *Nigerian Critical Election 2011*, Lanham, Lexington Books, pp. 203–228.

Moravscvik, A. (2002) 'In Defence of the "Democratic Deficit": Reassessing Legitimacy in the EU', *Journal of Common Market Studies*, Vol. 40, No. 4, pp. 602–624.

Moravscvik, A. (2004) 'Is there a "Democratic Deficit" in World Politics?: A Framework for Analysis', *Government and Opposition*, Vol. 39, No. 2, pp. 336–363.

Mudacumura, G. M. and Morcol, G. (eds.) (2014) *Challenges to Democratic Governance in Developing Countries*, New York, Springer International Publishing.

Musschenga, A. W. (2004) 'Identity-Neutral and Identity-Constitutive Reasons for Preserving', *Journal of Applied Philosophy*, Vol. 21, No. 1, pp. 77–88.

MyJoyOnline. (2017) 'UN Warns of Terrorism on Regional Scale in Africa', Available online: http://www.myjoyonline.com/news/2017/February-4th/un-warns-threat-of -terrorism-on-regional-scale-in-africa.php [Accessed 06/03/2017].

Navarro, J. (2010) 'The Creation and Transformation of Regional Parliamentary Assemblies: Lessons from the Pan-African Parliament', *The Journal of Legislative Studies*, Vol. 16, No. 2, pp. 195–214.

Ndlovu-Gatsheni, S. J. (2018) *Epistemic Freedom in Africa: Deprovincialization and Decolonisation*, New York, Routledge.

N'Diaye, B. (2011) 'Conflicts and Crises in West Africa: Internal and International Dimensions', in Jaye, T., Garuba, D. and Amadi, S. (eds.), *ECOWAS and the Dynamics of Conflict and Peace-Building*, Senegal, CODESRIA, pp. 27–44.

Neack, L. (2007) *Elusive Security, State First, People Last*, New York, Rowman and Littlefield Publishers Inc.

Nesadurai, H. E. S. (2015) 'Civil Society and Land Conflicts in Southeast Asia: Navigating Between National, Regional and Transnational Governance', in Fioramonti, L. (ed.), *Civil Society and World Regions: How Citizens Are Shaping Regional Governance in Times of Crisis*, London, Lexington Books, pp. 107–122.

News Ghana. (2015) 'Casamance Conflicts Renders Over 60,000 People Homeless', 25 August. Available online: https://newsghana.com.gh/casamance-conflicts-renders -over-60000-people-homeless/ [Accessed 24/04/2020].

New York Times. (1991) 'President of Mali is Reported Arrested', 26 March. Available online: http://www.nytimes.com/1991/03/26/world/president-of-mali-reported -arrested.html?mcubz=3 [Accessed 05/09/2017].

Ngongang, E. (2009) 'New Regionalism in Sub-saharan Africa: A means to Attract Foreign Direct Investment (FDI) and to Legitimate Democratic Governments', *African Journal of Political Science and International Relations*, Vol. 3, No. 1, pp. 15–26.

Nieuwkerk, V. A. (2001) 'Regionalism into Globalism? War into Peace?', *African Security Review*, Vol. 10, No. 2, pp. 6–18.

Nigerian Vanguard. (2013) '"Civilian JTF" Should not Fight', 31 July, Available online: https://www.vanguardngr.com/2013/07/civilian-jtf-should-not-fight/   [Accessed 14/04/2020].

Nossiter, A. (2012) 'Soldiers Overthrow Mali Government in Setback for Democracy in Africa', *The New York Times*, 22 March. Available online: https://www.nytimes.com/2012/03/23/world/africa/mali-coup-france-calls-for-elections.html [Accessed 06/02/2020].

Notaras, M. Popovski, V. and Howe, B. (eds.) (2010) *Democracy in the South: Participation, the State and the People*, Tokyo, United Nations Press.

Norris, P. (2012) *Making Democratic Governance Work: How Democracy Shape Prosperity, Welfare and Peace*, Cambridge, Cambridge University Press.

Nwajiaku, K. (1994) 'The National Conferences in Benin and Togo Revisited', *The Journal of Modern African Studies*, Vol. 32, No. 3, pp. 429–447.

Nzewi, O. (2014) 'Regional Parliamentary Assemblies: The Case of the Pan African Parliament's Search for Legislative Powers', *Journal of Asian and African Studies*, Vol. 49, No. 4, pp. 488–507.

Obadare, E. (2004) 'Civil Society in West Africa', in Glasius, M., Lewis, D., and Seckinelgin, H. (eds.), *Exploring Civil Society: Political and Cultural Contexts*, New York, Routledge, p. 136.

Obadare, E. (2004b) 'The Alternative Genealogy of Civil Society and Its Implications for Africa: Notes for Further Research', *Africa Development*, Vol. 29, No. 4, pp. 1–18.

Obadare, E. (ed.) (2013) *The Handbook of Civil Society in Africa*, New York, Springer.

Obadare, E. (2014) 'Dangerous Associations: Legal Homophobia and the Changing Politics of Civil Society', *African Regional Civil Society Research Network*, Vol. 8, pp. 6–8.

Obadare, E. (2015) 'Background on Civil Society and Development in West Africa: Issues Problems and Doubts that Just Won't Go Away', in WACSI (ed.), *Civil Society and Development in West Africa: Regional Perspective*, Accra, WACSI, pp. 12–21.

Obadare, E. (2016) *Humor, Silence, and Civil Society in Nigeria*, Rochester, University of Rochester Press.

Obasanjo, O. (1981) *My Command: An Account of the Nigerian Civil War*, London, Heinemann.

Obi, C. (2009a) 'Nigeria's Niger Delta: Understanding the Complex Drivers of Violent Oil-related Conflict', *Africa Development*, Vol. XXXIV, No. 2, pp. 103–128.

Obi, C. I. (2009b) 'Economic Community of West African States on the Ground: Comparing Peacekeeping in Liberia, Sierra Leone, Guinea Bissau, and Côte D'Ivoire', *African Security*, Vol. 2, No. 2–3, pp. 119–135.

Obono, O. (2015) 'The Role of Civil Society in Nigerian National Development', in WACSI (ed.), *Civil Society and Development in West Africa: Regional Perspective*, Accra, WACSI, pp. 146–157.

Ochieng-Springer, S. (2012) 'Democratic Governance within Regional Institutions: A Critical Analysis of the African Union and the European Union', Available online: http://www.academia.edu/5981842/Democratic_Governance_within_regional_institutions_A_Critical_analysis_of_the_African_Union_and_the_European_Union [Accessed 20/12/2014].

Ochonu, M. E. (2016) 'The Fulani Herdsmen Threat to Nigeria's Fragile Unity', *Sahara Reporters*, Available online: http://saharareporters.com/2016/03/08/fulani-herdsmen-threatnigeria%E2%80%99s-fragile-unity-moses-e-ochonu [Accessed 08/03/2016].

Odhiambo, M. and Chitiga, R. (2016) *The Civil Society Guide to Regional Economic Communities in Africa*, New York, Open Society Foundation.

Ojakorotu, V. and Adeleke, A. A. (2017) 'Nigeria and Conflict Resolution in the Sub-regional West Africa: The Quest for a Regional Hegemon?', *Insight on Africa*, Vol. 10, No. 1, pp. 37–53.

Okechukwu, I. and Dureke, B. U. (2010) 'WANEP Press Release', Available online: http://wanep.org/wanep/attachments/article/127/pr_jos_22_jan_2010.pdf [Accessed 27/02/2018].

Ola, P. (1979) 'Pan-Africanism: An Ideology of Development', *Présence Africaine*, 4e Nouvelle série, No. 112, pp. 66–95.

Olonisakin, F. (2004) 'Windows of Opportunity for Conflict Prevention: Responding to Regional Conflict in West Africa', *Conflict, Security & Development*, Vol. 4, No. 2, pp. 181–198.

Olonisakin, F. (2009) 'ECOWAS and Civil Society Movement in West Africa', *Institute of Development Studies Bulletin*, Vol. 40, No. 2, pp. 105–112.

Olonisakin, F. (2011) 'ECOWAS: From Economic Integration to Peace-Building', in Jaye, T. Garuba, D. and Amadi, S. (eds.), *ECOWAS and the Dynamics of Conflict and Peace-Building*, Daka, CODESRIA, pp. 11–26.

Olowu, D. (2003) 'Governance and Policy Management Capacity in Africa', in Olowu, D. and Sako, S. (eds.), *Better Governance and Public Policy: Capacity Building for Democratic Renewal in Africa*, Boulder, Kumarian Press, pp. 1–10.

Olowu, D. and Sako, S. (eds.) (2003) *Better Governance and Public Policy: Capacity Building for Democratic Renewal in Africa*, Boulder, Kumarian Press.

Onishi, N. (2000) 'Ivory Coast Ruler Declares Himself Winner', *The New York Times*, 25 October. Available online: http://www.nytimes.com/2000/10/25/world/ivory-coast-ruler-declares-himself-winner.html [Accessed 22/02/2018].

Oosthuysen, G. (1997) 'The Illegal Drug Trade in Southern Africa', A Report on International Conference, The South African Institute of International Affairs, Available online: http://dspace.africaportal.org/jspui/bitstream/123456789/29745/1/SAIIA%20Report%20no%203.pdf?1 [Accessed 13/02/2015].

Opoku, J. M. (2007) 'West African Early Warning and Early Response System: The Role of Civil Society Organisations', KAIPTC Paper, No. 19, September. Available Online:http://www.kaiptc.org/publications/occasional-papers/documents/occassional-paper-19.aspx [Accessed 20/3/2017].

Oppong, R. F. (2011) *Legal Aspects of Economic Integration in Africa*, New York, Cambridge University Press.

Ormston, R., Spencer, L., Barnard, M. and Snape, D. (2014) 'The Foundations of Qualitative Research', in Ritche, J., Lewis, J., Nicolas, M. C. and Ormston, R. (eds.), *Qualitative Research Practice: A Guide for Social Science Students and Researchers*, London, SAGE Publication Ltd., pp. 1–23.

Osumah, O. (2013) 'Boko Haram Insurgency in Northern Nigeria and the Vicious Cycle of Internal Insecurity', *Small Wars & Insurgencies*, Vol. 24, No. 3, pp. 536–560.

Paasi, A. (2009) 'The Resurgence of the "Region" and "Regional Identity": Theoretical Perspectives and Empirical Observations on Regional Dynamics in Europe', *Review of International Studies*, Vol. 35, No. S1, pp. 121–146.

Paasi, A. (2010) 'Regions are Social Constructs, but Who or What 'Constructs' Them? Agency in Question', *Environment and Planning A*, Vol. 42, No. 10, pp. 2296–2301.

Peace Insight. (2017) 'West African Network for Peacebuilding (WANEP- Burkina Faso', Available online: https://www.peaceinsight.org/conflicts/burkina-faso/peacebuilding -organisations/west-africa-network-for-peacebuilding-wanep-burkina-faso/ [Accessed 16/02/2018].

Peter, B. (2003) 'Governance Conditions, Roles and Capacity-building Needs in the Rebel-Held Areas of Southern Sudan', *Public Administration and Development*, Vol. 23, No. 2, pp. 125–139.

Pinfari, M. (2015) 'Transnational Civil Society and Regionalism in the Arab World: More of the Same', in Fioramonti, L. (ed.) *Civil Society and World Regions: How Citizens Are Shaping Regional Governance in Times of Crisis*, Lindon, Lexington Books, pp. 161–176.

Polanyi, K. (1957) *The Great Transformation: The Political and Economic Origins of Our Time*, Boston, Beacon Press.

Pouligny, B. (2005) 'Civil Society and Post-Conflict Peacebuilding: Ambiguities of International Programmes Aimed at Building 'New' Societies', *Security Dialogue*, Vol. 36, No. 4, pp. 495–510.

Premium Times. (2013) 'Borno Govt. to Train 5,000 "Civilian JTF" by 2015', Available online: http://www.premiumtimesng.com/news/top-news/147407-borno-govt -train5000-civilian-jtf-2015.html [Accessed 14/04/2020].

Pul, H. S. (2014) 'Civil Society and Conflict on Africa', *African Regional Civil Society Research Network*, Vol. 8, June 2014, pp. 1–4.

Punch, K. (2005) *Introduction to Social Research: Quantitative and Qualitative Approaches*, 2nd Edition, London, Sage Publication Limited.

Quayle, L. (2012) 'Bridging the Gap: An "English School" Perspective on ASEAN and Regional Civil Society,' *The Pacific Review*, Vol. 25, No. 2, pp. 199–222.

Reinold, T. (2019) 'Civil Society Participation in Regional Integration in Africa: A Comparative Analysis of ECOWAS, SADC, and the EAC', *South African Journal of International Affairs*, Vol. 26, No. 1, pp. 53–71.

Reuters. (2008) 'Factbox: Sierra Leone's Civil War', Available online: https://www .reuters.com/article/us-warcrimes-taylor-war/factbox-sierra-leones-civil-war-idUSL06 6107120080108 [Accessed 19/04/2020].

Reuters. (2011) 'Timeline: Liberia: From Civil War Chaos to Fragile Hope', Available online: https://www.reuters.com/article/us-liberia-election-events/timeline-liberia -from-civil-war-chaos-to-fragile-hope-idUSTRE7A62BN20111107   [Accessed 06/04/2018].

Richmond, O. P. (2006) 'The Problem of Peace: Understanding the "Liberal Peace"', *Conflict, Security & Development*, Vol. 6, No. 3, pp. 291–314.

Rozee, S. (2012) *European Union as Comprehensive Actor in Policing*, PhD Thesis, University of Dundee, Dundee.

Saha, S. C. (1999) *Dictionary of Human Rights Advocacy Organizations in Africa*, London, Greenwood Press.

Saharan Reporter. (2016) 'Adama Barrow Unseats Gambian President Jammeh in Shocking Victory', Available online: http://saharareporters.com/2016/12/02/ adama-barrow-unseats-gambian-president-jammeh-shocking-victory   [Accessed 27/07/2017].

Saidou, K. A. (2018) '"We Have Chased Blaise, So Nobody Can Resist Us": Civil Society and the Politics of ECOWAS Intervention in Burkina Faso', *South African Journal of International Affairs*, Vol. 25, No. 1, pp. 39–60.

Sajoo, B. A. (1996) 'Conditions of Liberty: Civil Society and its Rivals: Ernest Gellner', *Canadian Journal of Law and Society*, Vol. 11, No. 1, pp. 307–310.

Salih, M. A. M. (2013) 'African Regional Parliament: Legislature without Legislative Powers', in Costa, O., Dri, C. and Stavridis, S. (eds.), *Parliamentary Dimensions of Regionalisation and Globalisation*, New York, Palgrave Macmillan, pp. 150–165.

Sani, L. M. (2012) 'The Pan African Parliament', in Yusuf, A. A. and Ouguergouz, F. (eds.), *The African Union: Legal and Institutional Framework: A manual of Pan African Organisation*, Leiden, Koninklijke Brill, pp. 95–117.

SARS. (2017) 'SADC Treaty and Protocols', Available online: http://www.sars.gov.za/ Legal/International-Treaties-Agreements/Trade-Agreements/Pages/SADC-Treaty-and -Protocols.aspx [Accessed 02/06/2018].

Schleicher, D. (2011) 'What if Europe Held an Election and No One Care?', *Harvard International Law Journal*, Vol. 52, No. 1, pp. 109–161.

Scholte, J. A. (2005) 'Civil Society and Democratically Accountable Global Governance', in Held, D. and Koenig-Archibugi, M. (eds.), *Global Governance and Public Accountability*, Oxford, Wiley-Blackwell, pp. 87–109.

Scholte, J. A. (2011) *Building Global Democracy? Civil Society and Accountable Global Governance*, Cambridge, Cambridge University Press.

Scholte, J. A. (2012) 'A More Inclusive Global Governance? The IMF and Civil Society in Africa', *Global Governance*, Vol. 18, No. 2, pp. 185–206.

Scholte, J. A. (2015) 'Civil Society and Reinvention of Regions', in Fioramonti, L. (ed.), *Civil Society and World Regions: How Citizens Are Reshaping Regional Governance in Times of Crisis*, London, Lexington Books, pp. 11–32.

Schulz, M. (2011) 'The Role of Civil Society in Regional Governance in the Middle East', in Armstrong, D., Bello, V., Gilson, J. and Spini, D. (eds.), *Civil Society and International Governance: The Role of Non-State Actors in Global and Regional Regulatory Framework*, New York, Routledge, pp. 149–166.

Searcey, D. (2016) 'Boko Haram Falls Victims of a Food Crisis He Created', *New Yorker*, Available online: http://www.nytimes.com/2016/03/05/world/africa/boko-haram-food -crisis.html?_r=0 [Accessed 06/03/2016].

Semian, M. and Chromý, P. (2014) 'Regional Identity as a Driver or a Barrier in the Process of Regional Development: A Comparison of Selected European Experience', *Norsk Geografisk Tidsskrift-Norwegian Journal of Geography*, Vol. 68, No. 5, pp. 263–270.

SERAP. (2017) 'Ground-Breaking ECOWAS Court Judgment Orders Government to Punish Oil Companies Over Pollution', Available online: http://serap-nigeria.org/ ground-breaking-ecowas-court-judgment-orders-govt-to-punish-oil-companies-over -pollution.ngo/ [Accessed 26/08/2017].

Seth, S. (2011) 'Postcolonial Theory and the Critique of International Relations', *Millennium - Journal of International Studies*, Vol. 40, pp. 167–183.

Seyferth, D. (2014) 'Senegal: An End to One of Africa's Longest Civil Conflicts', *Atlantic Council*, Available online: http://www.atlanticcouncil.org/blogs/africasource/senegal -an-end-to-one-of-africa-s-longest-civil-conflicts [Accessed 06/04/2018].

Shaw, M. T. (2000) 'New Regionalisms in Africa in the New Millennium: Comparative Perspectives on Renaissance, Realisms and/or Regressions', *New Political Economy*, Vol. 5, No. 3, pp. 399–414.

Shaw, M. T. (2016) 'African Agency Post-2015: The Roles of Regional Powers and Developmental States in Regional Integration', in Levine, D. H. and Nagar, D. (eds.), *Region-Building in Africa*, New York, Palgrave Macmillan, pp. 109–126.

Shaw, M. T., Soderbaum, F., Nyang'oro, E. J. and Grant, A. (2003) 'The Future of New Regionalism in Africa: Regional Governance, Human Security/Development and Beyond', in Grant, A. J. and Soderbaum, F. (eds.), *The New Regionalism in Africa*, Aldershot, Ashgate, pp. 192–206.

Sliverman, D. (ed.) (2011) *Qualitative Research: Issues of Theory, Method and Practice*, 3rd Edition, London, Sage Publication Limited.

Smith, K. (2009) 'Has Africa Got Anything to Say? African Contributions to the Theoretical Development of International Relations', *The Round Table*, Vol. 98, No. 402, pp. 269–284.

Social Platform Website. (n.d.) 'Who We Are', Available online: http://www.socialplatform .org/who-we-are/ [Accessed 17/04/2017].

Soderbaum, F. (2002) *Political Economy of the New Regionalism: The Case of Southern Africa*, Gothenburg, University of Gotherburg.

Soderbaum, F. (2004a) *Political Economy of the New Regionalism: The Case of Southern Africa*, New York, Palgrave Macmillan.

Soderbaum, F. (2004b) 'Modes of Regional Governance in Africa: Neoliberalism, Sovereignty-Boosting and Shadow Networks', *Global Governance: A Review of Multilateralism and International Organisations*, Vol. 4, No. 10, pp. 419–436.

Soderbaum, F. (2007) 'Regionalisation and Civil Society: The Case of Southern Africa', *New Political Economy*, Vol. 12, No. 3, pp. 319–337.

Soderbaum, F. (2009) 'Comparative Regional Integration and Regionalism', in Landman, T. and Robinson, N. (eds.), *The Sage Handbook on Comparative Politics*, London, Sage Publication Limited, pp. 477–496.

Soderbaum, F. (2013) 'Rethinking Regions and Regionalism', *Georgetown Journal of International Affairs*, Vol. 14, No. 2, pp. 9–18.

Soderbaum, F. (2016a) *Rethinking Regionalism*, London, Palgrave.

Soderbaum, F. (2016b) 'Old, New and Comparative Regionalism: The History and Scholarly Development of the Field', in Borzel, T. and Risse, T. (eds.), *The Oxford Handbook of Comparative Regionalism*, Oxford, Oxford University Press, pp. 4–16.

Soderbaum, F. and Shaw, T. M. (eds.) (2003) *Theories of New Regionalism*, New York, Palgrave Macmillan.

Soderbaum, F. and Taylor, I. (2007) 'Introduction: Thinking about Micro-Regionalism in West Africa', in Soderbaum, F. and Taylor, I. (eds.), *Micro-Regionalism in West Africa: Evidence from Two Case Studies*, Nordiska Afrikainstititet, pp. 5–7. Available online: http://www .diva-portal.org/smash/get/diva2:240826/FULLTEXT01.pdf [Accessed 15/07/2015].

Söderbaum, F. (2003) 'Introduction: Theories of New Regionalism', in Soderbaum, F. and Shaw, T. (eds.), *Theories of New Regionalism*, London, Palgrave Macmillan, pp. 1–21.

Söderbaum, F. and Taylor, I. (2008) *Afro-Regions: The Dynamics of Cross-Border Micro-Regionalism in Africa*, Nordiska, Afrikainstitutet.

Spini, T. (2011) 'Civil Society and Democratisation of Global Public Space' in Armstrong, D., Bello, V., Gilson, J. and Spini, D. (eds.), *Civil Society and International Governance: The Role of Non-State Actors in the Regional Regulative Frameworks*, New York, Routledge, pp. 15–30.

Steady, C. F. (2011) *Women and Leadership in West Africa Mothering the Nation and Humanizing the State*, New York, Palgrave Macmillan.

Stets, J. E. and Burke, P. J. (2000) 'Identity Theory and Social Identity Theory', *Social Psychology Quarterly*, Vol. 63, No. 3, pp. 224–237.

Stierer, B. and Antoniou, M. (2004) 'Are there Distinctive Methodologies for Pedagogic Research in Higher Education?', *Teaching in Higher Education*, Vol. 9, No. 3, pp. 275–285.

Stoddard, E. (2017) 'Authoritarian Regimes in Democratic Regional Organisations? Exploring Regional Dimensions of Authoritarianism in an Increasingly Democratic West Africa', *Journal of Contemporary African Studies*, Vol. 35, No. 4, pp. 469–486.

Storey, A. (2015) 'Chronicle of a European Crisis Foretold: Building Neoliberalism from Above and Options for Resistance from Below', in Fioramonti, L. (ed.), *Civil Society and World Regions: How Citizens Are Shaping Regional Governance in Times of Crisis*, London, Lexington Books, pp. 33–47.

Tagola, A. (2015) 'From Community Development to Socio-Economic and Democratic Progress: Contribution of Malian Civil Society to National Progress', in WACSI (ed.), *Civil Society and Development in West Africa: Regional Perspective*, Accra, WACSI, pp. 128–137.

Taylor, I. (2003) 'Globalization and Regionalization in Africa: Reactions to Attempts at Neo-Liberal Regionalism', *Review of International Political Economy*, Vol. 10, No. 2, pp. 310–330.

Taylor, I. and Williams, P. D. (2008) 'Political Culture, State Elites and Regional Security in West Africa', *Journal of Contemporary African Studies*, Vol. 26, No. 2, pp. 137–149.

Thankur, R. and Langenhove, L. V. (2006) 'Enhancing Global Governance through Regional Integration', *Global Governance*, Vol. 12, pp. 233–240.

The Economist. (2000) 'Guiei Gone', Available online: http://www.economist.com/node /404141 [Accessed 22/02/2018].

The Economist. (2018) 'Child Marriage Persists in Africa', Available online: https://www .economist.com/graphic-detail/2018/09/25/child-marriage-in-africa-persists [Accessed 02/05/2020].

The Nobel Prize. (2011) 'Leymah Gbowee: Facts', Available online: https://www .nobelprize.org/prizes/peace/2011/gbowee/facts/ [Accessed 05/04/2018].

The Tide. (2017) 'Addressing Cases of Statelessness in Nigeria', Available online: http:// www.thetidenewsonline.com/2017/03/22/addressing-cases-of-statelessness-in-nigeria/ [Accessed 21/06/2017].

This Day. (2016) 'WACSOF: Re-strategising with ECOWAS for Regional Development', Available online: https://www.thisdaylive.com/index.php/2016/07/14/wacsof-re -strategising-with-ecowas-for-better-regional-devt/ [Accessed 11/05/2017].

Thonke, O. and Spliid, A. (2012) 'What to Expect from Regional Integration in Africa', *African Security Review*, Vol. 21, No. 1, pp. 42–66.

Tom, P. (2017) *Liberal Peace and Post-Conflict Peacebuilding in Africa*, London, Palgrave Macmillan.

Tom, P. (2018) 'The Fabric of Peace in Africa: Looking Beyond the State', *Canadian Journal of African Studies/Revue canadienne des études africaines*, Vol. 52, No. 3, pp. 408–409.

Tom, T. (2016) 'Peace in West Africa', in Richmond, O. P., Pogodda, S. and Ramovic, J. (eds.), *Dimensions of Peace: Disciplinary and Regional Approaches*, Basingstoke, Palgrave Macmillan, pp. 299–310.

Tracy, J. S. (2010) 'Qualitative Quality: Eight "Big-Tent" Criteria for Excellent Qualitative Research', *Qualitative Inquiry*, Vol. 16, No. 10, pp. 837–851.

Traoré, O. (2017) *Mapping of Civil Society Organizations in Peace & Security in West Africa*: An Unpublished Draft Report of the ECOWAS-European Union Peace, Security and Stability Project: EuropeAid/134834/D/SER/Multi.

UNDESA. (2019) *World Population Prospects: 2019 Highlights*, New York, United Nations.

UNDP. (1994) *Human Development Report*, New York, Oxford University Press.

UNDP. (2006) *Sierra Leone Case Study: Evaluation of UNDP Assistance to Countries Affected with Conflict*. Available online: http://web.undp.org/evaluation/documents/ thematic/conflict/SierraLeone.pdf [Accessed 19/04/2020].

UNECA. (1990) *African Charter on Popular Participation in Development and Transformation*. Available online: https://www.ircwash.org/sites/default/files/70 -UNECA90-7322.pdf [Accessed 10/01/2018].

UNECA. (2013) *ECOWAS at 40: An Assessment of Progress Towards Regional Integration in West Africa*. Available online: https://www.uneca.org/sites/default/files/ PublicationFiles/uneca_ecowas_report_en_web_v2.pdf [Accessed 01/02/2018].

UNICEF. (2016) *Conflict Sensitivity and Peacebuilding: A programme Guide*. Available Online: https://eccnetwork.net/wp-content/uploads/05-Programming -Guide-Conflict-Sensitivity-and-Peacebuilding-UNICEF-Nov-2016.pdf. [Accessed 12/07/2019].

UNICEF and UNFPA. (2018) *Child Marriage in West and Central Africa at a Glance*. Available online: https://www.unicef.org/wca/media/2596/file/Child%20Marriage %20in%20WCA%20-%20At%20a%20Glance.pdf [Accessed 02/04/2020].

United States Institute of Peace. (2007) 'Côte d'Ivoire: Ensuring a Peaceful Political Transition', Available online: https://www.usip.org/publications/2007/12/cote-divoire -ensuring-peaceful-political-transition [Accessed 20/02/2018].

UN News. (2014) '"Insecurity on the March Again" in Africa's Sahel Region, UN Relief Official Warns', Available online: http://www.un.org/apps/news/story.asp?NewsID =49386#.VOetYMtyaM8 [Accessed 20/02/2015].

UNOWAS. (2018) *Pastoralism and Security in West Africa and the Sahel: Towards Peaceful Coexistence*. Available online: https://unowas.unmissions.org/sites/default/ files/rapport_pastoralisme_eng-april_2019_-_online.pdf [Accessed 02/04/2019].

UNOWAS. (2019) 'Activities of the United Nations Office for West Africa and the Sahel', Available at: https://unowas.unmissions.org/sites/default/files/s_2019_549_e.pdf [Accessed 27/07/2020].

USAID. (2010) 'Early Warning and Response Design Support (EWARDS) Côte D'ivoire Conflict Assessment', Available online: http://pdf.usaid.gov/pdf_docs/Pnadx565.pdf [Accessed 20/02/2018].

USAID. (2016) 'Mitigating Electoral Violence through the National Early Warning System (NEWS)', Available online: https://www.usaid.gov/sites/default/files/documents/1860/ NEWS%20Fact%20Sheet%20Nov%202016.pdf [Accessed 24/02/2018].

UNCTAD. (2016) *Statistical Table on the Least Developed Countries 2016*. Available Online: http://unctad.org/en/PublicationsLibrary/ldc2016_Stats_en.pdf [Accessed 06/03/2017].

USAID. (2019) 'Mitigating Electoral Violence through the National Early Warning system (NEWS)', Available online: https://www.usaid.gov/sites/default/files/documents/1860/ NEWS_Fact_Sheet_Feb_2019.pdf [Accessed 10/09/2019].

USAID and WANEP. (2018) 'Preliminary Declaration', Available online: http://www .wanep.org/wanep/files/2018/Apr/WANEP_ESR_Preliminary_Declaration_-_Final _Press_Release_1.pdf [Accessed 02/04/2018].

US Embassy in Ghana. (2015) 'USAID Makes Award to the West African Network for Peacebuilding to Prevent Election Violence in the Region', Available online: https://

gh.usembassy.gov/usaid-makes-award-west-africa-network-peacebuilding-prevent
-election-violence-region/ [Accessed 04/04/2018].

Van Langenhove, L. (2004) 'Regionalising Human Security in Africa: UNU-CRIS Occasional Paper' (Paper for the UNU-TICAD III Follow-up Workshop, Tokyo 29–30. Available online: http://cris.unu.edu/sites/cris.unu.edu/files/O-2004-8.pdf [Accessed 30/01/2015].

Van Langenhove, L. (2012) 'Why We Need to "Unpack" Regions to Compare Them More Effectively', *The International Spectator*, Vol. 47, No. 1, pp. 16–29.

Vayrynen, R. (2003) 'Regionalism: Old or New', *International Studies Review*, Vol. 5, No. 1, pp. 25–51.

Verkoren, W. (2008) *The Owl and the Dove: Knowledge Strategies to Improve the Peacebuilding Practice of Local Non-Governmental Organisations*, Amsterdam, Amsterdam University Press.

Villalon, A. L. (1994) 'Democratizing a (Quasi) Democracy: The Senegalese Election of 1993', *African Affairs*, Vol. 93, No. 371, pp. 163–194.

Viljoen, F. (2012) *International Human Rights Law in Africa*, Oxford, Oxford University Press.

Vleuten, A. and Eerdewijk, A. (2014) 'Regional Governance: Gender and Transnationalism: A First Exploration', in Vleuten, A., Eerdewijk, A. and Roggeband, C. (eds.), *Gender Equality Norms in Regional Governance: Transnational Dynamics in Europe, South America and Southern Africa*, New York, Palgrave Macmillan, pp. 17–41.

VOA. (2016) 'One Million Remain Stateless in West Africa', Available online: http://www.voanews.com/a/million-remain-stateless-west-africa/3208401.html [Accessed 06/03/2017].

Voors, M., Van Der Windt, P., Papaioannou, K. J. and Bulte, E. (2017) 'Resources and Governance in Sierra Leone's Civil War', *The Journal of Development Studies*, Vol. 53, No. 2, pp. 278–294.

WACSI. (2009) 'Towards an ECOWAS of Peoples', A Paper Presented at the 3rd Annual East African Civil Society Organisations' Forum (EA-CSO Forum), From 20–21 March 2009, Arusha, Tanzania.

WACSI and WACSOF. (2014) 'Communique: 1st Annual West African Civil Society Conference', Available online: https://commonwealthfoundation.com/wp-content /uploads/2014/12/Communique%20%20%201st%20West%20Africa%20Civil %20Society%20Conference%20Accra%20-%20December%208-9%202014.pdf [Accessed 03/08/17].

WACSOF. (2003) *Charter of the West African Civil Society Forum (WACSOF)*, Accra, WACSOF.

WACSOF. (2008) *2008 Annual Report of WACSOF*, Abuja, WACSOF.

WACSOF. (2012) *A Report of the Workshop on the Restructuring and Reconstitution of the WACSOF Thematic Groups*, Held from 13th to 14th April 2012 at the Gombe Jewel Hotel, Abuja, Nigeria.

WACSOF. (2013) *2012 and 2013 Annual Reports of WACSOF*. Available online: http://www.wacsof.net/images/2013wacsofannualreport.pdf [Accessed 19/11/2018].

WACSOF. (2015) *2015 Annual Report of WACSOF*. Available online: http://www.wacsof .net/images/wacsof%202015%20anual%20report.pdf [Accessed 28/08/2017].

WACSOF. (2016) 'Communiqué of the 6th WACSOF People's Forum, 16 August 2016 Reiz Continental Hotel, Abuja, Nigeria', Available online: http://www.wacsof.net/ images/wacsof%206th%20biennial%20peoples%20forum.pdf [Accessed 01/09/2017].

WACSOF. (n.d.) 'Thematic Groups', Available online: http://www.wacsof.net/index.php/en/thematic-area [Accessed 01/05/2017].

WACSOF. (n.d.) 'WACSOF Wants NGOs to Register with its National Platforms', Available online: http://www.wacsof.net/index.php/en/news/others/press-briefing [Accessed 03/08/2017].

Wamai, E. N. (2011) 'UNSCR 1325 Implementation in Liberia: Dilemma and Challenges', in Olonisakin, F. Barnes, K. and Ikpe, E. (eds.), *Women, Peace and Security: Translating Policy into Practice*, New York, Routledge, pp. 52–65.

WANEP. (2002) *WANEP 2002 Annual Report*. Available online: http://wanep.org/wanep/files/ar/ar_2002_en.pdf [Accessed 21/09/2017].

WANEP. (2003) *WANEP 2003 Annual Report*. Available online: http://wanep.org/wanep/files/ar/ar_2003_en.pdf [Accessed 05/04/2018

WANEP. (2005) *WANEP 2005 Annual Report*. Available online: http://wanep.org/wanep/files/ar/ar_2005_en.pdf [Accessed 10/03/2018].

WANEP. (2006) *WANEP 2006 Annual Report*. Available online: http://www.wanep.org/wanep/files/ar/ar_2006_en.pdf [Accessed 07/02/2018].

WANEP. (2012) *Peace Education in Formal Schools in West Africa: An Implementation Guide*, Accra, West African Network for Peacebuilding.

WANEP. (2013a) 'Ghana', Available online: http://www.wanep.org/wanep/index.php?option=com_content&view=category&layout=blog&id=40&Itemid=58&limitstart=4 [Accessed 24/06/2019].

WANEP. (2013b) 'The Gambia: Organisational Structure', Available online: See WANEP's website: http://www.wanep.org/wanep/index.php?option=com_content&view=article&id=65:organizational-structure&catid=50:the-gambia&Itemid=90 [Accessed 24/06/2019].

WANEP. (2013c) 'WANEP Appoints New Liaison Officer for the ECOWAS Early Warning Directorate', Available online: http://www.wanep.org/wanep/index.php?option=com_content&view=article&id=460:wanep-appoints-new-liaison-officer-for-the-ecowas-early-warning-directorate-&catid=25:news-releases&Itemid=8 [Accessed 31/01/2018].

WANEP. (2014) 'The Ivorian Government Commends WANEP for its Contribution to Conflict Prevention and Peacebuilding in Cote d'Ivoire', Available online: http://www.wanep.org/wanep/files/2014/sept/Discours_R2P_8_septembre_2014.pdf. See the English version of the statement relating to WANEP. Available online: https://wanep.org/wanep/index.php?option=com_content&view=article&id=677:the-ivorian-government-commends-wanep-for-its-contribution-to-conflict-prevention-and-peacebuilding-in-cote-divoire&catid=67:slide-show [Accessed 02/04/2018].

WANEP. (2015a) *WANEP 2015 Annual Report*. Available online: http://wanep.org/wanep/files/2016/apr/ar_2015_en.pdf [Accessed 2/04/2018].

WANEP. (2015b) *Casamance Tendencies and Tensions: Transforming West Africa's Protracted Conflict*, WARN Policy Brief. Available online: file:///C:/Users/user/Desktop/ACADEMIC%20MATERIALS%20-%20ECOWAS/pb_casamance_dec_2015%20WANEP%20BRIEF.pdf [Accessed 24/04/2020].

WANEP. (2016a) *WANEP 2016 Annual Report*. Available online: http://wanep.org/wanep/files/2017/apr/ar_2016en.pdf [Accessed 03/10/2017].

WANEP. (2016b) '*WANEP News* Issue X, January–March 2016, page 2', Available online: http://www.wanep.org/wanep/files/2016/may/WANEPNews_x.pdf [Accessed 03/04/2018].

WANEP. (2016c) *The Strive and Strain in Civil Society Organisation in West Africa: The WANEP Story*. Available online: https://www.wanep.org/wanep/files/2019/Dec/OUR _STORY_Wanep_English.pdf [23/04/2020].

WANEP. (2017a) *WANEP 2017 Annual Report*. Available online: https://www.wanep.org /wanep/files/2018/Apr/WANEP_2017_English_Annual.pdf [Accessed 20/04/2020].

WANEP. (2017b) 'The Coordinated Election Situation Room (ESR) for Ghana 2016 General Election: Comprehensive Report', Available online: http://www .wanep.org/wanep/files/2017/mar/rp_coordinated_ESR_Ghana_.pdf [Accessed 02/04/2018].

WANEP (2017c) 'Violent Extremism: Armed Violence and Human Security in West Africa', in *WANEP Thematic Report* January–June 2017. Available online: http://wanep .org/wanep/files/2017/sep/THEMATIC_REPORT01.pdf [Accessed 21/09/2017].

WANEP. (n.d.) 'WANEP- Benin', Available online: http://wanep.org/wanep/index.php ?option=com_content&view=category&layout=blog&id=37&Itemid=54 [Accessed 14/02/2018].

WANEP and GPAC. (2017) 'Report of the Workshop on Early Warning and Response Practice', Available online: https://www.peaceportal.org/documents/130276236/ dd525e83-9b73-4d49-a6d7-c40d514554bc [Accessed 02/04/2018].

WANEP and IPCR (2010) *Report of 2nd Jos Dialogue Process, "Sustaining the Search for Peace in the Home of Peace and Tourism*. Available online: http://www.wanep .org/wanep/attachments/article/290/rp_2nd_jos_dialogue_process.pdf [Accessed 06/04/2018].

WANEP-Nigeria. (2019) 'Zonal Coordinators', Available online: http://www.wanepnigeria .org/index.php?option=com_content&view=category&id=9&Itemid=27 [Accessed 24/04/2019].

Wendt, A. (1992) 'Anarchy is What States Make of It: The Social Construction of Power Politics', *International Organization*, Vol. 46, No. 2, pp. 391–425.

Wendt, A. (1999) *Social Theory of International Politics*, Cambridge, Cambridge University Press.

White, D. J. (2002) *The United Nations System: Towards International Justice*, London, Lynne Rienner Publishers Inc.

Wiess, T. G., Seyle, D. C. and Coolidge, K. (2013) 'The Rise of Non State Actors in Global Governance: Opportunities and Limitations', One Earth Future Foundation Discussion Paper. Available online: http://acuns.org/wp-content/uploads/2013/11/gg-weiss.pdf [Accessed 17/02/2015].

Woods, D. (1992) 'Civil Society in Europe and Africa: Limiting State Power through a Public Sphere', *African Studies Review*, Vol. 35, No. 2, pp. 77–100.

World Bank. (2019a) 'World Bank in Benin', Available online: http://www.worldbank.org /en/country/benin/overview [Accessed 20/02/2018].

World Bank. (2019b) 'World Bank in Burkina Faso', Available online: http://www .worldbank.org/en/country/burkinafaso/overview[Accessed 20/02/2018].

World Court. (2010) 'SERAP *v Federal Republic of Nigeria and Universal Basic Education*: ECW/CCJ/APP/12/07; ECW/CCJ/JUD/07/10 (ECOWAS, Nov. 30, 2010)', Available online: http://www.worldcourts.com/ecowasccj/eng/decisions/2010.11.30 _SERAP_v_Nigeria.htm [Accessed 26/08/2017].

Yaya, S., Odusina, K. E. and Bishwajit, G. (2019) 'Prevalence of Child Marriage and its Impact on Fertility Outcomes in 34 Sub-saharan African Countries', *BMC International Health and Human Rights*, Vol. 19, No. 33, pp. 1–11.

Yin, K. R. (2009) *Case Study Research: Design and Methods*, 4th Edition, London, SAGE Publications Limited.

Yin, K. R. (2012) *Applications of Case Study Research*, 3rd Edition, London, SAGE Publication Limited.

Yukawa, T. (2018) 'European Integration through the Eyes of ASEAN: Rethinking Eurocentrism in Comparative Regionalism', *International Area Studies Review*, Vol. 21, No. 4, pp. 323–339.

Zajontz, T. and Leysens, A. (2015) 'Regionalism Revised: A Critical-Reflectivist Framework for Engaging the Changing Nature of Developing Regionalisms in Africa', *Politikon*, Vol. 42, No. 3, pp. 299–323.

Appendices

Appendix 1: List of Host Organisations for WACSOF

National Chapter	Host Organisation	Contacts
Benin	Plateforme des Acteurs de la Société Civile au Benin (PASCIB)	(+229) 21 30 10 89
Cote d'Ivoire	Club Union Africaine (CLUB-UA)	(+225) 051 924 33
Gambia	TANGO	(+220) 9995093 / 3995093 / 4390525
Ghana	Institute for Democratic Governance (IDEG)	+233 20-81-30-800
Guinea Bissau	Mouvement National de la Société Civil pour la Paix et la Démocratie (MNSCPD)	(+245) 590 93 77
Guinea Conakry	Association Mère Enfant (AME)	(+224) 60 52 45 26 / 62 13 79 433
Liberia	Liberia Education for All Technical Committee (Letcom)	(+231) 88 65 67 821
Mali	La Marche Mondiale des Femmes	00223 66 62 72 72 / 76 33 67 84
Cape Verde	SOS CAP VERT	+238 2647379
Nigeria	Civil Society Legislative Advocacy Centre (CISLAC)	(+234) 706 134 7269
Senegal	Organisation Nationale des Droits de l'Homme (ONDH)	(+225) 051 924 33
Sierra Leone	Institution for Governance Reforms	(+232) 78399388
Togo	PACJA-Togo	(+228) 22221731 / 90 24 66 67
Niger	Groupe de Réflexion et d'animation Multidimensionnelle pour 'Environnement et le Développement (G.R.A.M.E.D)	0227 92 36 26 78 / 00227 93 72 44 29
Burkina Faso	Le Centre d'information et de formation en matière des droits humains en Afrique	22670315919

Appendix 2: The List of Participants in the Study's Interviews

Participant by Number	Affiliation	Mode	Location	Year of Interview
Interviewee 1	CSO	Interview	Abuja	2016
Interviewee 2	CSO	Interview	Abuja	2016
Interviewee 3	CSO	Interview	Abuja	2016
Interviewee 4	CSO	Interview	Abuja	2016
Interviewee 5	CSO	Interview	Abuja	2016
Interviewee 6	CSO	Interview	Abuja	2016
Interviewee 7	CSO	Interview	Abuja	2016
Interviewee 8	CSO	Interview	Accra	2016
Interviewee 9	CSO	Interview	Accra	2016
Interviewee 10	CSO	Interview	Accra	2016
Interviewee 11	CSO	Interview	Accra	2016
Interviewee 12	CSO expert	Interview	Accra	2016
Interviewee 13	CSO expert	Interview	Ibadan	2016
Interviewee 14	Govt. official	Interview	Abuja	2016
Interviewee 15	ECOWAS Parliament	Interview	Abuja	2016
Interviewee 16	ECOWAS Parliament	Interview	Abuja	2016
Interviewee 17	ECOWAS Parliament	Interview	Abuja	2016
Interviewee 18	ECOWAS Parliament	Interview	Abuja	2016
Interviewee 19	ECOWAS Parliament	Interview	Abuja	2016
Interviewee 20	ECOWAS Commission	Interview	Abuja	2018
Interviewee 21	ECOWAS Commission	Interview	Abuja	2019
Interviewee 22	ECOWAS Commission	Interview	Abuja	2019
Interviewee 23	ECOWAS Commission	Interview	Abuja	2019
Interviewee 24	ECOWAS Commission	Interview	Abuja	2019
Interviewee 25	Donor Agency	Interview	Abuja	2016
Interviewee 26	International Alert	Interview	Skype	2019
Interviewee 27	International Alert	Interview	Skype	2019
Interviewee 28	Academic	Discussion	Coventry	2017
Interviewee 29	Academic	Discussion	Sweden	2018
Interviewee 30	CSO expert	Interview	WhatsApp	2018
Interviewee 31	CSO	Interview	Skype	2017
Interviewee 32	CSO	Interview	WhatsApp	2017
Interviewee 33	CSO	Interview	WhatsApp	2017
WPForum 2016	Public Forum	Observation	Abuja	2016
Interviewee 34	ECOWAS citizen	Interview	Dundee	2016
Interviewee 35	CSO	Interview/ e-communication	Email	2019

Appendix 3: The List of WANEP's Partners/Supporters

1. ACT Netherlands
2. African Women's Development Fund (AWDF)
3. Bread for the World
4. British High Commission – Ghana
5. Community House Church
6. CORDAID
7. CRS/WARO
8. Dreikonigsaktion der Katholischen Jungschen (DKA) – Austria
9. Dutch Government
10. Dutch Interchurch Aid
11. Eastern Mennonite University
12. ECOWAS
13. European Center for Conflict Prevention
14. European Union
15. FASTENOPFER
16. Finland Ministry of Foreign Affairs
17. Ghana Research and Advocacy Program (G-RAP)
18. Global Fund for Women
19. Global Partnership for the Prevention of Armed Conflict (GPPAC)
20. GTZ now GIZ
21. IBIS
22. IFOR/WPP
23. Mama Cash
24. Mennonite Board of Missions
25. Mennonite Central Committee
26. Mennonite Mission Networks
27. MISEREOR
28. New Field Foundation
29. NOVIB
30. Oxfam Great Britain
31. Oxfam USA
32. Ploughshare
33. The William and Flora Hewlett Foundation
34. Tides Foundation
35. UNDP Ghana
36. UNICEF
37. UNIFEM
38. Urgent Action Fund
39. USAID
40. War Child Canada
41. Westminster
42. Westminster-Fewer
43. Winston Foundation for World Peace

Source: WANEP (2016c:75–76).

Index

Note: Page numbers in *italics* indicate figures, **bold** indicate tables in the text, and references following "n" refer notes